Reason to Believe

THE ANTHROPOLOGY OF CHRISTIANITY

Edited by Joel Robbins

1. *Christian Moderns: Freedom and Fetish in the Mission Encounter,* by Webb Keane
2. *A Problem of Presence: Beyond Scripture in an African Church,* by Matthew Engelke
3. *Reason to Believe: Cultural Agency in Latin American Evangelicalism,* by David Smilde

Reason to Believe

Cultural Agency in Latin American Evangelicalism

David Smilde

UNIVERSITY OF CALIFORNIA PRESS
Berkeley · Los Angeles · London

University of California Press, one of the most distinguished university presses in the United States, enriches lives around the world by advancing scholarship in the humanities, social sciences, and natural sciences. Its activities are supported by the UC Press Foundation and by philanthropic contributions from individuals and institutions. For more information, visit www.ucpress.edu.

University of California Press
Berkeley and Los Angeles, California

University of California Press, Ltd.
London, England

Library of Congress Cataloging-in-Publication Data

Smilde, David.
Reason to believe : cultural agency in Latin American evangelicalism / David Smilde.
p. cm. — (The anthropology of Christianity ; 3)
Includes bibliographical references and index.
ISBN-13: 978-0-520-24942-4 (cloth : alk. paper)
ISBN-13: 978-0-520-24943-1 (pbk. : alk. paper)
1. Evangelicalism—Venezuela—Caracas. 2. Pentecostalism—Venezuela—Caracas—Case studies. 3. Christianity and culture—Venezuela—Caracas. 4. Men—Religious life. 5. Caracas (Venezuela)—Church history. I. Title.

BR1642.V4S65 2007
280'.409877—dc22 2006037487

Manufactured in the United States of America

16 15 14 13 12 11 10 09 08 07
10 9 8 7 6 5 4 3 2 1

This book is printed on New Leaf EcoBook 50, a 100% recycled fiber of which 50% is de-inked post-consumer waste, processed chlorine-free. EcoBook 50 is acid-free and meets the minimum requirements of ANSI/ASTM D5634–01 (*Permanence of Paper*).

For Carole Ann Gaiser,
mother and friend

Contents

Note on Translations and Names

All the translations of the primary material used here are my own. As the old Italian adage says, "translation is treason": one inevitably betrays some aspects of the original meanings in play. Here I have prioritized the semantic feel of my respondents' words over against literal meaning, looking whenever possible for the English-language equivalents of Spanish-language turns of phrase. This is an imprecise science, and I have tinkered with the translations until the end.

With the exception of people and places that are readily identifiable, all names have been changed to protect my informants. However, I have tried to maintain the character of Venezuelan names. These are of three basic types: traditional Spanish-language names such as José, names transliterated from English such as Jhony, and names wholly created anew such as Orent. In each case pseudonyms are of the same type as the original name. Some of my non-Evangelical respondents used only their nicknames. In these cases I developed nicknames with similar characteristics.

All photographs were taken by me.

Acknowledgments

This book represents the efforts, goodwill, and resources of so many people that I share William James's fear that if I acknowledge them all, my readers will say, "How could such mammoth moanings have released such a mouse?" But I'll risk it, as without the good faith and support of these people this book would not have reached fruition. Needless to say, they bear credit for its contributions and no blame for its shortcomings. The extent of my debts means that I will likely leave some important people unrecognized; I apologize if I have done so.

At Calvin College, Mary Stewart Van Lieuwen, Nicholas Wolterstorff, and Lambert Zuidervart first gave me a taste of the scholarly life. Dan Miller first inspired me with empirical facts. Guillermo Cook and Elsa Cortina first spurred my interest in Latin culture. My friends from that era, Steve Andries, Rick Devries, Ron and Jeanne Dewaard, Bob Dozema, Lisa Hoekstra, Brad Ipema, Brian Noordewier, and Tim Steigenga, remain my real or imaginary conversational partners. Tim has been a friend, adviser, and coauthor from the beginning of this project to the present.

At Chicago, Wendy Griswold saw potential and believed in this project before I did. Martin Riesebrodt pushed a trained philosopher toward a more historical, empirical perspective on sociology. Bill Parish used his analytic scissors to shred every misstep and guide my project toward more solid sociology. Most of what I know about sociology came from the first-year sequence in social theory with Donald Levine. Without his confidence and guidance I would not have entered, stayed in, or finished Chicago's program. I am still motivated by Jim Coleman's flat-footed approach to sociological research and debate. Dan Levine, adviser and friend, has consistently pushed me to maintain my empirical grounding and has inspired me with his unwavering commitment to the people we study. Phyllis Levine was a friend and inspiration in so many ways, before and after her untimely death. My friends from my Hyde Park years—James and Gracia Farrer, Grace Kao and Jeff Rubingh, Chenoa Flippen and Emilio Parrado, James Schulman, David and Mary Blair-Loy, Kara Joyner, Emily Barman and Julian Go, and Penny Edgell, Richard Lloyd, and Jeremy Straughn—continue to provide valued support and friendship.

In Venezuela, numerous colleagues provided essential support. At the Universidad Católica Andrés Bello, Anitza Freitez, María Di Brienza, Luis Pedro España, and Luis Ugalde facilitated my work in important ways. Alberto Gruson discussed my research design and logistics any number of times over endless cigarettes and coffee. *¡Gracias, hombre!* Iván Gil graciously led me out of innumerable computing crises. At the Universidad Central de Venezuela, Luisa Betancourt, Cecilia Cariola, Beatriz Hernández, Luis Lander, Margarita López Maya, and Heinz Sontag and provided important assistance and direction. I could not have carried out the research without the help of Rafael Lugo, Keison Carrillo, Pedro Cedeño, Carlos García, Valdehmar Pérez, Antonio González, Jose Angel, and Vicente Mente. Francy Fonseca, Joanna Falcon, Venus Romero, Elizabeth Cherry, and my wife, María Romero, were long-suffering research assistants. Bryan Froehle was key to getting this research off the ground in Venezuela.

Scott Mainwaring, Andy Abbott, David Sikkink, David Yamane, Lyn Spillman, Barry Schwartz, and Joe Hermanowicz provided key support that facilitated the transition from graduate student to junior faculty member. Jeff Goodwin, John R. Hall, Steve Warner, and Rhys Williams have been supportive mentors.

In Athens, Carolina Acosta and Guillermo Alzuru, Ignacio Aguerrevere and María Teresa Michelangeli, José Álvarez and Daniela Melis, and José López and Marirosa Molina have been a family away from family, providing unconditional support and lots of good times.

The following people have commented or provided key advice on all or parts of this book project: Mary Blair-Loy, Mark Cooney, Jeanne Elders Dewaard, James Farrer, Sujatha Fernandes, Tom McNulty, Ann Mische, Dawne Moon, Andrew Perrin, Paul Roman, Ron Simons, Alejandro Velasco, Al Young, Melissa Wilde, and Barry Schwartz. A couple of people require specific mention. Sharon Erickson Nepstad, Steve Vaisey, and Rich Wood read the whole manuscript and provided thousands of words of commentary that greatly sharpened the argument. Courtney Bender and Paul Lichterman each worked through the conceptual argument twice, providing incisive but generous comments that pushed me in new directions. Participants of the Georgia Workshop on Culture, Power and History have vetted or inspired any number of ideas developed here. The students in my 2006 graduate seminar in the sociology of religion—Nichole Arnault, Chudamani Basnet, Lauren Buechner, Michallene McDaniel, Bryan Nichols, and Erin Winter—were the last to comment on the manuscript. William Finlay provided sage advice on the publishing process every step of the way.

This book has benefited from presentations before social scientific audiences at Calvin College; the University of California, San Diego; the University of Chicago, Duke University, the University of Florida, the University of Georgia, Northwestern University, the University of Notre Dame, the University of Pennsylvania, Princeton University, the Universidad Católica Andrés Bello, the Universidad Central de Venezuela, and the Universidad Externado de Colombia, Bogotá. It has also benefited from presentations at annual meetings of the American Sociological Association, the Association for the Sociology of Religion, the Eastern Sociological Society, and the Latin American Studies Association.

I have been blessed with ample financial support for this project. My first visit to the field was made possible by a Tinker Fellowship from the University of Chicago's Center for Latin American Studies. An International Predissertation Fellowship from the Social Science Research Council got me to Venezuela for an extended stay and pilot studies. I carried out the main data collection while on a U.S. Department of Education Fulbright-Hays Dissertation Abroad Fellowship. My first slugs at making a dissertation into a book came as a residential fellow at Notre Dame's Helen Kellogg Institute of International Studies. I finally gained the time to finish the manuscript through a one-semester fellowship from the University of Georgia's Willson Center for the Humanities and Arts. Brent Berlin provided a secret hideaway at the university's Latin American and Caribbean Studies Institute during this final stage. My colleagues in the Department of Sociology at the University of Georgia have consistently supported research quite different from their own.

Reed Malcolm of the University of California Press showed enthusiasm for this book project from the beginning and graciously attended to the timing needs of a pretenure assistant professor. Rose Vekony and Sheila Berg provided crack editorial assistance. Some parts of this book are revised from previous publications. Part of chapter 5 appeared in my article "Popular Publics: Street Protest and Plaza Preachers in Caracas," *International Review of Social History* 49, suppl. 12 (2004): 179–95. Another section of that chapter appeared in "Skirting the Instrumental Paradox: Intentional Belief through Narrative in Latin American Evangelicalism," *Qualitative Sociology* 26, no. 3 (2003): 313–29 (© Springer Science and Business Media). Parts of chapter 6 and appendix C were published in my article "A Qualitative Comparative Analysis of Conversion to Venezuelan Evangelicalism: How Networks Matter," *American Journal of Sociology* 111, no. 3 (2005): 757–96 (© 2005 by The University of Chicago; all rights reserved).

Friends and family made this project possible by providing support for an adult who was not financially viable until his late thirties. My wife, María Romero, has been an integral part of this project—from her role as a wonderful partner and mother of my children to her toleration of yet another evangelization by one of my informants to her help formulating my methods. Most of what I know about indirect interviewing strategies came from my discussions with her. My beloved daughters, Yara and Annelies, have never known life without this project. I can only hope one day they will forgive all the times they sobbed at the door of my home office pleading, "Papaaaa! Quiero jugaaaar!"

My father, Edward Smilde, first got my sociological imagination churning. Long summers spent in the mountains of central California without television or telephone, long trips meandering across North America with nothing but interest as our guide, and long conversations about life, family, and religion developed in me a love of mind, travel, and people. Choosing the dedication for this book was easy. No person is more responsible for its completion and any good that may come from it than my mother, Carole Gaiser. Only by having my own children have I begun to understand her love and her dedication. Most of this book, indeed my life, has been created in dialogue with values she imparted to me. My stepfather, Geoff Gaiser, and my siblings, Susan and Paul Holwerda and John and Julia Smilde, have always been there without hesitation. In Venezuela, Dalia Romero and Fernando Freites were my first hosts in Caracas; they introduced me to their family and allowed me to make it mine. Carmen Montilla and Robinson Romero, Nelson Romero, Mireya Romero and Domingo Uzcátegui, Vicente Romero and Clenin Morales, Fabio Romero, Carlos Romero, and Mariela Hernández welcomed a gringo into the family. Sanity, cognitive clarity, and desperately needed exercise have been provided by (at last count) nineteen nieces and nephews.

My most solemn debt is to all those working-class Venezuelans who were able to trust an anomalous stranger long enough to share their victories and defeats, joys and sorrows—all while knowing their risk and effort would be of no direct benefit to them. I can only hope this book will make good on their trust by contributing to the creation of a more just world that is more respectful of people like them.

PART ONE

Beginnings

CHAPTER 1

Making Sense of Cultural Agency

CAN PEOPLE DECIDE TO BELIEVE?

Jorge was born in the Afro-Venezuelan coastal region of Barlovento and as a child moved with his family to Petare, the massive group of barrios at the eastern end of Caracas. At fourteen he dropped out of school to work and help his mother support eleven brothers and sisters. During Jorge's formative years, Petare evolved from a slum with grinding poverty into a slum with grinding poverty, drugs, and violence—a process Jorge's family experienced in concrete and tragic terms. When Jorge was in his late teens a feud between some of his brothers and other *malandros* (delinquents) led the latter to invade Jorge's family home to seek revenge. They beat, kicked, and stomped his brother to death on the kitchen floor at Jorge's mother's and sisters' feet. In a not unreasonable panic, his mother quickly sold the house and the family dispersed, moving in with kin or friends in various parts of Barlovento and Caracas. With an older brother, Jorge lived for several years in and out of the homes of kin, in flophouses, and occasionally in the street. They worked odd jobs, occasionally stole, and always partied heavily. Jorge eventually fell in love, and he and his partner lived together.

Jorge started to work stably and had three children with his partner, along with her child from a previous union. However, after a few years of routine, he began to use drugs again. His marriage grew increasingly conflictive as his drug use depleted scarce household resources. To make up the difference, he started robbing people in the street—using his handgun not only to steal people's money but also their jewelry, clothes, and shoes for later resale. He used the money to buy food for his house full of children—as well as drugs for himself. He got to the point of pulling out his gun instead of his billfold at the cash registers of neighborhood *abastos* (small mom-and-pop grocery stores). After narrowly surviving an ambush in which the brothers of a man whose shoes he stole tried to kill him and after listening to a cassette that a friend's Evangelical sister had given him, Jorge decided he wanted to change. He went with his friend to the sister's church where they both "accepted the Lord." When he told his wife about it and said he wanted her to come to the church, she asked him if he was serious. Jorge answered, "I sure am. I want to change this life I'm leading." In my first interview with Jorge, about a year after his conversion,[1] he explained, "I was against the wall. I was cornered and I didn't know what to do." When I followed up five years later he was still attending the same church and was leader of its youth group. Jorge and his wife eke out a living for their family of seven selling cleaning products door-to-door, and Jorge occasionally works on government maintenance crews.

Jorge is typical of converts to Evangelical Protestantism in Latin America insofar as his conversion was undertaken as a solution to persistent life problems—what Andrew Chesnut (1997) has aptly called states of "dis-ease." Evangelicalism has grown by leaps and bounds in Latin America since the mid-twentieth century but especially in the past twenty-five years. According to recent estimates, one-tenth of the population of traditionally Catholic Latin America—some fifty million people—belong to a Protestant denomination (Jenkins 2002). While initial analyses of this boom amounted to shrill accusations of cultural imperialism or laments over a shift toward otherworldly escapism,[2] empirically grounded research revealed Evangelicalism is a means by which poor Latin Americans address the challenges they are confronted with.

1. I agree with the criticism that the term *conversion* denotes a rapid and radical transformation that rarely occurs in individual religious change (Comaroff and Comaroff 1991; Stark and Bainbridge 1987). However, alternatives also stack the conceptual deck. *Affiliation* directs our attention away from belief and personal experience and toward the organizational dimension of experience. *Recruitment* places agency with the organization or movement rather than with the person who joins. The term *commitment* means personal assent to the meaning system. Here I simply use the term *conversion* and rely on my substantive descriptions to make clear that I consider the extent and rhythm of change empirical questions.

2. Much of this research refers to a purported invasion of *las sectas* (Albán Estrada and Muñoz 1987; Consejo Episcopal Latinoamericano 1982; Gamuza 1988; Silleta 1987). For an overview of this debate in Latin America as a region, see Stoll 1990. For an overview of Venezuela, see Smilde 1999.

In other words, it serves as a form of cultural agency through which they can gain control over aspects of their personal and social contexts. Probably the best-known challenge is substance abuse. Researchers have argued that whereas alcohol traditionally facilitates peasant norms of reciprocity in rural areas, in the context of urban poverty it frequently reaches debilitating levels and can fade into drug use. This, in turn, can exacerbate poverty and family conflict. Numerous researchers (Annis 1987; Brusco 1995; Chesnut 1997; Flora 1976; Mariz 1994; Martin 1990; Stoll 1990) have argued that Evangelicalism provides a solution to problem drinking. It prohibits drinking—as well as drugs, tobacco, and gambling—and provides an alternative social network not based on alcohol consumption. This network also supports individuals trying to overcome addiction and monitors their progress. Backsliding can result in church discipline and the disapprobation of fellow members.

According to researchers, individuals also convert to address conjugal conflict. The challenges of impoverished urban life often lead patriarchal ideals to transform into a male prestige complex referred to as *machismo* (Brown 1991; Brusco 1995; Smilde 1994). The *machista* male frequently consumes in the street resources that should be directed to the home. And his search for female conquests produces conflict with a wife no longer willing to tolerate the patriarchal double standard. Women suffer not only from *machista* men but also from a lack of culturally legitimate opportunities to participate in extrahousehold organizations. Fieldwork has shown that participation in Evangelicalism leads men to focus on the domestic sphere (Brusco 1995; Burdick 1993; Flora 1976), confirms male headship while providing a new basis for female autonomy (Brusco 1995; Burdick 1993; Smilde 1997), and provides women with a form of participation that is relatively nonthreatening to the men who aspire to control them (Brusco 1995; Flora 1976; Smilde 1994). Most of this scholarship has been based on fieldwork carried out with women; inferences are made primarily on the basis of data on women's perspectives. In chapter 4 I address these issues, among others, using data collected among men.

Another reason for conversion to Evangelicalism is violence. In the context of dictatorship, war, and other forms of political conflict Evangelicalism can function as an effective means for withdrawal from situations of violence. By becoming Evangelical, the individual is effectively extracted from extended violent interaction: he or she is no longer considered a threat or an opportunity by either side (Annis 1987; Martin 1990; Stoll 1990, 1993). Research in urban contexts shows a similar phenomenon in the case of urban violence: conversion to Evangelicalism provides men with a way to step out of conflict-ridden situations (Brusco 1995; Burdick 1993). The crime wave in Latin American societies in the 1990s has only increased the importance of this issue for Latin America's poor, as well as for Evangelicals. I want to mention one final finding of research on Latin American Evangelicalism: religious participation can provide networks of support for rural-to-urban migrants (Roberts 1968). These networks provide information on employment, recommendations, small loans, and other forms of assistance and are therefore key to socioeconomic survival and advancement among the popular sectors (Lomnitz 1977). Without such networks individuals face reduced life chances. In addition to an environment of solidarity, the rigorous norms for personal behavior in Evangelicalism serve as credentials for honesty and hard work in an unstable environment in which work is often day-to-day and one never knows when social support will be necessary (Annis 1987; Mariz 1994; Martin 1993; Roberts 1968).

These portrayals of Evangelical conversion and participation as a form of cultural agency have gone far toward undermining simplistic criticisms of this movement as an "opiate of the masses." However, these portrayals are "instrumentalist" insofar as they explain the adoption of a religious meaning system and form of practice as a means of obtaining nonreligious rewards. Some of the literature speaks openly in these terms. Elizabeth Brusco (1995: 146 ff., 222) sees Evangelicalism as "a form of female collective action" in that it is "an intensely pragmatic movement aimed at reforming those aspects of society which most affect [women's] lives." Cecilia Mariz (1994: 121) speaks of conversion as "a cultural strategy in poor people's attempts to improve their lives." When taken by themselves, statements such as these make one wonder why religion is involved at all.

I originally took up this study because although I could understand positive this-worldly effects of religious belief, I could not understand positive this-worldly effects as *reasons for* religious beliefs. Many of the authors I was reading seemed to feel the same tension and concluded their work with disclaimers moderating the instrumentalist tone of their arguments. Thus Mariz (1994: 59) writes that the "cultural strategies" she found might actually be "unintended consequences." Sheldon Annis (1987: 141) concludes his book on conversion as a form economic maximization thus: "Yet one need only attend prayer in any village church . . . to know that Protestantism means far more than just rationalizing economic gain." And David Martin (1991: 82–83), in an article on Evangelicalism and entrepreneurship, argues, "People don't convert for economic gains. But when they come they are happy to thank the Lord for his blessings" (see also Berger 1990: ix).

I entered the field with the idea that religious conversion was undertaken for religious reasons, not for the nonreligious rewards resulting from belief and practice. Nevertheless, from my first days in the field it became clear that my respondents did not support this assumption. My first field trip was to Colombia. During my first week in Bogotá, I interviewed the pastor of a large Evangelical church on the city's north side. As I waiting for the pastor I struck up a conversation with his secretary about her becoming an Evangelical. She said that she and her family left the Catholic Church for Evangelicalism when they moved from a small town in the Amazon to Bogotá. When I asked why, she left me speechless by saying they had arrived with little money and without family or friends and decided that "the economic and spiritual fruits [of Evangelicalism] were better." As my fieldwork continued, such anomalies accumulated: time and again people unabashedly said they had converted because of the perceived economic, social, and personal gains. Jorge, for example, openly communicated his conversion history in terms of an *intentional* project of self or family reform. He unapologetically spoke of conversion as a way to address pressing life problems. He presented it that way to his wife. He presented it that way to me, the interviewer.

Of course, it is hardly news that people intentionally change aspects of their lives in order to address the challenges they face: they get married or divorced, return to or drop out of school, move or stay put, apologize or take stands. But adopting a set of *beliefs* in order to address the pressing challenges of everyday life is different. Can people really *decide* to believe in a religion because it is in their interest to do so? This explanation for adopting religion raises a number of thorny issues that must be addressed if we are to understand the growth of Latin American Evangelicalism and any number of other cultural phenomena in contemporary social life. One need only conduct a quick internet search on the phrase "you gotta believe!" to find a wide range of inspirational books, tapes, music, and speeches that urge people to "believe" in order to overcome addiction, win the big game, increase sales, or defeat injustice. In each case there is the suggestion not only that it is important to believe you can succeed but also that you can decide to adopt that belief.

There is a complex relationship between intention and belief here that is poorly understood.

WHY DOESN'T EVERYONE DECIDE TO BELIEVE?

Aurelio is forty years old but could easily pass for fifty-five. He lives with his mother and sister in the same *rancho* where he grew up and has a permanent grumbly, beleaguered demeanor. During our two-hour interview, he readily told me about a decade of defeats, his collection of regrets, and the serious problems he still confronts. Two years before our interview he had organized residents to close off their sector of the barrio with locked gates to which only the residents would have keys. This is one of a number of ways that residents of Caracas's barrios have found to reduce crime and violence. However, the prospect of gates often causes conflict with those who benefit from disorganization through involvement with the drug economy; and neighborhood organizers are frequently the targets of violence. Indeed, in Aurelio's barrio just one year before his initiative, a neighborhood activist had been brutally murdered in the middle of the night by hooded gunmen. With this in mind, Aurelio was reluctant about his leadership role in this tense process. He expressed resentment at his neighbors for what happened when drug-dealing neighbors opposed to the gate brought in a malandro to rough him up. None of the neighbors who supported installing the gate defended him. Instead, he says, "everyone ran into their houses to hide and watch the fight."

At about the same time Aurelio learned that his partner of six years was pregnant with her lover's child. They separated as a result, but he has not seen another woman since. They still have occasional sexual encounters, though she is living with the child's father. The combination of neighborhood conflict and relationship breakdown hit him hard. In his terms, he got "skinny, skinny, skinny." In the Venezuelan ethnophysiology of suffering, being *gordo* (fat) means health and success while being *flaco* (skinny) means hardship and affliction.

One of the issues that brought his relationship to an end was gambling. For many years Aurelio was the president of a sports club he founded. The members had created and painted a volleyball court in the parking lot of a hospital just down the street from their neighborhood. However, when neighborhood malandros started using the parking lot to do drugs, the hospital closed it off. This was just the last of several setbacks for a sports club in a city with virtually no green space. Aurelio disbanded it and soon thereafter started betting on horses. This pastime rapidly became an obsession that consumed all his resources. He told me that he got to the point that he would have to leave cash at work, or he would lose it all playing the horses. On the few occasions when he made money gambling he generally used the windfall to buy a crate of beer to drink with neighbors and candy for the neighborhood kids. The financial drain caused conflict with his partner. It also prevented any significant accumulation. Aurelio said his whole family has "vices" and pointed to the decrepit state of their rancho as evidence. Nobody in the family works together, he complained, everyone pulls in their own direction. But he is no exception. "I can find money for vices, even if it means a loan," he said in self-deprecation. "But for my mother, my pockets are empty."

One of Aurelio's good friends is an Evangelical with whom he likes to talk about the Gospel. This friend helped Aurelio through the breakup of his relationship and the conflict over the gate. Aurelio reads the Bible on his own but does not think he could become an Evangelical like his friend. He explained, "I like the Gospel, but I'm not going to tell you that I'm prepared to become an Evangelical because I like women a lot, I like booze. I'm not going to lie to anybody." Why has Aurelio not become an Evangelical? His case seems overdetermined: he has experienced acute danger and personal conflict, is beleaguered by money-consuming vices, suffers enduring poverty, and is dismayed with his neighbors, his family, and himself. Yet he has not become Evangelical. When I followed up five years later he was still living in largely the same way. If Aurelio, like Jorge, could simply decide to believe, he could overcome his gambling problem, save money, contribute to his household, overcome his fear of violence, and very likely find a new partner.

The issue can be broadened. A large percentage of the population of all Latin American countries suffers from one, a few, or all of the problems Evangelicalism reportedly addresses. Nevertheless, even in those countries with the largest Evangelical populations, such as Brazil, Chile, and Guatemala, only a relatively small percentage of the population has converted. Why? We can go further. If people in Venezuela or anywhere could simply decide to believe, the implications would be vast. Few people would be depressed, family conflict would be resolved, crime and violence would end, and low self-esteem would be history. Even in the direst of situations, a person could conceivably adopt the belief that he or she is well off and the luckiest person alive. Of course, this is not the world we live in; conflict, dysfunction, and sorrow are constants of the human condition. Yet most analyses of cultural empowerment would lead us precisely down this path.[3] So we are left with another question: if people can decide to believe, why doesn't everyone do so?

EVANGELICALISM AND SOCIAL CHANGE IN LATIN AMERICA

The growth of Evangelicalism in Latin America has received widespread attention and, unsurprisingly, has been given widely differing assessments. Neo-Marxist scholars see cultural movements such as Latin American Evangelicalism as symptoms rather than solutions. Religious movements, in this view, clearly manifest discontent with conditions of inequality, poverty, and suffering, but they are backward looking and inconsequential as solutions. Manuel Castells has provided the most recent version of this theory in his trilogy, *The Information Age.* In his view transportation and communication technologies have reconstructed modern society away from nation-states and toward global networks of dominant classes that are shadowed by excluded masses. The latter have no place in the network society, yet their traditional ways of life are threatened and undermined by it. Chapter 2 outlines changes such as these in Venezuelan social structure since structural adjustment began in 1983. In Castells's analysis marginalized peoples create reactive identity movements that look to reestablish and reaffirm local identities. However, these movements are poorly situated to facilitate any gain in agency among the marginalized and are therefore largely irrelevant and superfluous. In this view poverty and underdevelopment are the result of social structure, not culture. If certain types of culture correspond to poverty, this is because poverty creates the culture, not vice versa.

The neo-Marxist argument corresponds to the flat-footed common sense of most intellectuals when they confront the phenomenon of

3. I frequently use the term *empowerment* as a subset of *agency*. By "agency," I mean a form of practice in which an individual or social actor's autonomy and control are for the most part increased. I use *empowerment* for more concrete cases in which it is relatively clearer that autonomy and control have been increased.

singing, praying Evangelicals holding their hands high in the middle of Catholic Latin America: Evangelicalism is an expression of futility at best, cultural imperialism at worst (see note 2). The title of Christian Lalive D'Epinay's book *Haven for the Masses* (1969) could hardly be more eloquent. Most versions of this argument, however, are abstract critiques based on impressionistic fieldwork. And they sit uneasily with people like Jorge who seem to be empowered by their religious participation. People like Jorge, and findings like those described in my discussion of his case above, are more consistent with perspectives that highlight the role of culture in social change.

Neoconservative scholars have long pointed to cultural differences when seeking to explain the differential success of development between the United States and in Latin America. Far more advanced at the end of the eighteenth century, Catholic Latin America was eclipsed during the nineteenth and twentieth centuries by the Protestant North in terms of economic growth and political development. Edward Banfield, Samuel Huntington, Lawrence Harrison, and many others have argued, in various ways, that "development is a state of mind." Latin American culture, in this view, lacks the values of personal initiative and responsibility, freedom and peacefulness, and is tied down by a heritage of particularism and patron-client ties of loyalty. From this perspective, culture is an autonomous factor that determines who prospers. While the culture of Latin America has been seen as a hindrance, neoconservative scholars are hopeful that this "new reformation," this dramatic growth of Evangelical Protestantism, is a sign that change is coming (Berger 1990; DeSoto 1989; Martin 1990, 1991; Sherman 1997). This perspective is generally accompanied by the view that neoliberal reforms—such as reductions in state budgets, regulations, and price controls and the opening of national industries and markets to global competition—*generate* values conducive to societal development. "Research that provides evidence of the influence of cultural factors on development prospects is valuable for reinforcing the emerging shift toward neoliberalism in development thinking," wrote Amy Sherman (1997: 17) in her book *The Soul of Development*.[4]

But there is a tension in the neoconservative view that brings us back

4. The idea that the withdrawal of government programs can facilitate culture more suitable for capitalism and democracy is, of course, not confined to debates on third world development. The 1996 welfare reform law in the United States was called the Personal Responsibility and Work Opportunity Reconciliation Act. The guiding idea was precisely that

to the questions of whether people can decide to believe and, if so, why not everybody does. The attempt to use the rise of Evangelicalism to support the effectiveness of neoliberal development policies sits uncomfortably with the desire to portray culture as an autonomous factor in development. As Howard Wiarda (2001) has pointed out, if culture is a key independent variable in explaining which societies successfully adopt neoliberal capitalism, then the fact that Latin America is still far and away a Catholic majority leads to the conclusion that for the foreseeable future neoliberal reforms would be ill advised. Neoconservative support for neoliberal reforms only works if, in some way, neoliberal reforms themselves produce cultural change—a difficult position if you are trying to argue that previous development regimes failed precisely because "culture matters" (Harrison and Huntington 2000). But several authors have pushed forward with this argument. Harrison (2000: 171) gives seven recommendations for how to change culture in order to facilitate progress, including "religious reform." Otto Reich (1983: 40) writes that states can facilitate a "culture of responsibility" by "establishing a fertile context for private initiative." And in the introduction to *The Culture of Entrepreneurship*, Bridgett Berger (1991: 1) argues that given the right context entrepreneurs produce culture. "Any culture is available to any group at any time, provided external conditions (as well as social values, practices, and norms) permit and encourage new patterns to unfold and take root" (6). This position depends on a view in which human actors like Jorge can decide to adopt new beliefs and practices that will help them adjust to their life circumstances.

Applying the neo-Marxist and neoconservative perspectives on social change to the growth of Latin American Evangelicalism makes clear that each lacks an adequate sociology. On the one hand, neo-Marxist pessimism would focus on Aurelio but completely dismiss Jorge. It depends on an abstract determinism that is critical, yet overlooks the increasing power of cultural mobilization among Latin America's popular sectors. Popular religious movements, ethnic indigenous movements, and subaltern nationalist movements are changing the face of Latin American society in ways that are difficult to reconcile with the abstract determinism of Castells and others. On the other hand, neoconservative triumphalism would point to Jorge and ignore Aurelio. It depends on a decontextualized voluntarism that assumes people can always maximize their social

welfare discouraged values of individual responsibility whereas welfare reform would encourage them.

situations by selecting from an infinite repertoire of culture.[5] It thereby distracts attention from the dominant if unintended ground-level effects of global restructuring: unemployment, poverty, crime, violence, substance abuse, drug trafficking, and family conflict. If we hope to understand the significance of Latin American Evangelicalism for social change, we need to develop a conceptualization of agency, culture, and social structure that will allow us to understand the simultaneous coexistence of Jorge's transformation and Aurelio's dysfunction.

THE ARGUMENT

In this book I develop an explanation that contradicts the neo-Marxist perspective by arguing that Evangelical conversion is not a reactive response to identities lost but a forward-looking, intentional project of self- or family reform.[6] Put differently, I answer the question of whether people can decide to believe by portraying Evangelical belief and practice as a form of *imaginative rationality* through which people get things done in this world. "Imaginative" should not be taken here as a synonym for false, insincere, or ungrounded (Anderson 1983; Chakrabarty 2000; Lakoff and Johnson 1980). To the contrary, by "imaginative rationality" I mean humans' ability to get things done by creating concepts.[7] Part 2 of this book shows the way in which the Evangelical men I worked with imagine their social world as well as their own religious practices and how this facilitates their action. Chapter 3 looks at how my informants use Evangelical meanings to conceptualize problems of substance abuse, crime, and violence in such a way that they can overcome them or at least address their pernicious effects. Chapter 4 examines how my informants use Evangelical meanings to address issues of personal development and social life such as unemployment, family, and conjugal conflict. Each of these chapters provides a clear view of how marginal men can address pressing life issues, recurring sources of dis-ease, by becoming Evangelical. Chapter 5 looks directly at the first question posed in this book: can people decide to believe? I argue that they can. First I argue that there is

5. Several contributors to Sommer 2006 point out parallel issues, arguing that the term *cultural agency* easily fits into a logic of abandonment by the state as a concomitant of *cultural autonomy*.

6. My argument on this point parallels Richard Wood's (2003) argument in *Faith in Action* but at a more micro level.

7. I use the terms *concepts* and *meanings* throughout this book instead of the term *schemas* as I have elsewhere (Smilde 2004), precisely to undermine the distinctions between cultural and everyday or scientific concepts.

no natural distinction between religious and nonreligious goals; this common distinction always depends on the religious meanings used to conceptualize it. Thus in the meaning system of Venezuelan Evangelicalism, seeking to address pressing problems of self- or family reform through religious practice is no more instrumental than seeking eternal life through religious practice. Then I argue that the men I studied had good reason to believe in Evangelical projects. The Evangelical meaning system not only helps me address the problems they face; it also provides a repertoire of meanings with which to understand the success and failure of Evangelical projects. Finally, I argue that the Evangelical meaning system provides narratives through which Evangelicals "remember" their conversion experience as one in which it was God acting, not them. These narratives, in effect, minimize the believer's responsibility for conversion and thereby increase the interpretive validity of that new identity.

My analysis of imaginative rationality is fully consistent with the neoconservative view that people can adopt culture that helps them to address their problems and maximize their situations. However, my analysis in part 3 complicates the matter by challenging the idea that "any culture is open to any group at any time." Put differently, I answer the question of why not everybody believes by arguing that a cultural innovation such as religious conversion depends on *relational imagination.* What the men I studied can imagine and when they can imagine it largely depends on their relational context.[8] Conversion to Evangelicalism depends on structural contexts that facilitate exposure to a particular meaning system or do not hinder cultural innovation. Chapter 6 shows that young men in Caracas are often spurred to imagine alternatives by contact with household members embodying those alternatives. Alternatively, they are often prevented from imagining alternatives by contact with household members who maintain traditional meanings. Indeed, over the past twenty years of economic and political reform in Venezuela, relatively few people have coped with the breakdown of their way of life by means of religious change. More common strategies run from the benign—such as reduced consumption and informal street selling—to the malignant—such as consumption and distribution of drugs, involvement in crime, and abuse and violence. In chapter 7 I push further into relational imagination through extended attention to two men who find themselves at the intersection of competing networks that provide alter-

8. See Al Young (2004) for a similar argument regarding young African American men in Chicago's inner city.

native strategies. Reinterviewed five years later, these men reveal their wrenching struggles to extract themselves from networks that lead to participation in the complex of drugs, crime, and violence. These cases also delve more deeply into how family, friends, and particular meanings affect the ability of individuals to imagine alternative futures.

In chapter 8 I push toward a relational, pragmatic theory of cultural agency, returning there to the theoretical issues introduced at the beginning of part 2. Drawing on pragmatist, feminist, and postcolonial theories, this perspective seeks to skirt the Scylla of abstract determinism while avoiding the Charybdis of decontextualized voluntarism and thereby to allow us to understand more clearly how and when people get things done with culture.

CHAPTER 2

The Venezuelan Context

Confronting *La Crisis*

A TALE OF THREE CITIES

One of the few places you can still perceive the colonial past in Caracas is the downtown Plaza Bolívar. Colonial Spanish authorities always located a plaza at the center of the city, and here it is inevitably named after "the liberator," Simón Bolívar. Caracas's Plaza Bolívar has a triumphant equestrian statue of Bolívar at its center and is surrounded by a wrought iron fence. There are eight entrances—one at each corner and one in the middle of each side. A tiled walkway leads from each entrance to the statue of Bolívar, and another walkway encloses the plaza's perimeter. This creates eight neatly manicured gardens with large trees that provide shelter to squirrels and sloths. Old men sit around the perimeter on the cement base of the iron fence. At the northeast corner of the plaza, but in the plaza itself, people—mostly old men—congregate to listen or wait their turn to stand up and weigh in on current events, religion, or philosophy. Beside them is the seventeenth-century Caracas Cathedral, where Bolívar was baptized.

Caracas was founded by Diego de Losada in 1567. Lack of either natural resources or an exploitable indigenous civilization assured that Caracas would not be one of the main cities of the Spanish colonial system, and much of the territory now called Venezuela was largely overlooked in favor of Peru and Mexico. However, Caracas became the moderately prosperous commercial center of the region's agricultural production centered on cocoa cultivation in the interior. For this modest colonial province, the eighteenth century was the most successful period; it was also the high point of the Catholic Church's influence in Caracas and the larger Venezuelan society (Watters 1933). By the beginning of the wars of independence in the first decades of the nineteenth century, the most important edifices and institutions of Caracas were Catholic (González Casas 2002). This should not be interpreted as evidence that Caracas was the capital of a comprehensively Catholic nation. Many areas of what is now Venezuela were never fully evangelized. In fact, after unsuccessful attempts to "reduce" nomadic Indian tribes and incorporate them into Catholic civilization in the sixteenth and early seventeenth century, the archbishopric of Caracas ceded the entire eastern region of the country to the archbishopric of Puerto Rico for a century and a half. Venezuela in general, and Caracas in particular were backwaters in the Spanish colonial effort.

The revolutionary battles of the first decades of the nineteenth century ravaged the colonial institutions that existed, including the Church. Whereas in Colombia the Church became one of Simón Bolívar's main tools for reunification, in Venezuela religious pluralism was an issue from the first decades of independence. Among liberals religious toleration was seen as key to receiving the recognition of non-Catholic Europe and the United States, as well as to receiving the European immigrants they thought would be key to progress (Watters 1933). Anticlericalism had been an important part of the independence movement in Venezuela, and Bolívar's attempt to increase the profile of the Church in La Gran Colombia was one of the reasons for Venezuela's secession. Throughout the nineteenth century liberal reformers supported religious toleration and other measures as means to check the Church's social power. There was continual civil war between conservatives and liberals, as well as regional battles between *caudillos* (de facto political leaders) and bands of mercenaries over territory.

A liberal elite that sought to reduce the influence of the Church largely undermined colonial institutions in the nineteenth century, and anticlericalism is still inscribed on Caracas's geography. If you walk to the west from the Plaza Bolívar one comes immediately upon the gleaming white Palacio Federal Legislativo built by Antonio Guzmán Blanco—the president-cum-dictator who brought the first modern influence to Caracas's architecture and planning. Influenced by French and English modernity, he constructed imposing edifices meant to project national unity and enlightened rationality. The ceiling of the Congress building's impressive gold-plated dome is painted with a scene from the Battle of

Carabobo—the decisive battle in Venezuela's drive for independence from Spain. Guzmán Blanco tore down a number of colonial churches and replaced them with government ministries, theaters, and plazas for a cosmopolitan bourgeoisie. He also sought to replace the tight colonial street design with wide-open boulevards.

Despite Guzmán Blanco's modernizing efforts, by the end of the nineteenth century Venezuela was one of the poorest, most indebted countries in Latin America and had yet to gain full political control over its territory. All this would change, of course, with the onset of oil exploitation (see Coronil 1997; Levine 1973). During his twenty-seven-year dictatorship (1908–35), Juan Vicente Gómez was able to strengthen the state dramatically through oil revenues and was the first Venezuelan leader to achieve full political domination over the territory. While his rule was ruthlessly personal, using state control of Venezuela's resources to buy loyalty and foreign concessions to prevent the development of a bourgeoisie not loyal to him (Coronil 1997; Pérez Schael 1993), he succeeded in making Venezuela into a nation-state. His death in 1937 was followed by ten more years of authoritarian rule, then a three-year democracy that was overthrown by the military—bringing on a decade of military rule by General Marcos Pérez Jiménez.

If you walk down the east side of the Congress building and enter the Capitolio subway station you can take a train east two stops to the Agua Salud station. There you will be in the heart of the 23 de Enero. This is the biggest, most ambitious housing project in Latin America: forty-one (or fifty-nine, depending on how you count the double- and triple-wing structures) fifteen-story buildings, together containing nine thousand apartments. This complex was the centerpiece of Pérez Jiménez's "war on ranchos," in which he looked to overcome poverty and backwardness through modern housing developments. The Venezuelan architect Carlos Raul Villanueva designed the apartments with moderate living space but generous common spaces in which the public could interact. In the 1990s the 23 de Enero was an outpost of modernity where nonelites still believed in community activism and revolutionary movements still thrived. However, almost five decades after their construction this modernist megaproject bears witness to the decline of Venezuela's modern promise. The buildings themselves are in various stages of dilapidation, and most of the common spaces have themselves been made into what Venezuelans refer to as "barrios"—squatter's settlements of self-constructed, usually brick "ranchos" in different stages of "autoconstruction." Some of these barrios are among the most violent in Caracas.

The 23 de Enero now looks like an artfully designed, decaying modern neighborhood filled in with swirls of informal rancho settlements. Depending on how you measure it, between 40 and 60 percent of the dwellings in Caracas are of this type: ranchos in barrios or public housing units in the midst of barrios (United Nations Development Program 2000).

Pérez Jiménez was forced into exile in 1958 as a result of growing opposition to his increasingly brutal dictatorship among elite sectors, the Church, and the general populace. But the democracy that followed continued his project of state-led modernity (Coronil 1997).

If you return to the subway and travel east five stops to the Bellas Artes Metro station, you will be confronted with the enormous Parque Central complex. The complex consists of two fifty-six-story glass towers constructed during the 1970s and 1980s where numerous government ministries and agencies are located. Around these buildings are eight forty-four-story buildings—seven dedicated to apartments and one to a hotel. These ten buildings are conjoined by a multilevel shopping center with breezy openings to the street, small shops, and grocery stores. Parque Central tells a similar tale of fading modernity. Elevators are in perpetual disrepair, paint is falling off the outside of the buildings, and the dirty labyrinth of parking and shopping below has become a favorite place for pickpockets and thieves. In 2004, as if to add insult to injury, a small fire on the thirty-fourth floor of Parque Central East turned into an uncontrollable blaze because sprinkler systems had not been maintained. The fire consumed ten floors and had to be extinguished by military helicopters.

If you return to the Metro and continue east to the Chacaito–Altamira corridor, you will find a completely different context. The mirrored glass–clad office buildings and shopping malls with small nondescript entrances leading to atrium interiors provide a world apart of efficiency and affluence. After an hour inside one of these buildings it is easy to forget that you are in the so-called third world. When friends or family visited me in Caracas they usually would not even notice the decaying downtown area as we passed by it. But they would be impressed by the glitter and advertisements of the Chacaito–Altamira corridor and would inevitably ask, "Is this downtown?" It was an entirely appropriate question for a historical juncture when economic and even political power was increasingly moved from the modern institutions of the state located downtown to those postmodern institutions tied in to global flows of capital and political influence. To the north and south of this main cor-

The Parque Central complex from Barrio San Agustín in January 2006. The east tower is being reconstructed after the 2004 fire.

ridor you will find residential gated communities—each apartment complex or subdivision with its own security guard. During the fieldwork for this book, I lived in just such a building. It was one of a group of five apartment complexes completely surrounded by barbed wire and with two guarded gates. In addition, each individual complex had its own security guards. Lush green spaces, swimming pools, and a view of the mountains made it a peaceful place apart. The Venezuelan historian Margarita López Maya (2004) calls these commercial and residential spaces "bubbles of modernity in an ocean of insecurity."

At either end of the Caracas valley you will find massive areas of barrios called Catia to the west and Petare to the east. Up all the hills north and south of the modern downtown area you will find barrios as well. These barrios teem with people living in catacombs of informal squatters houses locally referred to as ranchos. While some of these neighborhoods are more than fifty years old, the rule of law does not extend far into them, and drug and crime networks usually have the upper hand.

In *A Tale of Two Cities* Charles Dickens describes the dramatic contrast of poverty and wealth existing side by side in London's industrial revolution of the mid-nineteenth century. At the turn of the millennium, Caracas makes for an altogether more complex story. With its colonial past almost imperceptible, Caracas has three cities that coexist: the decaying modern city, the affluent context of global networks, and the marginalized informal city. Under the aegis of oil revenues, an ambitious and grandiose modern city was built on the ruins of a poor, weak, and fractured colonial society. But by the 1990s this modern city struggled for relevance—overshadowed by the ever-increasing power of the global networks of capital and influence, overwhelmed by the massive informal city. Members of the latter were never fully incorporated into modernity and are even more marginalized from global postmodernity. This book focuses on one set of cultural strategies members of the informal city use to gain agency over their lives in postmodern Venezuela.

FROM MODERNITY TO POSTMODERNITY

With Pérez Jiménez ousted from office by a military coup with broad popular support, democracy was reestablished in Venezuela and a new constitution written by political elites who above all aimed to ensure the stability and the continuance of the regime; there was a consensus among them that the previous democratic experiment had been undermined by the intensity of conflict between conservatives and liberals. In the following decades they maintained legitimacy among the population by using the state's oil wealth to attend to both the consumption demands of the majority and the accumulation demands of private capital (Crisp, Levine, and Rey 1995; Karl 1995; Lander 1995; Navarro 1995; Neuhouser 1992; Salamanca 1997). The achievements of Venezuela's modern period were considerable. Annual growth in the gross domestic product averaged 5 percent between 1958 and 1980. Immunization drives and health care development dramatically increased life expectancy, lowered infant mortality, and led to a threefold increase in population between 1950 and 1990. A country that was 50 percent rural and illiterate in 1950 was almost 90 urban and literate by 1990 (Salamanca 1997). Table 1 demonstrates that in this modern period Venezuela went from a poor, sick, and uneducated population to a relatively prosperous nation in full demographic transition.

The elite-pact democracy of 1958–98 maintained political legitimacy on the one hand by elections in which the public could participate and on the other by the establishment of autocratic parties and the formation of pacts and commissions by which elites and organized interests could guarantee a disproportional voice in policy making and electoral options. Given that this period was characterized by the breakdown of democracies in Chile, Brazil, Argentina, and a number of other Latin American countries, Venezuela's stability is remarkable. Social life was comprehensively dominated by the state. The private sector was supported by state contracts, incentives, and protections; and political parties developed clientelist networks of patronage down to the most micro of levels. Incipient civil associations were usually co-opted by political parties; those that remained autonomous usually became mere machines for obtaining state resources (Lander 1995). The Catholic Church had a significant if not strong social presence, focusing mainly on education and disproportionately on elite sectors. Non-Catholic religions experienced little growth.

Venezuela's state-led modernity began to unravel in the early 1980s with the drop in oil prices and resulting fiscal crisis. While the currency was first devalued in 1983, successive governments postponed structural change as long as possible, until in 1989, under the guidance of the International Monetary Fund, a severe structural adjustment package was implemented. In 1996 another round of structural reforms were pushed through. The economic figures after 1980 are sobering. Through the 1980s and 1990s the percentage of the government's budget dedicated to paying interest on foreign debt steadily increased. Per capita growth for the decade of the 1980s was –3.2 percent. In the 1990s it was –0.3 percent (Ocampo and Martín 2003). And this economic decline changed the labor market. As work became more "flexible" workers progressively lost collective bargaining rights, social security, and health benefits (Barrantes 1997; Cariola et al. 1989; Cartaya and D'Elía 1991). As can be seen in Table 2, the real story is not so much unemployment but remuneration. Between 1981 and 1997 unemployment almost doubled, but more significantly, in 1997 real wages were 37 percent of what they were a decade earlier. The figures in the table, dramatic as they are, hide the magnitude of the socioeconomic decline in the 1980s, as 1985 is the first year data are available. From 1981 to 1988 average family income declined by 43 percent. Among the bottom 10 percent it decline by more than 50 percent (Cartaya and D'Elía 1991: 43). Thus increased poverty and inequality is not explained by unemployment but rather the growing number of the working poor (Cartaya and D'Elía 1991: 72).

Of course, the economic decline hit some much harder than others. Table 2 clearly reveals the decline of Venezuelan modernity and the bi-

Table 1. Venezuela's Demographic Transition

	Population (millions) and Intercensal Growth Rate	%<12	Crude Birthrate[a]	Infant Mortality[b]	Life Expectancy[c]	Illiteracy	HEC[c]
1930	3.12 (11%)	—	28.4	152.4	34.0 ('26)	—	—
1940	3.71 (19%)	—	35.7	116.6	42.8	—	75.17
1950	4.97 (34%)	43.5	43.7	75.0	51.8	50.5%	69.87
1960	7.35 (48%)	45.7	45.9	53.9	58.5	36.7%	61.23
1970	10.28 (40%)	45.6	40.1	49.3	66.0	23.5%	56.21
1980	15.02 (46%)	40.7	32.8	43.3	65.1/70.6	15.1%	48.64
1990	19.33 (29%)	38.2	29.9	24.2	66.7/72.8 ('85)	9.9%	45.7
1998	23.24 (20%)	34.0	25.3 ('97)	21.4	72.7	7.0%	42.52

SOURCES: *Statistical Abstract of Latin America;* Chen and Picouet 1979; *U.S. Census Bureau International Data Base.*

[a] Determined by the number of live births per thousand, midyear population.

[b] Number of deaths per 1,000 live births.

[c] Number of years a child born can expect to live (figures divided by slash represent separate numbers for male and female).

[d] Index that combines several health, education, and communications indicators. Index measures the scaled percentage decrease necessary to bring the United States and Venezuela to equality.

Table 2. Evolution of Selected Economic Indicators

	Government Interest Payments (as % of federal budget)	Urban Unemployment (as % of workforce)	Evolution of Real Wages (100=1990)	Poverty (% of households)	Poorest 40% (% of national wealth)	Richest 10% (% of national wealth)	Caracas Murder Rate (per 10,000)
1981	5.9 ('80)	6.8	—	22	20.2	21.8	15
1986	11.4	12.1	187.1	27	16.3	28.9	11
1990	16.0	11.0	100.0	34	16.8	28.4	28
1992	16.6	7.8	98.8	33	16.4	28.1	41
1994	16.7	8.7	75.9	42	16.7	31.4	59
1997	21.9 ('96)	11.4	69.7	42	14.7	32.8	38

SOURCE: *Statistical Abstract of Latin America.*

furcation of Venezuelan society into a globally networked minority and a marginalized majority. In 1981 the poorest 40 percent of Venezuela's population and the richest 10 percent earned roughly the same percentage of Venezuela's overall wealth. However, by 1997 the top 10 percent earned more than twice as much as the bottom 40 percent.[1] The rate of poverty and indigence has progressively increased (Ocampo and Martín 2003: 236). While Venezuelans of all social classes refer to this period as *la crisis* (the crisis), it is worth noting that similar processes occurred in most Latin America countries (Portes and Hoffman 2003). Indeed, in the period 1975–95 the increase in inequality in Latin America was surpassed only by that experienced in the former Soviet republics (Ocampo and Martín 2003).

As is usually the case, the state's capacity to alleviate the effects of economic disruption declined at the same time that demand increased. Vanessa Cartaya and Yolanda D'Elía (1991) argue that it is not so much the decline in state resources that explains declining state contribution to equity. Rather, the institutional breakdown of the Venezuelan state has meant inefficient and ineffective use of these resources and prioritization has not been based on need. Job cuts have come not where they are needed but where state workers are not organized. As a result, organized labor has effectively fought to maintain state institutions that are ineffective and duplicate the missions of other agencies. Cartaya and D'Elía describe the process as follows:

> The struggle over distribution [of state resources] . . . ended up protecting the strongest instead of the weakest, reinforcing in this way the strong process of economic concentration. In addition, the social safety net deriving from the labor market weakened as the structure of this market changed and as the labor movement worked to preserve their privileges. The better part of the movement consisted of public employees—not exactly the poor. (1991: 115)

During Venezuela's oil-funded modern period, state provision of benefits to the poorest sectors of society tended to flow through clientelist ties rather than institutional channels. So when the resources that flowed through these ties dried up, there were few institutional means and little organizational experience with which the poorest strata of the popula-

1. These figures go far toward explaining the process of political polarization that would develop during the presidency of Hugo Chávez.

tion could have demanded their fair share of the shrinking pie (Cariola et al. 1989: 40).

This economic decline seriously undermined the legitimacy of the state and Venezuelan society in general. The announcement of austerity measures in February 1989 resulted in El Caracazo, several days of rioting, looting, and marshal law. López Maya (1997) argues that this was the beginning of a "cycle of protest" that saw more than four thousand demonstrations between 1989 and 1993. In 1992 two attempted coups by nationalist sectors of the military failed but resulted in hundreds of deaths. Opinion polls throughout the 1990s made it clear that the general populace saw corruption as the number one cause of la crisis. The year 1993 saw the destitution of President Carlos Andrés Pérez for misuse of state funds, and another former president is still being investigated for corruption carried out through exchange controls. Corruption was and undoubtedly still is a problem: a study carried out during the period of this study rated Venezuela as the most corrupt country in Latin America (*El Nacional,* June 2, 1996). However, focusing on corruption as the source of la crisis rather than a manifestation of it or at most a catalyst misses the dynamics of global restructuring.

Venezuelan modernity was stitched together in the second half of the twentieth century not only through oil revenues but also by becoming an imagined community founded on a teleological myth of future social welfare. Progress in the form of giant construction projects was everywhere, and any individual who had not benefited could be assured that well-being would arrive in the future. La crisis has largely undermined this national project as a unifying cultural framework for the population. Luis Ugalde and colleagues, in their exploration of violence in the 1990s, argue that it represented a cultural watershed:

> From a cultural point of view, [El Caracazo] was a cathartic expression of the unresolved contradiction between an optimistic national image—encouraged and formed by political and economic elites—and the new pessimistic socioeconomic scene that undermined the basic principles of that image.
>
> The national image saw redistributive paternalism and egalitarian morality as the model for public decisions and consumption as the goal of personal and family fulfillment and contained a naive optimism in which the future was a mythical place of well-being—all made inevitable thanks to oil profits.
>
> [But] the new economic scene saw an exponential drop in living standards, a deepening of class differences, an intensification of the exhibition-

> ism and ostentation of Venezuela's new rich, a continuing process of concentration of decision-making power in the hands of small party cadres, and the loss of confidence in the institutions and men who control the political system. (Ugalde et al. 1994: 42)

At the time of this study few people believed in the promise of an egalitarian Venezuelan modernity. A largely disillusioned and marginalized majority struggled through the worst of times, preoccupied with basic social reproduction. The globally networked classes worried about the decline of Venezuelan modernity but were largely resigned to the "inevitable" economic logic of structural reform and dulled by the fact that for many of them, these were the best of times.

SURVIVAL STRATEGIES AND NEW SOCIAL ACTORS

The decline of Venezuelan modernity has atomized the lower classes. Just as the benefits typical of modern Venezuela were experienced by the lower classes as the goodwill of patrons, the problems most characteristic of the socioeconomic crisis—declining wages and work conditions, unemployment, and unmet nutritional needs—are now experienced not as structural issues but as individual- or household-level predicaments to be addressed through "survival strategies" rather than concerted political action (Barrantes 1997; Cariola et al. 1989; Ugalde et al. 1994). C. Cariola et al. (1989) outline three basic strategies. The most obvious is a decrease in consumption. Families reduce the quality and quantity of the food they eat, the clothes they buy, their investment in housing, education, transportation, and household goods. Alternatively, they seek to find additional sources of household income. This strategy includes the main provider having more than one job—for example, waiter during the day and cab driver in the evening—and more members of the family working. Increasingly, households with the father as sole provider have given way to ones in which women and children work for wages too. Often this work is in the informal sector, including licit activities such as local commercialization of goods or household production of food such as cakes or empanadas as well as illicit activities such as prostitution or drug distribution. Similarly, stability for navigating uncertain income comes from cultivating ties of reciprocity and solidarity, usually family ties (Barrantes 1997; Cariola et al. 1989; Gutiérrez 1990). Finally, Ugalde et al. (1994: 30) point to the increase in forms of escape such as gambling, substance abuse, crime, and violence—each of which can fulfill the double role of providing escape and providing the illusion of financial solvency if you win at gambling, successfully sell drugs, or pull off a robbery. All these survival strategies constitute ways that members of the informal city attempt to maintain or regain a sense of agency with respect to their immediate life circumstances.

Alongside these survival strategies new forms of political mediation have developed. The state/parties hegemony and political pacts that once ensured stability no longer have the resources to address the demands of an increasingly diverse, urban population fully connected to the mass media (Crisp, Levine, and Rey 1995; Karl 1995; Lander 1995; Navarro 1995). More and more new social movements—environmental action groups, neighborhood associations, women's groups, labor unions, religious associations, among others—are forming new spaces for political life that do not pass through the mediation of the party-state complex and do not justify themselves in terms of "the programmatic political rationality that was traditionally offered to the country as the path to the construction of a modern society" (Uribe and Lander [1988] 1995: 23). Cariola et al. (1989: 131) argue that Venezuelan political discourse has bifurcated: "On the one hand, there is a neoliberal discourse that . . . doubts the state's ability. On the other hand, if more timidly and with less social and political power, there is a discourse that criticizes the party-state relationship on the part of small, independently organized groups and movements and which promotes a model for the organization of society that is based on solidarity and looks to improvements in quality of life considered in integral terms" (see also Barrantes 1997: 119). Although these new social actors may not be significant in terms of numbers, they possess "symbolic effectiveness" (Uribe and Lander 1995). Through the mass media or through public demonstrations, a relatively small movement can affect public opinion (López Maya, Smilde, and Stephany 2002).

But of course the new social movements and associations hardly fill the gap left by the restructuring of the state and the withdrawal of political parties from social life, as they have largely formed among the middle and upper-middle classes among whom they are referred to as *la sociedad civil.* Those who are most acutely affected by the restructuring—the popular sectors—are precisely those who lack the resources and experience to effectively organize at a collective level and tend to cope through individual and household-level survival strategies (Lander 1995: 88). Indeed, the immense obstacles confronting the development of associational life within Venezuela's popular sectors are well documented.[2] But it is here that Evangelicalism has been exceptional in its success. The class distribution of Evangelical groups is similar to the overall class distribution of the population. However, their particular strength—what they can do that nobody else does—is their ability to attend to these hard to mobilize sectors that have been left without a voice. Evangelicalism is just one of a number of different forms of popular mobilization that have grown among the popular sectors.

Evangelical groups in Caracas are what Manuel Castells (1997) would call "reactive movements of communal resistance." In his view such groups occurring among those marginalized by the global network society seek to reestablish their place in the world and preserve their threatened way of life. But in this book I seek to understand Evangelicals on their own terms. Doing so reveals that, in contrast to Castells's analysis, Evangelicals clearly develop "project identities." In other words, they clearly develop a proactive sense of agency with which they can change aspects of their life circumstances. Evangelical meanings provide individuals with a way to get a cognitive fix on the processes that are affecting their lives, gain control over their selves, reformulate social relationships, and overcome obstacles to associational mobilization. Thus Evangelicalism provides not only an individual and household-level survival strategy but also a collective response to la crisis.

EVANGELICALISM IN VENEZUELA

While Protestants have been present for centuries in Venezuela, their presence was long confined to small immigrant communities who brought their religion with them. Real penetration of foreign Evangelists began in the mid-twentieth century with the establishment of Presbyterian missions

2. The School of Social Psychology at the Universidad Central de Venezuela has as its principal research focus the problems of establishing nongovernmental organizations in the popular sectors (see Wiesenfeld and Sánchez 1995).

in Caracas and missionaries associated with the Scandinavian Free Church tradition in Maracaibo. Presbyterian missions never really took off; they still account for only a handful of churches in the Caracas area and concentrate their efforts on the prestigious Colegio Americano (see Ríos Troconis 1986). Growth really only began with the period of urbanization after midcentury but was still modest because of the relative peace and prosperity of that period. As late as 1990 David Martin (1990) could point to Venezuela as an example of a highly secularized society in which Evangelicalism was making little progress. The chapter on Caracas in a 1984 book on Latin American cities written by a North American missionary, John Maust, is titled "Caracas, Venezuela: Secular City." Maust writes, "You wonder if success didn't dull the people's spiritual sensitivities. Something must explain why, proportionally, the city's evangelical church ranks among the smallest in any Latin [American] city" (55). Indeed, until the end of the 1980s Venezuela provided relatively infertile ground for Evangelical growth compared to other Latin American countries. But it has been dramatic since then as the percentage of population that considers itself Evangelical roughly doubled in the decade of the 1990s.

Venezuelan Evangelicals are primarily Pentecostals. Not only have Pentecostal churches and denominations led Evangelical growth in the past two decades; non-Pentecostal churches have grown to the extent that they have adopted aspects of Pentecostal doctrine, meanings, and forms of worship. The essential elements of Pentecostalism are spirit baptism, the belief that the Holy Spirit can enter the body and possess the individual and thereby take hold of his or her life; faith healing, the belief that God will heal the physical ailments of those who truly believe in his power; perfectionism, the belief that moral perfection is a goal for this life; and premillennialism, the belief that Jesus will return and usher in a millennium of Messianic rule (Dayton 1987). Pentecostals are more enthusiastic and less fundamentalist than North American Evangelicals. In most churches faith healing and speaking in tongues are the norm, and being "born again" is taken for granted. Venezuelan Evangelicals do not dislike the term *Pentecostal* and often incorporate it in the names of their churches. However, they prefer to call themselves Evangélicos, denoting their (professed) prioritization of the Gospel,[3] or Cristianos, denoting

3. For this reason, I refer to them as Evangelicals instead of Pentecostals. Apart from the usual ethnographic desire to use emic terms whenever possible, it also avoids distract-

their "Christocentrism" (and implicitly delegitimizing Catholics as not truly Christian). They see themselves as attempting to return to the religiosity of the primitive churches and closely follow the Epistles of Paul. Traditional Pentecostalism of the type analyzed here has recently been accompanied by the growth of *neo-Pentecostal* churches that cater to the upper-middle and upper classes.[4] During the time of this study, Evangelicals constituted approximately 5 percent of the population in Venezuela, evenly distributed among social classes.[5] The image of Evangelicals being largely a phenomenon of the lower classes is both correct and misleading as it is generally used. Members do come primarily from the lower sectors but not disproportionately so. It is predominantly a lower-class phenomenon because most Venezuelans are lower class.

Bryan Froehle points out the strong affinities between Pentecostalism and notions common in popular Catholicism—such as the intervention of the spirit in everyday life in both positive and negative ways. The strong influence of Afro-Venezuelan culture on the popular conscience should also be kept in mind. The image of the trickster self—as the individual caught between countervailing tendencies—is central to the Venezuelan ethnopsychology (Austin-Broos 1997). Venezuela's magical, spiritist religious traditions as well as increasingly popular new age religions all focus on liberating individuals from nondescript negative energies or harnessing them for their benefit (Pollak-Eltz 1994). Pentecostal Manichaeism is an easy extension of this religious logic. The Pentecostal self is one that can protect itself from negative spiritual influences—now seen as originating with Satan—by maintaining communion with God in ritual and conduct. As with the trickster, it is a process in which the individual is continually placed in novel predicaments. But in the Pentecostal context the solution is not clever improvisation but rather the continual search for communion with God through prayer, worship, and scrupulous observance of Evangelical norms. Another reason for the success of Pentecostal forms of Protestantism is their organizational adaptiveness. In most Pentecostal organizations the requirements for becoming a pastor are nothing more than the demonstrated ability to evangelize and the individual's "testimony": his or her recognized reputation for exemplary behavior and appearance of being controlled by the Holy Spirit.

---

ing variation between the term used in the analysis and the term used in the interview data. The Spanish word *Evangelio* translates in English as "Gospel."

4. For a discussion of the growth of neo-Pentecostalism throughout Latin America, see Cleary 1997.

5. Paul Freston (2004) now puts the figure at 7 percent.

Holy Spirit Pentecostal Evangelical Church in the downtown neighborhood of El Silencio.

Pentecostal organizations, therefore, have an almost unlimited ability to meet demand. Furthermore, it is thought that if the spirit is truly present, then God will provide. Therefore, Evangelists frequently go out or are sent out with virtually no financial support and are forced to find ways to attract followers. As Jaime Banks, leader of one of the largest autochthonous Venezuelan Pentecostal denominations, told me, if an individual truly has the spirit, "he can sit on a street corner using a milk can and stick as a drum" and attract a following.

As Froehle (1997) argues, Pentecostalism has spread largely through the mission efforts of individual churches and small-scale organizations rather than well-financed large-scale initiatives from transnational organizations. As a result Pentecostalism in Venezuela is rather disarticulated. Nevertheless, the image of a collage of intolerant, competing, even warring factions is not accurate. Non-Catholic Christian groups that accept the doctrine of the Holy Trinity are, in most cases, remarkably civil and cooperative with each other. The Pentecostal Evangelical Confraternity of Venezuela (CEPV) is an umbrella group for most Pentecostal Evangelical churches; the Venezuelan Evangelical Council (CEV) gathers together most Pentecostal organizations along with Baptists and Free Church organizations to pursue common interests. In addition, in most urban centers of any regional importance the Fraternity of Evangelical Pastors generally functions as the most important local governing body.

TWO CHURCHES

This book is based on three years of participant observation centered on a large Pentecostal Evangelical church in Caracas. During the time I participated there, Emmanuel Church had about five hundred members—although nobody seemed to know for sure. It began in the late 1950s with the efforts of Puerto Rican Baptist missionaries. However, the congregation quickly became dominated by "manifestations of the spirit" and escaped the control of the missionaries, breaking away and moving to its current location. After slow but steady growth in the 1960s there was a struggle for control of the church with about half of the members wanting to follow the "Jesus only" United Pentecostal movement that rejects the Holy Trinity. The leader of those who did not want to follow the movement, Pastor Antonio González, maintained control of the church and the building. Slow but steady growth continued through the 1970s and 1980s but became explosive growth in the 1990s. The church developed a federation with the Emmanuel name, which by the late 1990s gathered together more than one hundred churches that were either spawned by missionaries from the "mother church" or came to affiliate with the organization.

The mother church is located in downtown Caracas next to the Nuevo Circo bullfighting ring and the Nuevo Circo bus terminal. The area is one of bars, flophouses, brothels, liquor stores, lottery ticket and horse betting kiosks, and other small businesses that cater to travelers and those who work or scam in and around the seedy bus terminal. In the hundreds of visits I made to the church during my fieldwork, I witnessed countless street robberies, fistfights, and bottle fights, as well as police chasing, beating, or shooting at supposed criminals.

From the back door of the church on any given evening you can look across the street into the vacant lot to watch a homeless person construct a lean-to out of cardboard, a young man do drugs, or a couple of malandros making secret plans. Almost without fail at some point during the church service, a drunk stumbles in from the street and either just observes or starts to make a scene up front near the stage, saluting the pastor, dancing, or pretending to be possessed by the spirit. Usually one or two of the *hermanos*[6] proudly suggest that the individual sit down to listen to the service. Occasionally he or she accepts the invitation and may even receive a prayer at the end. But sometimes the drunk continues to disrupt the service and is brusquely escorted to the door by one or two young hermanos waiting for the opportunity. The small city block on which the church is located serves as a turnaround for the bus terminal, so every couple of minutes a bus comes by, making a deafening racket that drowns out the preaching and, depending on the wind, sends a cloud of diesel fumes through the paneless windows.

The church itself is easy to miss unless one is looking for it or passes by during a service for it has no sign with its name on it. Inside there is a large sanctuary with four large sections, each with about twenty well-crafted homemade wooden pews. With a mixture of affection and derision, members refer to the building as *el ranchón* (the big rancho) not only because of its undecorated, slightly dilapidated appearance but also because it is in a perpetual state of change—typical of the progressive construction that characterizes popular Venezuelan architecture. Periodic surpluses are invested in building supplies, which are used whenever a group of church members put themselves to constructing a new wall, painting, putting up a new roof, and so on. When I started attending Emmanuel Church in spring 1996 the new high aluminum roof had already been put up. But the walls had not yet been raised so the old, low, leaky roof was still in use. In one corner, next to the pulpit and stage, was the pastor's office—a small one-room affair with two desks and a window, which, when opened, afforded a view of the sanctuary. On the other side of the stage was another makeshift cubicle in which two secretaries worked. Between the office and the stage was a door that used to lead to a damp storage space where the assistant pastor had a small library with about a hundred books he used for the church's Bible institute and a small desk on which sat an old computer a member had donated. Above the sanctuary were twelve ceiling fans hung from the rafters with improvised iron construction bars bent into hooks at each end. Some of them worked well. Others menacingly gyrated at each link, with a resulting loss of rhythm and effectiveness. Nobody else seemed to be bothered by the whirling danger looming above, but I studiously

6. *Hermano* means "brother" in Spanish and is the most common term Evangelicals use to refer to each other. In English, because of its use in African American slang, the term does not capture the same meaning, so throughout this book I use the Spanish.

avoided sitting below the fans for the first year of my fieldwork. After a year or so, beyond any conscious decision, I too forgot and freely sat below them. Also hanging from the rafters were fluorescent light fixtures of the type meant to fit into a hung ceiling, looking absurd in their isolation. On top of the pastor's office were a couple of dozen old rusting classroom desks stacked on top of each other. In marked contrast to the dilapidated, improvised, "backstage" feel of most of the sanctuary were eight twenty-inch Peavey amplifiers strategically placed throughout. I thought the amplifiers provided remarkable sound and at dull moments occasionally tried to calculate how much they must have cost, but members and leaders frequently criticized them, arguing that the church deserved something better. Toward the back of the sanctuary there were several rooms without ceilings that could be used for discussion or storage purpose, as well as the inevitably dirty bathrooms with plumbing in various stages of disrepair. The "prayer circle," however, had a ceiling, as well as benches incorporated into the walls. The floor and walls were nicely tiled in light blue. This space functioned twenty-four hours a day, seven days a week, as space for members to get together, pray, and share testimonies.

During the course of my research, the old roof was finally taken down, and the walls were raised and given a fresh coat of paint. On each side the last stretch upward was no longer cement block wall but aluminum siding. On the street side the members who had put up the siding had accidentally put it on the outside of the eave troughs, with the result that when the troughs overflowed during the torrential downpours of the rainy season, those sitting on that side would get splattered. In December 1996 Pastor Antonio proudly announced to the congregation, who enthusiastically applauded, that the Lord had blessed them and that a new hung ceiling would be installed. However, this never happened because other opportunities appeared. In 1997 the owner of the two storefronts next to the church offered to sell, and Pastor Antonio quickly bought the space. In 1997 and 1998 hermanos, both paid and volunteer, built a three-story edifice in the space. By the end of my research the first-floor space, destined for new offices, was still used to store construction materials. The second floor, on the other hand, had been made into half a dozen small classrooms for Sunday school. The only ventilation for the whole floor came from two windows in the one classroom next to the street, whose door was usually closed. The other classrooms quickly became stifling hot when more than a few people congregated in them. But

Emmanuel Church in 2006. The back one-third of the building, including the prayer circle, has been demolished for construction of a new subway line. It will subsequently be rebuilt.

I never heard anybody complain. The top floor served as a large meeting place, with good ventilation, and also as a space to deposit extra building materials. Here the young men's Sunday school class met, as well as the Bible Institute during the week. The outside of the church also received a coat of stucco and paint (and later a new rock facade). A large sign with the church's name was put up for a while, but when the letters started falling off, it was taken down and a replacement was not sought. A year after the old roof was finally taken down, the large columns that supported it and blocked the view of the pulpit from some seats were finally knocked down with sledgehammers. Once, while making conversation with Pastor Juan at the back door of the church, I mentioned that I admired the fact that they devoted more attention to internal organization and activities than to the building, something rare among Venezuelan organizations. He responded that they did not care about a beautiful building: "We're getting ready [slap of the hands and upward motion] to go to Heaven."

The church holds services every night except Thursday when the Sunday school teachers meets to go over the next Sunday's lesson guide.[7] The Monday night service is led by the Lady's Society. The Tuesday night service is led by the Men's Society. On Wednesday is the prayer service the first hour of which consists of individual prayer, after which the pastor preaches for half an hour and takes prayer requests. Friday night is Bible study, also led by the pastor. The Saturday night service is led by the Young People's Society. On Sunday there is a morning service lasting from approximately 9:00 A.M. to 1:30 P.M. and an evening service of praise that begins around seven o'clock with singing led by a member of whatever association is in charge of the service. Then come prayer and announcements, a sermon, an offering, prayer requests and prayer, and a final altar call for anyone who wants to "receive the Lord" that night. In theory the prayer circle is open every night for vigils—all-night sessions of prayer and testimony sharing. On Fridays and Saturdays dozens of members usually attend the vigil (when it becomes too large, they move to the sanctuary). During weekdays, a handful of people attend at best, frequently no one. In those cases the live-in janitor closes the church door for the night. The most important service, of course, is on Sunday morning. It officially runs from 10:00 A.M. until noon. But there are usually people in the sanctuary already in the early-morning hours, having spent the night in the church in "vigil." From around 7:30 to 9:00 A.M. this vigil moves from the prayer circle in the back to the front of the sanctuary. Around 9:00 or 9:30 someone starts to lead singing from the stage, which goes on for the next hour or so. By 10:30 one of the elders of the church offers words of inspiration, followed by a call to break into Sunday school groups. The men go to the back of the church to get solid wood dividers painted light green—some of which have blackboards on them. They quickly fashion between six and eight makeshift classrooms in which Sunday school was taught. If the weather is nice, the older gentlemen go to the grassy field bordering the Avenida México a block up from the sanctuary. When the annex was done, most of these classes met in the new classrooms on the second and third floors. During my fieldwork, the classes were taught by individual members using photocopied materials obtained from the Church of God, headquartered in Cleveland, Tennessee. I sat in on innumerable Sunday school classes and found them extraordinary spaces of discourse where biblical concepts were applied

7. These guides are photocopied from a book of guides published by the Church of God. However, this is the result of Pastor Antonio's and other leaders' appreciation of their content rather than any official contact with that organization.

directly to the issues confronting members of Caracas's marginalized majority, discussed and argued over. After Sunday school Pastor Antonio makes announcements and delivers a sermon. Singing follows. On weekends the singing often continues, getting faster and faster and eventually leading some people into spirit possession—revealed either by uncontrollably dancing, speaking in gibberish, or collapsing backward into the arms of other members. However, this rarely happened on Sunday mornings. The pastor then places an altar call for those who would like to accept Jesus, or those with ailments, followed by a prayer in which he touches the foreheads of those who respond to the call. The service concludes anytime between 1:00 and 2:30 P.M. Unlike the church I grew up in, where a fifteen-minute deviation in either direction would produce complaints, I do not recall even one discussion of the length of services. Indeed, I suspect that if you had asked anybody the next day how long service had lasted, they would be hard-pressed for an answer.

During the services, the pews are roughly divided between men in the two blocks on the right side and women in the two blocks on the left side. Occasionally married couples separate to sit on different sides. The official reason for this gender separation is to facilitate concentration. However, the distinction is not enforced, and couples or families sitting together on one or the other side or individuals sitting on the side of the other gender is rarely commented on. Rather the two sides of the sanctuary are like two poles of a continuum, each dominated by one gender. Pastor Antonio occasionally mentions with pride that in Emmanuel Church there are approximately as many men as women. In fact, I found that during the weeknight services men often outnumbered women; at the Sunday services women usually outnumbered men. When asked about this phenomenon, one of the assistant pastors said it could be attributed to the location of the church. He pointed out that if you watch the street during the day, the great majority of those circulating in the area were men. And at night almost all were men. This he attributed to the primary commercial activities of the area—bars, brothels, and auto repair shops—as well as its dangerousness, especially at night. It is difficult to know whether it is a result of the greater numbers of men in the church, or source of attraction, but it is also worth pointing out that in Emmanuel Church one sees relatively less possession by the spirit and relatively more Bible study than in other Evangelical churches. At minimum this supports arguments regarding the elective affinity between women and "the spirit" and men and "the Word" (Weber 1978: 488–90). Members are expected to participate in whichever association corresponds to them, the Young People's Society, the Lady's Society, or the Men's Society. However, if it is well known that work or family commitments impeded participation, an individual is not pressured to join in.

Evangelical practice is not limited to church services. Sunday afternoons are spent by active members in various mission projects—visiting hospitals or a neighbor whose baby died, bringing food to a senior, or circulating through downtown handing out pamphlets and witnessing to people in the streets. And this activity continues during the week, as permitted by other commitments. For example, noon services at the downtown Plaza El Venezolano are run and maintained by the Christian Coalition Front—a group of three or four men led by Pablo Costa and a couple of other rotating members who make decisions about who is going to preach, the next move in the ongoing struggle to obtain permits for the plaza services, and any other logistical problems that arise. About half of the regular attendees and preachers in the plaza are from Emmanuel Church. The other half are members of other Evangelical churches who for reasons of work or residence are in the downtown area around noontime. A service with one of the more gifted preachers such as Ramiro can bring a crowd of two hundred people. During vacation periods or when a less gifted preacher is present, only a handful of people will listen. Much of my initial participant-observation was conducted at these daily plaza services. This I found to be a fascinating crossroads of Evangelicals and interested sympathizers, meeting in an unofficial context that permitted the free exchange of ideas and a prominent public space that lent itself to moralizing on politics and social issues. I quickly became friends with Ramiro and Enrique. Not only were they my age, but they also shared my interest in social and political issues. In this they were not typical Evangelicals, but as will become clear throughout this book, fellow members by no means considered them atypical. Indeed, almost every member is atypical in some way.

Emmanuel Church and Pastor Antonio have a leadership role among Caracas Pentecostal Evangelical churches. In 1996 Pastor Antonio was in the second year of his presidency of the CEPV, which he helped to found some years earlier. Also, the church's central location made it a convenient place to hold CEPV meetings or campaigns and other activities cosponsored by several churches. More informally, it was frequently visited by Evangelicals from other churches in the area. Given this leadership role, its location in the downtown area, and its large size, I decided to gain experience in a more typical smaller church in a barrio.

After visiting several small churches that for various reasons did not seem suitable, I began to participate in Raise Your Voice to the Lord Church (hereafter referred to as RYVL Church). I became acquainted with the church through Augusto Pinedo, a member who on his own initiative organizes and almost singlehandedly carries out services in the plaza next to the subway station in Petare. With bus stops all around it, the plaza is a crossroads for members of the enormous group of barrios named Petare, at the eastern end of the Caracas valley. Augusto preaches every day from 4:00 to 6:30 P.M., even leading the singing despite his hoarse and raspy voice. He took me to his church one Sunday morning in February on a harrowing motorcycle ride, and I visited frequently over the next eight months.

Walking to the church from the Petare subway station means walking past a bus turnaround and up a road that winds through the lower part of Petare toward Guarenas, a satellite community of Caracas. The sidewalks are usually so cluttered with street sellers' stands and people waiting for buses that it is much easier to walk in the street. There, large buses roar through the streets, never slowing down for the pedestrians who scatter like chickens in front of a farmer's pickup. Walking up the road one passes a cemented-in trash dump, made for two large dumpsters. But there are no dumpsters, and the perpetual pile of garbage quickly rots in the tropical heat, resulting in a permanent stench in the area. The highway runs parallel on one side and barrios rise up from the other side. People are everywhere, coming and going, standing around talking, or waiting for public transportation. The third barrio from the subway station is Barrio Miranda, as indicated by an arch over the entrance to the area. It has one narrow street going down and then up the hill. Branching off of this are countless walkways leading to ranchos farther up the hill and not contiguous with the street. One side of the street is used for parking, and there is one lane for driving. Frequently, and more commonly as one gets to the end of the street, an individual will leave a car in the middle of the street until someone honks or starts yelling insults for it to be moved. At the bottom of the dip on the left is RYVL Church.

The church has approximately one hundred members that pack into the first floor of a three-story rancho in one of Petare's barrios. It originated by splitting from a "free" Evangelical church that did not observe the strict norms of Pentecostal Evangelicals. They met for a while in a sanctuary lent to them by a Lutheran church. When the Lutheran church sold the building, RYVL Church purchased its current location.

The pastor and core group of members are actually from Las Minas de Baruta, another group of barrios on the other side of the city. But most of the rest are from various barrios in Petare. Like Emmanuel Church, RYVL Church also does not bear any external signs that it is a church. The first floor has a small stage with a pulpit and fold-up chairs for the congregation. The left side has ten rows of four fold-up chairs reserved for men; the right side has the same number of rows but with five chairs each reserved for women. They too have services every night and twice on Sunday, using a scheme similar to Emmanuel Church. Sunday morning services are usually packed, and the poorly ventilated building is stifling. The second floor has a makeshift office with a desk for the pastor and several spaces in which Sunday school classes meet. The third floor has a kitchen and more meeting spaces.

I found virtually no differences at the level of individual members between RYVL and Emmanuel Churches. There were perhaps more families in this church but also a solid constituency of young men coming from problems with substance abuse and delinquency. The social class composition was the same, although even more homogeneous than Emmanuel Church. Whereas the latter had a few members from humble origins who had become professionals or had made money in small business, members of RYVL Church were uniformly from the lower working class. RYVL Church did, however, reveal the more rigorous organization made possible by its small size. Services began and ended more or less at the same time each week. The brief survey I carried out with extreme difficulty in Emmanuel Church was done easily in the smaller church. And all of the ten respondents to my interviews showed up the first time for our appointment. At Emmanuel Church I frequently had to persist through three or four broken or missed appointments to succeed in carrying out an interview.

After several years of being independent, RYVL Church joined with a Venezuelan denominational organization called the Peniel Church. In addition to providing a support network and access to materials, such as indoctrination booklets and Sunday school guides, the affiliation also enabled Pastor Vincenzo and several young people to receive theological training in the denomination's Bible Institute. Both the Emmanuel and the RYVL Churches are typical in the sense that they are members in good standing of the Evangelical organizations mentioned above and would be accepted by most people who consider themselves Evangelical. They each have some small doctrinal peculiarities—in RYVL Church, for example, women wear veils during services. But pastors and members regard these differences as insignificant and do not see the need to debate them with other churches.

ETHNOGRAPHIC PERSPECTIVE

I began my work with each of these churches by attending services—as I did at about a dozen other churches in and around Caracas. This generally led to conversations with members, which in turn led to an introduction to the pastor. Above all, Evangelicals are meaning makers who want to let others know about their new way of being in the world. Thus having a foreign sociologist come to their church as part of his research was generally the cause of celebration and enthusiasm. Anybody who has done fieldwork with Latin American Evangelicals knows that one of the first questions an ethnographer is asked is, "Are you a Christian?" Having grown up in a highly religious enclave of Dutch immigrants in western Michigan and still being a believing if not very observant Christian, I always answered, "Yes." This inevitably created a certain misunderstanding as for them this meant an Evangelical just like them. As it turns out, however, I grew up in a mainline Protestant congregation, originally became interested in Latin America through liberation theology, and abide by few of the behavioral norms observed by Venezuelan Evangelicals. I did little to highlight the differences between my beliefs and practice and theirs but never lied if asked. This did not require much effort on my part, as the very idea that I might differ on key points of doctrine was rarely even imagined.[8]

No ethnography is "objective" in the classic positivist sense. Rather, its subject matter is the unique result of interactions between a particular ethnographer and particular informants (Nepstad 2004). The currently fashionable trend of identifying one's "biases" provides no solution. When this identification is treated as a way of controlling for "distortions" in order to get closer to objective reality, it merely sneaks the positivist impulse through the back door. More useful, in my view, is ethnography that describes scenes in which particular informants with particular characteristics interact with each other in concrete settings of

8. There were a few times when my differences with my informants were exposed. As the resident *sociólogo* I was invited to be a regular contributor to an Evangelical radio talk show focusing on social issues and reluctantly assented. The first show went fine as it treated suicide and I gave a summary of the difference between alienated and anomic suicide. The situation deteriorated in my next two appearances, however, as I argued that evolution was compatible with Christianity and then argued that homosexuality had always existed, was not increasing, and that the proper Christian attitude to it was based on the Apostle Paul's message that "the most important of these is love." While I had worked hard to make my view palatable, the producer stopped the interview several times to see if I she had heard me correctly. She eventually finished the tape but never played it on the air. She never invited me back either.

which a particular ethnographic researcher is an integral part. Descriptions of ethnographic perspective, then, only provide a first step toward that goal. The characteristics of the ethnographer should not be seen as limitations or biases but simply characteristics that affect the reality that was created and therefore the generalizations that can be made. My religious upbringing—including religious education from first grade through college—not only gave me quick entrée into my research sites but also a background in the religious ideas and practices my informants worked with, as well as some direction regarding creative tensions in the meaning system. In that sense I think my ethnography might penetrate the meanings and practices more than other ethnographies do. However, my familiarity with the discourse meant that I might not have had the analytic distance that a lifelong agnostic or person of another faith tradition might have had.

Even after three years of participant observation, I never became "one of the people" and was always treated as something of an anomalous stranger—a status that generated suspicion among some, interest among others. As important as my status as a white foreigner was my class status as a Ph.D. candidate with a car, living in an upper-middle-class part of Caracas. Most of the people I studied had not completed high school. Some of them could not read. Many of them lived on the equivalent of a couple of dollars a day. For example, while on average Emmanuel Church would have five hundred or so people attending church on Sunday mornings, there were generally only ten to fifteen cars there. I initially considered many manifestations of class and educational differences to be cultural differences, as virtually every aspect of "otherness" I confronted was subconsciously interpreted as a symptom of backwardness. This view changed radically by the time I was done with my fieldwork and even more as I wrote the dissertation that would become this book. By far the most important impact on my view was having two children with my Venezuelan wife while living in Caracas. This fundamentally changed my engagement in Venezuelan society insofar as it truly pushed me from observer to participant. Participating in a world of doctors, nurses, preschool teachers, breast-feeding advocates, and other parents gave me a project in common with other Venezuelan adults. Having to communicate, cooperate, negotiate, and fight about something vitally important to me destabilized the categories with which I experienced Venezuelan culture. The degree of creativity, responsibility, knowledge, and effectiveness I encountered undermined once and for all the implicit culture-of-poverty views I had gone into the field with. It is not that I finally comprehended the other. Rather, I found myself playing intellectual catch-up, humbled by Venezuelan social skills and wisdom and deeply questioning my own assumptions about parenting. These experiences affected my interpretation of my data, moving me from a presupposition of otherness that needed to be tolerated to a presupposition that my informants and respondents were people searching for the same things, using the same basic tools, as every other human being.

One other characteristic of my interaction with the field has an important impact on the final product. This is a book by a man, about men, as men. Within the first month of my fieldwork I found myself developing a rapport with two Ramiro and Enrique, who were close to me in age, shared my interest in social activism, and were each raising children at a time when I was beginning my own family. Committed to an approach to ethnography that begins with lived experience and is grounded in bodily location (Bender 2003; Smith 1990), I cultivated these relationships. Of course, our rapport and common interests never came close to bridging our otherness. However, it gave us occasion to collaborate and address similar issues together—a process that more often than not highlighted contradictions in our ways of addressing these issues. In seeking to complement this participant observation with in-depth interviews, my grounded focus on male informants turned into a necessary focus on male respondents. The life history interviews I had in mind often focused on highly personal subject matter that could only be addressed one on one. Pilot interviews showed that doing one-on-one interviews with a woman behind closed doors was not an acceptable practice among this population. Even if it had been, establishing with women the rapport I would need to cover sensitive personal issues such as sexuality and relationship problems was unlikely.

While this means generalizations from my data must be made with care, it provides an important opportunity. Research on women and religion, as well as on women and development, has generated so much interest precisely because it facilitates an analytic move away from abstract theologies and teleologies and toward lived practice, grounded meaning making, and relational reasoning. This book replicates many of the findings of these subdisciplines but in a study of marginal men in Caracas. As such, it provides an important extension of their empirical reach. I will have more to say about this in chapters 5, 6, and 8.

PART TWO

Imaginative Rationality

RATIONALITY IN THE SOCIOLOGICAL STUDY OF CULTURE

The question of whether people can decide to believe not only affects our understanding of Evangelicalism and empowerment in Latin America; it runs through the center of contemporary sociological research on culture and religion. In the past twenty-five years approaches that portray people as strategic actors who consciously choose their meanings have reinvigorated the sociology of culture and religion after the decline of the modernization and secularization theories of the 1950s and 1960s. However, these approaches are increasingly being criticized as reductionist, incoherent, or incomplete by scholars who recommend a return to emphases on religion and culture as autonomous symbolic systems that cannot be reduced to instrumentally rational action. In what follows I look more closely at this debate and point toward the alternative path taken in this book.

CULTURE PRACTICE AS INSTRUMENTAL RATIONALITY

Much contemporary sociology of religion focuses on religious and cultural practices as forms of agency that are chosen by people according to the challenges they confront. Stephan Warner (1993) has portrayed this as a paradigm shift in the social scientific study of religion. In the old paradigm, based on the European experience of secularization, scholars saw meaning as the main function of religion and predicted that, in modern pluralistic contexts, religion would become increasingly abstract and privatist. In the new paradigm, in contrast, scholars see empowerment as religion's main function and regard religious pluralism as the norm. Whereas formerly researchers of religion concentrated on the construction of meaningful universes and the maintenance of the plausibility of deviant beliefs, researchers in the new paradigm pay attention to what religion *does* for its adherents. So, for example, women become involved in conservative religion to ensure the commitment of wayward spouses. Ethnic minorities see religious participation as a way to preserve ethnic identity and develop self-help networks. And groups on all sides of the political spectrum fight their battles through religion. Thus middle-class white Christians formed the core of the Christian conservative movement, African American churches were key in the civil rights marches, and religious congregations currently play a key role in gay communities and their struggles.

Perhaps the most striking direction taken in this new paradigm is the rise of the rational choice approach. Led by Rodney Stark, Lawrence Iannacone, Roger Finke, and others, the rational choice approach applies the basic tenets of neoclassical economic theory to religious phenomena.[1] While not suggesting that people only seek material self-interest, rational choice scholars see individuals maximizing interests in salvation as well as other religious goods through participation. This allows them to use conceptual tools from market analysis, organizational sociology, resource mobilization, network analysis, and deviance studies with remarkable results. In this approach, rather than a teleological given, secularization is seen as the result of monopoly markets in which religion becomes out of touch with consumer demand. Vibrant religious economies such as that of the United States result from deregulated religious markets in which religious firms compete for clients with their particular religious products. At a more micro level, religious experimentation is considered a normal desire, and rational choice sociologists look for the networks that facilitate or impede experimentation.

Equally influential in actual empirical studies of religion, however, has been the language of "strategies" coming from practice theory. Throughout the 1970s and 1980s Anthony Giddens (1979), Pierre Bourdieu (1977), and others reworked concepts of structure and agency in ways

1. The literature here is large. A good overall survey of the approach can be found in Stark and Finke 2000.

that were widely influential in the empirical study of culture and religion. And in contrast to the more voluntaristic approaches of exchange theory and symbolic interactionism, practice theory emphasizes structure as an important and determining force. In contrast to older debates between material and ideal factors, practice theory does not distinguish between symbolic and material structures. Structure is seen as reaching down into the subjectivities of individuals. However, it never fully determines social process and is always fragile. Practice generally reproduces structure, but practice can change structure through improvisation. In these emphases on the power of structure, as well as on inequality and conflict, practice theory is quite different from the rational choice perspective. However, the rationalistic model of action it uses is fundamentally similar. In practice theory, argues Sherry Ortner (1984: 151), "the model is that of an essentially individualistic, and somewhat aggressive, actor, self-interested, rational, pragmatic, and perhaps with a maximizing orientation as well." In practice theory culture and religion are seen as improvised and used by strategically calculating actors. Here ideas and subjectivities were deemphasized in favor of default portraits of strategic actors. For example, in his classic analysis of the Kabyle of Algeria, Bourdieu (1977: 133) says religious and magical beliefs are actively "misrecognized": "The whole truth of magic and collective belief is contained in this game of twofold objective truth. The group lies to itself producing a truth whose sole meaning and function are to deny a truth known and recognized by all, a lie which would deceive no one, were not everyone determined to deceive *himself*."

Other trends have also facilitated a view of culture as something people use in action rather than something that acts upon them. The "sociology of culture" movement has steered away from emphases on deeply held beliefs that consistently influenced behavior in favor of an antisubjective emphasis on culture as publicly available codes and discourses that people marshal to their own ends. Ann Swidler (1986) conceptualizes culture as a tool kit of resources that people can use to pursue their ends. Wendy Griswold (1987) offers a "cultural diamond" in which a "cultural object" can be distinguished from those who produce the object, those who receive it, and the social world in which it arises. The goal of antisubjective approaches is to move beyond ambiguous concepts of culture and ethereal assertions of culture's causal importance (Wuthnow 1987). Here as well the implicit model of the social actor is that of the rational maximizer. Rather than culture consisting of cognitive templates that affect actors behind their backs, culture is seen as external to actors and providing resources that could be used in conflict or other life projects.

What all these approaches to culture and religion have in common is that they explain culture in terms of instrumental rationality.[2] That is to say, culture is portrayed as a means for achieving some goal external to it. This trend has considerable strengths. It explains the vibrancy of religion and other cultural discourses in the postmodern period. It does not recur to oversocialized views of actors determined by unconscious cultural structures. Nor does it rely on views of culture as an opiate of the masses or other form of alienation. Its Achilles' heel, however, is a reductionism that undermines the autonomy of culture and religion. Put differently, it contradicts the analytic existence of what it is trying to explain. Bourdieu's critics, for example, argue that if "misrecognition" were an accurate portrayal of collective belief, it would be hard to understand how culture could ever have enough of a grip on people to affect their behavior (Calhoun, LiPuma, and Postone 1993; see, more recently, Smith 2003). And in Warner's analysis of the new paradigm, a revealing tension creeps in. Despite highlighting the new focus on empowerment and the "uses" of religion, Warner (1993: 1070) points out that practitioners of the new paradigm seek to avoid reductionism by acknowledging, "the empowerment functions of religion are latent." That is to say, the empowerment functions are not the overt purpose of religious participation but unintended consequences. This certainly addresses the concern for reductionism. However, it is not actually compatible with the main tenet of the "new paradigm." If the empowerment functions are latent, unintended consequences, what a religion does for adherents cannot enter into the individual's preference hierarchy and cannot therefore be the basis of rational action. The concept of rational action is not intelligible if actors are unaware of their interests (Smelser 1997; Stark and Bainbridge 1987).

Nevertheless, the instrumentalist perspective is still the leading perspective in the empirical study of religion and culture. Most studies, to great profit, openly explain religious and cultural phenomena in terms of instrumentality and leave their theoretical doubts for a disclaiming footnote or aside proclaiming that culture cannot be reduced to instrumental rationality—similar to those noted by Mariz, Annis, and Martin (6–7).

2. Ironically, the rational choice approach fits this description least as it has a clear theory of religious rewards. In the rational choice approach, religion is seen as providing explanations that no other source can. However, here as well the nature of these explanations is largely held constant and not relevant, and religious behavior is portrayed through an unconstructed, literal view of rational action.

CULTURE PRACTICE AS SUBSTANTIVE RATIONALITY

Instrumentalist perspectives have received important challenges that seek to tame its reductionist impulses. Christian Smith (2003: 145) argues that for all its empirical achievements, a convincing account of human motivation is still missing from contemporary sociology of religion and culture, with the result that utilitarian presuppositions of the rational choice approach have become the default portrayal. Smith agrees that human beings can be portrayed as selfish and self-centered but denies that this means this selfishness must predominate or that we must portray individuals in terms of *homo economicus* (31–32). He argues that "humans are not at bottom calculating, consuming animals, they are moral, believing animals" (114). Inspired by the philosopher Charles Taylor, Smith sees human morality as a series of second-order beliefs and norms that stand independent of and beyond the first-order level of desires, inclinations, and choices. The contents of this second order are themselves shaped by "moral orders." Humans necessarily develop belief systems regarding themselves and the worlds they live in; and these beliefs, at their most fundamental, are nonempirical. Moral beliefs provide a worldview, a moral order that affects all of our less fundamental beliefs and determines our desires and interests. For Smith, there are no extracultural interests:

> The idea of cultural tools nicely highlights the potential of strategies of action to be put to use to achieve various purposes. What the image tends to obscure, however, is the essential narrative constitution and ordering of culture. Tools are mere practical instruments for manipulating the physical world. Cultures, however, are epics, dramas, parables, legends, allegories. The meanings and motivations of culture are matters not finally of practical accomplishment but emplotted moral significance. (2003: 80)

Smith's theory provides a clear alternative to the rational choice model insofar as it returns us to the primacy of meaning and moral interests. But he also seeks to steer clear of approaches that portray culture as an autonomous and determinative deep structure. His is a looser view of culture as narrative. Indeed, humans, for Smith, have the capacity to step back, reflect, and shape the moral orders they are socialized into, but of course they can never fully escape the web of culture.

Jeffrey Alexander (2004) is motivated by a similar concern but comes up with a somewhat different approach. Alexander criticizes the "weak program" of the sociology of culture, which exclusively treats culture as a dependent variable to be explained by determination from noncultural factors such as self-interest, social institutions, or social networks. He argues that an alternative is emerging—a "strong program" of "cultural sociology" in which the autonomy and independence of culture is highlighted. The strong program is based on the idea that culture can be analytically uncoupled from nonsymbolic relations. Doing so one can use the tools of hermeneutics and structuralism to demonstrate the internal coherence and meaning of culture, the fact that it is not infinitely malleable, and the way it can have an important impact on nonsymbolic social life and structures.

In contrast to Smith's argument against "extracultural interests," Alexander's position is indebted to Durkheim's dualistic split between symbolic and nonsymbolic reality. In previous work Alexander (1988) outlined a theory of agency in which action has two basic dimensions: interpretation and strategization. The former amounts to understanding, the latter to practical, utilitarian action. Both occur at the same time in the same acts (312). Interpretation can involve both "typification" and "invention." Typification involves the placing of experience under the realm of existing categories; invention refers to the creation of partially new categories when existing ones do not fully fit (314). Strategization refers to that element that escapes the idealist framework, and practical action "certainly occurs only within the confines of understanding, but within the terms of clearly understood events it introduces the strategic considerations of least cost and most reward" (314). Hence Alexander succeeds in adding strategic and normative strands in a multidimensional theory of action.

Smith and Alexander provide powerful alternatives to research based on the assumption of instrumental rationality, clearly reasserting the autonomy of culture as well as its causal efficacy. They, in effect, reaffirm the importance of substantive rationality—practice in which cultural values, norms, concepts, and categories have a preponderant and determinative role in the selection of both ends and means (Levine 1985). But how can we make sense of cultural agency from these perspectives? How can we make sense of the clear cases of cultural empowerment among Latin American Evangelicals? How, for example, can we make sense of Jorge's conversion? Smith could see Jorge as a moral, believing animal that steps back, reflects on, and decides to alter his moral framework in order to enact new moral commitments. But what would bring him to do so? Smith could argue that Jorge would be experiencing his states of dis-ease as a moral malaise and therefore seeks to address it through religion. But Jorge openly states that he became Evangelical in order to overcome a life of drugs, crime, and marital conflict. And he displays an openly calculating perspective on what he is trying to change. Furthermore, the way he describes the changes in his life and how they validate his religious belief system hardly seems "nonempirical."

Alexander could portray Jorge as inventing, partially re-creating, his preexisting categories of understanding, with strategic interests determining which direction that invention goes. But seeing invention as a subcategory of "interpretation" does not render the sense of disjuncture we see in the empirical data. It certainly does not work behind Jorge's back as "unconscious reason," "feelings of the heart," or "fearful instincts" (Alexander 2003: 3). How, with Alexander's cultural sociology, can we understand reflective action on and through, culture rather than rational action limited by the cultural unconscious? Smith's and Alexander's portraits seem more adequate for understanding cultural continuity than cultural change, religious tradition than religious conversion. Conceivably, these approaches could be pushed beyond this. But when they are, they start looking a lot like the instrumentalist perspectives they want to move past.

WORKING TOWARD AN ALTERNATIVE: IMAGINATIVE RATIONALITY

The contradiction between scholars who see cultural practice as a form of instrumental rationality and scholars who see cultural practice as a form of substantive rationality is certainly not new. Nor is the sense of purpose that animates them. While Immanuel Kant saw his attempt to carve out a moral realm that worked on principles different from rationalistic science as a way to preserve human freedom, the British utilitarians he was responding to saw their rationalistic science of morals as a way to undermine aristocratic authoritarianism. While Émile Durkheim saw the preservation of a collective, moral realm independent from individual instrumental action as the key to keeping society together, his Marxist foils saw their materialist theories of culture as a means to undermine bourgeois mystification of class conflict and injustice (Levine 1995). Today, while Smith and Alexander see themselves preserving a realm of human behavior from reductionist impulses that undermine human dignity and freedom, Swidler, Stark, and others working from instrumentalist perspectives see themselves revealing the everyday creative agency involved in cultural practices. But understanding cases of cultural empowerment such as the dramatic growth of Latin American Evangelicalism demands an alternative that builds on the strengths of each of these approaches while avoiding their pitfalls. The approach I develop here accepts the need for a more robust concept of culture but tries to preserve the consciously calculating, strategic dimension of the instrumentalist perspective.

The issue, of course, is a version of the classic dilemma of structure versus agency. How can a structure have power over actors if they can freely choose whether or not they will be guided by it? When applied to culture as structure, the issue becomes whether we can affirm cultural autonomy and cultural agency at the same time. Instrumentalist perspectives sacrifice cultural autonomy and thereby undermine their explanandum. Perspectives affirming substantive rationality cordon off culture from instrumental action but thereby make agency through culture hard to understand. My portrayal follows the lead of Mustafa Emirbayer and Ann Mische (1997) in using a pragmatist approach that overcomes the dualism of meaningful moral order and self-interested rational action by seeing culture as the product of creative intelligence confronting problematic situations. While scholars such as Bourdieu and Giddens have focused on the way agents inevitably modify structure as they carry it out, Emirbayer and Mische seek to expand our understanding of the more reflective, creative moments of agency. People encounter problems, create new projects to address them, and then reflectively evaluate the success of these projects. This is the process I refer to as *imaginative rationality.*

In the next three chapters I portray Evangelical practice as a form of imaginative rationality through which men from Caracas's informal city address the challenges they face in their social context. Imaginative rationality is a way to get things done by creating concepts. People create concepts by combining and attaching existing, usually well-known images to inchoate objects of experience. They thereby gain a cognitive fix on these experiences that facilitates action with respect to them. Chapters 3 and 4 present portrayals of Evangelicals who use religious images to create concepts that identify the causes and character of substance abuse, crime, violence, family conflict, and other persisting life problems and thereby facilitate their solution. In chapter 5 I show that the inchoate experience requiring conceptualization can be religious practice itself. Put differently, I argue that the Evangelicals studied here not only construct first-order concepts about the way the world works; they construct second-order concepts about how they construct those first-order concepts—in other words, how they became Evangelical, how their religious practice works, and which motivations are appropriate for its practice. There is no universal distinction between appropriate and inappropriate goals of religious practice. These distinctions are located in concrete historical, biographical, and even interactive contexts. For believers, the success of religious concepts in foretelling consequences is what validates them. I show also that Evangelicals' conversion narratives are religious conceptualizations of the way religious conversion itself works. In the conclusion I develop more fully this pragmatic theory of cultural agency.

CHAPTER 3

Imagining Social Life I

Confronting Akrasia, Crime, and Violence

Participant observation in hundreds of services and events, as well as with church members in everyday life over the course of three years, left me with little doubt that hardship and suffering have permanent seats in Venezuelan Evangelical discourse. Exhortations to gain control of one's life through Jesus Christ were mixed with warnings of what will happen if one backslides from the Way, were interspersed with testimonies about God's power to resolve intractable problems and impossible situations. My findings agree, then, with the dominant social scientific interpretation that Latin American Evangelicalism is a religion oriented toward those experiencing sustained life problems, or dis-ease.

There is good reason to maintain a critical distance from the discourse of suffering. Because Evangelicalism, like all forms of revival Christianity, has a "once was lost, but now am found" narrative at its center, it is entirely plausible to believe that it might have little to do with any biographical facts of adherents but rather serves as a means to shore up charismatic capital. Pentecostals may well exaggerate suffering and hardship of their past for the purpose of demonstrating Joblike purification or to demonstrate by "how far they've come" that they have God on their side. After nine months of participant observation, I had serious doubts about many of the stories. Some of my key informants, such as Ramiro, seemed like such solid individuals that I could not imagine them having dark and troubled pasts. I fully expected that by spending time with and rigorously interviewing them, contradictions would surface as the truth emerged. In a grant proposal I wrote

Table 3. Frequencies of Conversion-Precipitating Problems

Life Problem	Number of Occurrences (% of Evangelical respondents with problem)
Substance abuse	24 (44%)
Gambling	2 (04%)
Violence	18 (33%)
Economic difficulty	8 (15%)
Self-improvement	8 (15%)
Emotional difficulty	8 (15%)
Conjugal conflict	11 (20%)
Family problems	7 (13%)
Peer social life	7 (13%)
Health	2 (04%)
Concern about the afterlife	2 (04%)
Other	4 (07%)

just before I began my structured interviews I stated my expected findings: my respondents' narratives were ex post constructions that functioned to provide them with spiritual authority. I thought I would be able to demonstrate that culture can facilitate action by distorting the past. Nevertheless, despite using a methodology designed to break through narrative constructions of the past by uncovering concrete details about life events (see appendix B), I found that among most of the men I interviewed conversion did indeed follow important life problems. Table 3 provides a summary of the problems encountered through life histories that coincided with the conversion period. These frequencies would likely be much different among female respondents as the declining viability of the patriarchal role especially affects men and likely leads them to have more problems with substance abuse, crime, and violence. On the other hand, women often experience the worst manifestations of these issues when they have abusive, unfaithful husbands who contribute little to the household.

The Evangelical meaning system provides my respondents and informants with metaphors they can use to conceptualize or imagine their social context, the problems that afflict them, and the means for overcoming them. Metaphors work by taking images from a better-know "source domain" and applying them to an inchoate "target domain."[1]

1. I am following common scholarly usage that seeks to maintain simplicity by using the term *metaphor* even when referring to metonymy, synecdoche, simile, and other tropic forms of classification (see Fernandez 1991).

For Venezuelan Evangelicals, the supernatural—as reflected in the Bible, as well as common sense and traditional Venezuelan spirituality—is the source domain from which they draw images used to predicate a specific target domain: problematic elements of their social lives. Put differently, Evangelicalism provides adherents with action-oriented metaphors that elucidate dimly understood problematic elements of their lives. Of course, these concepts are at clear variance with those that social scientists would use for the same purpose. But they can actually work better for certain purposes—such as overcoming the sources of dis-ease described in this chapter and the next.

AKRASIA: ALCOHOL, DRUGS, AND GAMBLING

A little more than 40 percent of the Evangelical men interviewed here were experiencing serious difficulties with alcohol, drugs, or gambling when they became Evangelicals. Male culture in Venezuela is a drinking culture. Given persisting patriarchal norms proscribing male-to-male expression, drinking is one of the few ways men have to achieve the emotional openness necessary for bonding with other males. Alcohol is present at most social events in general and at virtually all social activities men engage in. Any given night of the week around the working-class areas of Caracas one sees innumerable bars and restaurants, frequently open-air, with men sitting around tables drinking *tercios*—one-third-liter bottles of beer. Waiters generally leave the empty bottles on the table when they bring another round. While the explicit purpose of this technique is to be able to count the bottles at the end of the sitting instead of running a tab, it also renders testimony to macho tolerance of alcohol. A good night's drinking can result in a table with dozens of empty bottles. Men also get together and drink in the street. Especially in the barrios where small abastos sell beer, a few men get together and buy rounds, or someone buys a crate of thirty ten-ounce bottles to share. Drinking provides a forum for male bonding, and buying rounds reaffirms important norms of reciprocity.

Drug use and gambling are also widespread among the working-class and marginal sectors. Drinking in the street is frequently accompanied by discreet cocaine consumption. And drinking in someone's house may be accompanied by any number of different types of drugs. Among adolescents and young men, drug consumption may be the sole activity. As well, gambling in the form of the lottery and especially betting on horses is an extremely important social activity among men. When I carried out my interviews with non-Evangelicals I had to work around Saturday and Sunday mornings when many would not want to miss the horse races. Men get together at their favorite Centro Hípico (bar with off-track betting), watch races together on television, or gather around a radio. Bets are made through officially affiliated kiosks, unofficial dealers, or simply with each other.

The common denominator of drinking, drugging, and gambling is that they offer a break from the stress of everyday life. In Venezuela, as elsewhere, each has an antistructural, antivirtue character that permits a feeling of freedom from the social context and a sense of individual autonomy. While such feelings are important for most people at least some of the time, they are much more important much more of the time for men who daily live the humiliation of unstable employment, the discomfort of poor living conditions, and the hopelessness of fulfilling cultural ideals of the efficacious patriarchal male. Aurelio, one of my non-Evangelical respondents, admits to having a gambling problem. "I do it," he says, "to clear my head!" Eric, an Evangelical from Emmanuel Church, says, in retrospect, that he drank to forget about his marital problems: "You know, sometimes, with alcohol, you look to it as an escape. When your wife says, 'No, I don't want anything to do with you, you'd go to the bar on the corner to drink. You'd go and you'd think so that you could forget your problems." When done in moderation, drinking, drugging, and gambling are affordable means of recreation and relief from daily life. To members of the popular classes, golfing, boating, exotic travel, and fitness clubs are confined to the television screen. Furthermore, the lack of parks, recreational facilities, and green space of any kind in Caracas seriously limits possibilities for organized or impromptu sports activities.

However, these behaviors also have in common the possibility that, rather than affordable breaks with everyday life, they can become serious impediments to it. Any one of them can become the central activity in a person's life or result in destructive binges—however infrequent. And this generally results in a desire to stop or reduce the destructive behavior coupled with the inability to do so. I call this situation akrasia, or weakness of will. Akrasia amounts to a pattern of self-deception in which the individual's overall preferences take a backseat to more immediate preferences. While in general the person would like to lead a sober life, at any given moment, having a few drinks or consuming drugs is a decision that seems to only affect the here and now and the global preference is not focused on. While in general an individual might prefer to be fiscally sound, in any particular case he chooses to bet on horses. Individuals experiencing akrasia experience a sense of dis-ease insofar as they are living at odds with their global preferences (Ainslie 1992, 2001).

Persisting bouts of drinking, drugging, and gambling can, in turn, sap a person's attention and resources from other life commitments and deaden the normal controls on behavior that keep him from perpetrating or being the victim of violent or antisocial behavior. Let us look at these effects in more detail. First, time spent with the guys drinking on the corner, buying and doing drugs, or watching and betting on horses is time that is not spent on other dimensions of life such as bonding with spouse and children, maintaining a household, or taking technical school courses that could lead to improved job prospects. Alberto converted after years of drug abuse. When I asked him about the changes in his life, among other things he said, "I dedicate time to my kids. I dedicate time to my family, my mom, my dad, and I go all day long without needing any vice." At another point in the interview, he said, "When did I ever think about having kids? Never. I didn't have time for sex. All my time was for drugs. Drugs during the day, drugs at night . . . " Vincenzo had stopped drinking in the first years of his marriage. "But when my marriage ended," he said, "I started again. I mean, I didn't have anybody to keep me from doing it. I didn't care because I didn't have anyone telling me not to . . . so it was 'yeah sure, let's hit the bottle today.' Every night it went on until 11:00 at night. I'd go home without eating dinner, eat whatever was cold there, and go to work [in the morning]." When his children started living with him, he continued his lifestyle: "Shoot, I didn't respect them either! I didn't care if they were there. I'd be drinking and having people over, women, and a bunch of friends. My conscience had been blinded."

Excessive drinking, drugging, or gambling can quickly deplete financial resources needed for paying the rent, buying groceries, making home improvements, or other capital accumulation. Drinking frequently involves buying rounds and may involve buying high-status, and costly, liquors such as Scotch whiskey. In addition, the loss of control resulting from drinking can lead a man to spend more freely than he normally would. Drug, especially cocaine, use is especially difficult on financial resources. As is true in most contexts, illegality means informal, high-risk distribution networks that can result in extraordinary prices. Losing at gambling frequently leads to the downward cycle of trying to win back losses. Winning, on the other hand, is generally regarded as a windfall that is used to place more bets or to splurge on friends and neighbors.

Vincenzo had a decent income from his home workshop subcontracting to sew belts and handbags but failed to accumulate capital because of his constant partying: "I worked for so many years. I made so much money with that lady [the contractor] . . . and my house wasn't painted, didn't have floors. I had a little black-and-white television, a washing machine that I had bought and nothing else. I had just built the house, mounted the toilets, a bed for sleeping, and that's it!" The problem is even more serious for those with drug or gambling problems. The larger sums of money involved in these activities means that other sources of income need to be pursued. In the best cases this means the person needs to consume already scarce social capital. Agustín said that before becoming Evangelical, he spent at least half the salary he earned in a meatpacking plant betting on horses: "What I earned I would spend on horses and I would lose it. Then I would have to borrow money in order to be able to buy groceries for my wife and kids."

But in the worst cases, especially common among drug users, family members are objects in the search for the money necessary to maintain a habit. Alberto had spent time in jail for a street robbery. Once out he continued his drug use. When I asked if he had to rob in order to keep up his habit he said, "I would say to her [his wife], 'If you don't give me money, I'll rob for it. And if I rob, I'll go to prison again.' I had her blackmailed and she would give me money."

Ugeth was a crack user before he converted. He lived with his wife and teenager in a room in his parents' home. Because he spent most of his small salary on crack he would not have money to contribute to the household in which he lived. When he did not bring home money on payday, he would have to make up lies to explain to his wife: "I'd tell her lies. I'd say, 'Oh, such and such happened.' But she knew that I had consumed it [in drugs]. I'd say, 'I didn't get paid. This week they didn't pay me. I'll get paid next week.'" This explanation seemed to disarm his wife, but his drug problems had greater impact on his status with his parents, the owners of the house. When Ugeth's son had a fight with and threatened Ugeth's sister, who also lived in his parents' house, his parents decided that Ugeth had to leave and his sister could stay. Ugeth felt that this was because he did not contribute as much as his sister to the household: "I couldn't contribute more money to the household. So they got me on my weak flank. I mean, since I had problems because of my drug use, I didn't have any authority there [in the household] anymore." Ugeth never suffered legal consequences for his criminal activity but did suffer consequences with his family. Many other drug users and gamblers end up in jail or dead because of criminal activity undertaken to maintain their habits. José Gregorio said that drugs are what led him into crime and eventually prison: "I mean it obliged me to rob. It obliged me to commit crimes, to the point of even robbing my own family in order to consume drugs."

Drinking and drug consumption disengage the individual's normal prudence and self-control, leading him to engage in behavior he might ordinarily avoid. Drinking increases the likelihood of arguments and physical violence with other men or with a spouse. Inerio saw alcohol as the cause of his problems with women and violence: "When I had my wits, as they say, I was even-keeled. But when . . . I was drinking beer and had had a couple, I would lose all control with women . . . [and] I got in a lot of fights. I would ask for it. It was really incredible. Alcohol really brought me a lot of problems."

Drinking and drug use caused marital problems for Martín. He usually treated his wife decently if not exactly respectfully, but when he drank and used drugs he became abusive. When he told me this I asked him to elaborate. He answered:

> Sometimes I would force her [to have sex]. Or sometimes I would abuse her just for fun. I'd give her a slap or a kick, just for fun, to see how she cried, whatever. That was then. Later when I sobered up, the next day, [I would say to her,] "Hey, I was drunk. I didn't know what I was doing." I would be sorry. But in the moment, I don't know, just to unload, to bother her, to fight . . .

Of those who were involved in crime at the time they converted, all were drug users. Their drug use not only provided a reason to seek easy money but also would be used to build the courage to carry it out. Miguel Vicente's answer to my question about what problems his drug use actually caused him bears this out: "It would give me courage, strength to commit crimes. If I were going to go rob a business, first I would have to consume drugs because by myself I wouldn't be able to."

On the other hand, substance abuse frequently lessens the users' caution, leaving him open to being victimized by a social milieu that takes advantage of any weakness. Iván converted after a serious drinking problem. In the two years before he became Evangelical, twice he got so drunk at the beach that he passed out and woke up hours later without his belongings, identification, or money. He blames himself: "I should never say that I was robbed. I was the one who would leave my things lying around." José Gregorio ended up shot in the leg when he was drunk and careless: "I was buying liquor, and when I opened my jacket they saw my gun. So they followed me and took my gun from me and I was pretty drunk already. When I tried to defend myself, they shot me with my own gun."

The akrasia characteristic of problematic drug use, alcohol consumption, and gambling, as well as the loss of self-control during consumption, is understood by Evangelicals in supernatural terms. Ugeth explained how his drug consumption got progressively worse as he moved from marijuana to crack cocaine: "It's the Enemy. If you offer him a space, the Devil will come on in. He grabs a man's jugular and destroys him." Andrés said that his drug use and gambling went together. Like many people in this context, he thought he could predict which lottery numbers would appear by finding trends in the numbers from previous days and weeks. He spent inordinate amounts of time doing drugs, smoking, and studying lottery drawings. "The Devil himself puts all that in your messed-up head so that you're blinded," he explained. "And that's where his demons take over."

Akrasia is resolved by Evangelical conversion in a very direct way. Drinking, taking drugs, and gambling are all explicitly defined as contrary to the Evangelical lifestyle. Abstinence from them is seen as both a cause and an effect of being an Evangelical and tantamount to maintaining communion with God. And when one is in communion with God, in this view, God "takes control" of the person and keeps dangerous influences at bay. In chapter 5 I take a closer look at the logic through which Evangelicals see this. Beyond ideological tendencies, the substance abuser or gambler participates in a social group in which many people have had similar problems, in which there is a discourse of caring, and in which the meaning system is continually reaffirmed through discourse and ritual (Wuthnow 1994).

VIOLENCE

In the 1990s Caracas became one of the most violent cities in the world's most violent region. Numerous sources have pointed to inequality, drug trafficking, and impunity as the most important determinants of the crime wave sweeping Latin America—and Caracas has all of these in abundance (Briceño León and Perez Perdomo 2002; Fajnzylber, Lederman, and Loayza 1998; Ugalde et al. 1994). Ugalde et al. (1994) argue that one of the effects of the February 1989 riots was to demonstrate the power of violence and legitimize its use. Table 2 shows that the murder rate jumped after 1989—reaching a high point in 1994 that was quadruple the rate of thirteen years earlier. According to Ugalde et al., violence provides a fantasy of power and control in the face of declining life prospects. The process of atomization in the working classes has also likely played a role. Criminologists now argue that one of the most important predictors of the level of crime in a neighborhood is "collective efficacy"—the feeling, among residents, that they can monitor and sanction members of the neighborhood that do not belong to their own households (Sampson, Morenhoff, and Gannon-Rowley 2002). In neighborhoods with high collective efficacy, neighbors sanction those who break laws and norms because they feel other neighbors share their views and will support their action; in neighborhoods with low collective efficacy, they look the other way, because they do not trust their neighbors and fear retaliation. The downward cycle of impoverishment in Venezuela has diminished this sense of collective efficacy as neighbors compete for resources, work longer hours, and lack the economic well-being needed to overcome immediate self-interest (Barrantes 1997; Ugalde et al. 1994). In fact, many young people involved in crime feel an atmosphere in their neighborhood that compels them to act out, in contrast to, for example, the school environment (Duque and Muñoz 1995).

I originally had distinguished violence from crime, and being a perpetrator from being a victim, but examination of the data led me to see them as parts of one social logic and therefore more usefully examined together. Violence is almost always an extension of criminal acts or involvement in crime networks. And while crimes such as burglary are not carried out through violence, the type of crime that most worries Venezuelans of all classes is violent street crime such as robbery. And while some victims are not perpetrators, all perpetrators are potential victims. We can, however, distinguish between violence that works through the logic of vendetta and violence that is essentially random. In each case Evangelicalism provides adherents with tools to withdraw from or confront the situation.

THE LOGIC OF *CULEBRA*

A common misconception of violence in Latin America is that it is event based, random, and confrontational (see, e.g., Linger 1993). It is an understandable projection of the upper-middle-class fear of being the victim of arbitrary street violence. But Venezuela's institutional vacuum, more specifically, its for all practical purposes absent justice system, means that violent conflict works through the logic of honor and vendetta (Nisbett and Cohen 1996). Such violence is neither random nor sudden. It generally extends through time between individuals and groups who know each other. In popular Venezuelan parlance, vendetta is poetically referred to as *culebra* (snake). Here a humiliation, betrayal, or other interpersonal problem leads one person to assault or kill another. The victim or members of the victim's network—family members or other members of a gang or drug distribution network—must then seek revenge by victimizing someone in the network of the perpetrator. Knowing this, the people in the latter network frequently plan a preemptive strike against those in the opposing network. The result is often a series of killings Venezuelans call a *cadena* (chain) that may take numerous lives and continue indefinitely.

In the car on the way to an Evangelical workshop that Ramiro and Enrique were organizing for young people in a Caracas bedroom community, I had the tape recorder rolling and on the dashboard. Ramiro, as was his custom, carried on an unsolicited, running monologue about the Gospel, being Evangelical, and being poor in Caracas. He was talking about the problems of young people and started to explain the logic of the culebra through a story from his personal experience.

Ramiro: Noooo. I was part of a cadena that only broke after seven dead. It broke after seven dead and when all the others [involved] went to prison or fled, had to leave the sector.

David: What do you mean by "cadena"?

Ramiro: A cadena is like this. Let's say, for example, you being from my sector, I trust in you because you're a man of your word. I give you some drugs. And then you, thinking you're smart *(vivo),* don't want to pay me. So then I give you a deadline to pay me and you don't respect it because you think you're bad too—maybe you're armed too. So then I go and sneak in your house at night and kidnap you with a mask on. I pull you out of your house and I do something really evil to you—I shoot you so that you die bleeding. I don't kill you neatly but rather kill you in a malicious way so that your friends will see and will respect the group. The gang has to seek revenge itself and doesn't inform the authorities. He who informs the authorities is nothing; he's a chicken. You can't let the authorities know about this because the authorities don't enter here. "Here we resolve things ourselves." We used to say, "like gentlemen: to lead, lead." That is the saying.

So in the cadena that I'm telling you about, they killed one of our friends. [First] they stole some drugs from him. It was the brother of a guy who I would hang out with, Pablito Berli. Pablito's brother didn't want to say anything since he knew them [the ones who had stole the drugs from him]. So then some guys came and said to him [Pablito], "Hey, the guys that stole the drugs from your brother are at the bus stop, the same ones that robbed him. Are you going to let it go?" And they handed him [a gun]. I had a .45, another guy had a .38, and another had a 7.65, and he said, "Which one do you want to go settle the score with?" He said, "Let's go with the .38 because it doesn't jam up on me." And he went with another guy who had a .357 magnum. They went to the bus stop and shot him nine times. And the guy's [the guy who was shot] friends took him to the hospital. When my friend told me about it, I said, "Pablito, if you left that guy alive, prepare yourself because there's going to be a massacre here." I knew what was coming.

... So the guy survives.

David: The one who was shot nine times!

Ramiro: The one who was shot nine times. In the hospital he tells his friends. He doesn't say anything to the authorities. What he says is "They robbed me," that's the slogan—"they robbed me." So he says to his friends, "Look, the ones who shot me were X, X, and X"—the names of the guys. I was in Bonaire [working]. So then they come and kidnap the one [Pablito's brother] who they had taken the drugs from. They kidnap him and kill him in an alleyway. The woman I was living with didn't say anything because she knew that I would come back because he was my friend. Since she knew what I was like she said, "No, no, no, don't tell him." So then when I had a week off [and came back to Venezuela], I found out and said, "Why didn't you call me? Why didn't you tell me?" So the friend who I hung out with a lot [Pablito], that was the brother he was closest to and he was consumed by anger. [Some friends came to him and] told him, "The guys that killed your brother were in a bus that just went by." They went and got on the bus and killed the two guys. As it turned out, those two guys had nothing to do with it. We were in even bigger trouble since we had started a problem with some other people [from another barrio] up farther. I say "we." I was in Bonaire, but I knew what was going on. When I came back on vacation again, they would tell me, "They killed X." Another kid that lived in the barrio with us [Augusto] started fronting[2] for the guys. And one Saturday at two o'clock in the afternoon, two guys with pistols came down with the guy who had been shot who could walk again. He pointed to Augusto and the guy grabbed him and bam, bam, bam, bam, bam, bam, they unloaded the two pistols on him. They killed him right there in our barrio. So [our] guys go over there and kill a guy up there. Then they come back and start selling

2. A "front" is the individual who stands lookout for a drug operation. He is the first contact for potential customers and warns sellers inside when police or potential aggressors are near.

again while I was in Venezuela. And they kill another [one of our] guys. Then I left again because I was only home for a week and then I would leave again. Later they shot another friend of mine, one who I used to give drugs to sell. They shot him and almost killed him. He survived by the grace of God. Then they shot Alejandro, another one. Then they killed another guy who had nothing to do with it all, that was number six. He was a manager of an insurance company. Some shooting started, and he ran out to grab his kid who was outside, and bring him in. When he got in he had been shot two times and didn't even know it. He died as they were taking him to the hospital. That was number six. Then the guys went up there again, kidnapped a guy up there and they kill him up by Buenavista. Seven dead.

. . . So when I get back [from Bonaire, Pablito] had left. My other friend had left too. The other brother was put in prison. Everyone went to jail. Those who weren't in jail were dead. Those who weren't dead had to leave the barrio. Everything calmed down. And the gang from up above was slowly all killed. In the end that cadena resulted in seven murders. Those are problems that still, I mean, I'm a Christian, but if those guys [the others involved] see each other, they come up shooting. In fact, they've killed each other in prison. Carlos, for example, was killed in prison, as part of the same culebra. We call it a "culebra." A culebra is something that you have to kill because it can't remain alive. And since a culebra is long, the problem is long. [Laughs] So you have to kill each [motions with hands to show loops in a snake's body] one to eliminate the problem. But since we [those who live in barrios] all know each other, we're family, we all live together, we defend each other. So then I convert to the Gospel.

David: Was that after the problem was over or during it?

Ramiro: During the problem. The problem got so serious that I converted to the Gospel.

Ramiro's explanation of the logic of culebra was replicated by numerous other interviewees and fits well with recent theorizations of the violence of honor and vendetta. Perhaps the most revealing portrayals have been in Latin American cinema, including the Venezuelan movie *Gluesniffer: Law of the Street* (Schneider 1999) and the Brazilian *City of God* (Meirelles and Lund 2002). Culebras often start with drug dealings, but they go far beyond the drug economy, and drugs need not be involved at all. A simple insult or strange look can be enough to initiate an act of violence and begin a culebra. Ramiro added the following at the end of his story:

They always begin for some reason. Maybe I'm from a different sector than you and my girlfriend is from your sector. And maybe you don't like me be-

> cause that girl is highly sought after there and who do you think you are coming and picking up our women. And a problem starts. [Or maybe] you looked at me funny, or you threatened me. So the next time you came to my sector I shot you. Simple and insignificant stuff—that's the way the Devil tangles up humans.

While Ramiro understands the startling fact of insignificant affronts leading to significant violence through Evangelical concepts, from a sociological perspective, Richard E. Nisbett and Dov Cohen (1996: 5) argue that it is part of an economy of reputation and honor: "An insult means that the target is weak enough to be bullied" (cf. Castillo 1997). Thus an insignificant slight may result in further abuse if it is left unanswered. In a context without effective institutional justice, one must rely on one's reputation.

In practice, few people actually rely on cultivating an image of being the toughest on the block. The more typical combined strategy can be seen in the following scene. One afternoon when I arrived at Barrio El Samán to conduct interviews, Andrés and I stopped to talk to some neighbors standing around a local abasto. As is often the case, this abasto was a neighborhood gathering place. Standing nearby as we talked with neighbors was the local drunk whom everyone seemed to know. Seeing me, he stumbled over to introduce himself, saying, as if to make it clear right from the start, "Nobody messes with me, and I don't mess with anybody." The drunk's two-part proclamation was simply a less adorned version of the message beneath a good part of the verbal banter and humor characteristic of members of this environment. In my interviews with non-Evangelicals I presented respondents with conflict situations and asked them what they would do. Respondents often first pointed out their peaceful dispositions but went on to say that when attacked they "go crazy" and do not care what happens as long as they get their licks in (see Bourdieu 1977). As Nisbett and Cohen (1996) demonstrate, in an environment where one cannot rely on institutions to guarantee safety and integrity, one must rely on one's reputation. You must be seen as someone who should not be crossed. But you should also be seen as someone who does not cause problems for others.

Russell Hardin (1995: 121, 153) argues that the original violence may be insignificant when compared to the violence produced by preemptive strikes. If an individual fears attack from another, it is rational to try to preempt that attack by striking first. "You have to strike first, otherwise the bull will take you away on its horns," said one of the malandros Duque and Muñoz (1995: 57) interviewed. The great majority of violence in the barrios is preemptive and is experienced as a form of self-defense (Castillo 1997; Duque and Muñoz 1995). As the Venezuelan saying goes, "You have to kill the culebra before the culebra kills you." This being the case, it is also important for people in certain situations to be able to attach to themselves signs that they will not strike, in order not to draw a preemptive strike. For most members of the popular classes in most contexts, it is in their best interest to cultivate a reputation for minding their own business and not causing problems for others.

For those who, because of involvement in drugs, crime, or some contingent misfortune, have not succeeded in maintaining the equilibrium cultivated by the drunk of El Samán, another solution must be sought. Having victimized or, ironically, having been a victim, one may be exposed to (further) attack. In the broadest terms, one's options are to fight, negotiate, or exit. Fighting usually leads to a continuation of the problem. Direct negotiation is rarely a possibility, but by lying low, and avoiding the problem, it may blow over. Alternatively, one may simply move away to live with relatives, or, as Ramiro did, convert to Evangelicalism. It is generally known that an Evangelical cannot participate in acts of violence and thus is no longer considered a threat. And since he has opted out of the dominant economy of meaning, he is on a different playing field and not "settling the score" with him does not cause his rival lack of esteem. In the prestige logic of vendetta, even pretending to convert is an utter failure and therefore would entail no further action. As such, a convert is likely to be the target neither of an offensive attack nor a preemptive strike. Inerio was telling me how when he converted in his hometown of San Cristóbal, near the Colombian border, he had an ongoing problem with a family that had swindled him of some money he had invested to open a small store:

> I was planning on seeking revenge for that money, and I had a revolver, a .38 I had bought. And I always had some negative thoughts about going and, well, let's say kill one or two [members] of that family. That's what I thought. I would plan it all out. They lived in a house and I thought about going there and, well—[After converting] one thing I had to do—first because that is what God wanted—was to ask forgiveness of all my enemies. They were my archenemies, but God took care of it *(hizo la obra)*. I went there and humbled myself before them. And God took care of it wonderfully. When they saw me, they were surprised because they, I mean, I couldn't even go near their house because they had promised that if I came near them, lead would fly. They were going to shoot me. And I was willing to do the same.

Bartolo converted after living a life of drugs and violence. Telling about his first weeks as an Evangelical, when he faced his neighborhood unarmed for the first time since childhood, he explains how, in his view, God helped him confront the situation:

> I stayed in the *blòque* [public housing apartment building], and I could see how the Lord confronted me with one of my enemies. We used to not even be able to see each other from a distance. [God] confronted me with each of them personally, and I was able to preach to almost all of them. I was at peace and I saw how God freed me from my problems.

Each of these men had an ongoing problem with others that implicated him in the logic of culebra. Inerio's problem is incipient. Both parties are on notice, and he is the one thinking of initiating violence. In Bartolo's case, enemies are coordinated on violent conflict and therefore could make or suffer a preemptive strike. Conversion to Evangelicalism gave both Inerio and Bartolo confidence that they could face their enemies without carrying out or facing a preemptive strike.

AVOIDING AND CONFRONTING STREET VIOLENCE

Crime and violence regularly take first place in opinion polls on public concerns. A group of Venezuelan sociologists have argued that far from a hysterical panic, this concern is based in reality. They carried out a study of victimization based on their own random sample survey rather than official crime statistics, with alarming results: "[The results of our victimization survey] show that the fears of Caraqueños are not unfounded. . . . Three out of every ten of the city's inhabitants have been victim of a violent act [in any given year], and four of every ten have witnessed one" (Briceño León et al. 2002). These figures would likely be much higher for members of the popular sectors. In addition to being more exposed to the poverty, drugs, and institutional vacuum that facilitate crime, they live in spatial conditions that invite crime. Barrios spring up without centralized planning and generally are chaotic mazes navigable only by those who live there and are host to innumerable dark corners where malandros can lie in wait for victims. Outside the barrios, Caracas's streets are frequently so dark that nook and corners are not necessary. Where lighting exists and is working, it is often poorly located. And problem areas arise where the streetlights are in disrepair or where thieves have stolen underground cables. In addition, most people in the barrios are without cars and must use public transportation, exposing them to danger as they wait for buses or walk to their homes from the bus stop. The sum total is that members of Venezuela's popular classes are continually exposed to situations in which they are potential victims of crime. The combined threats of material loss, humiliation, and physical harm are enough to produce obsession with crime among the middle class. Briceño León et al. conclude that everyday conversation in Caracas has been "taken over" by victim narratives and discussion of strategies of how to avoid victimization (Zubillaga and Cisneros 2002). We can assume that it is even more of a concern for those in the popular classes. Evangelicalism helps these individuals in several ways. It provides the feeling of God's protection, the perception that potential attackers respect and fear "the saints," and a set of tools with which to engage attackers.

Evangelicals develop a confidence in God's protection that permits them to go about their daily routines. During my life history interviews, I asked respondents whether they had felt fear for their physical integrity in each of the months we were covering in the interview. I had the following exchange with Renlón, who lived in a violent barrio in the southwest part of Caracas.

"Fear?" He responded as if the question were so obvious he wasn't sure if he had heard me right. "Yeah, of course."

"Yeah? When? At some point in particular?" I asked.

"Well, your normal fear of malandros when you go up,[3] your normal fear. But being in the Gospel, all that fear is gone because God is with you. God protects you."

Fredy explained how he got over his fear in the following terms: "I have my trust placed in the Lord. I trust that he who is with me is more powerful than the one [the Devil] who is with them." Carlos Gómez explained that he still is sort of scared when he "goes up" but feels that God guides him: "The Lord [says,] 'Go this way.' Yeah, he's the one who guides you. And after three years, thanks to God, we will have been here three years and never, nothing [no problems with crime]."

Evangelicals believe—and it seems to be true to a significant extent—that potential attackers have respect for and fear of them because they

3. He says "up" here in reference to entering his barrio. Most barrios in Caracas rise up the hillsides surrounding the valley, where the city is located. "Going up" is synonymous with exiting formal society where there is at least a semblance of rule of law and entering informal society where there is an almost complete absence of rule of law. "Going down" refers to the opposite.

Main street of Barrio San Agustín.

have God on their side. Almost all Venezuelans of the popular classes, whether or not they practice religion, believe in the Christian God and Bible. And popular Catholicism is a religion in which sacred places and objects receive their due respect. Thus a Bible-toting Evangelical is an image that frequently instills enough insecurity in would-be attackers to prevent an assault. In the violent context of Caracas, this is one explanation for conspicuous Bible toting among Evangelicals.

To conduct fieldwork at RYVL Church in Petare, I had to walk about a kilometer from the Metro station to the entrance to Barrio Miranda and then about a hundred meters into the barrio to get to the church. It was a moderately dangerous walk inasmuch as the barrios there had once experienced a lot of violence, but at that time the violence was in an ebb. The main road hosted a lot of petty crime but also a lot of heavy pedestrian and bus traffic. In the beginning, this walk made me nervous. After my second visit, I was outside the church socializing and pretending to enjoy my ice cream while I thought about my walk back to the subway station. Nervous, but not wanting to reveal it, I struck up a conversation with Augusto Pinedo, the plaza preacher who had originally brought me to the church.

"What's this area like?" I asked. It was a question that anybody from that context understood to refer to personal safety.

"Well, there are lots of *malhechores* (ne'er-do-wells), but they don't do anything to us." With the last phrase, he motioned back and forth between where we were standing in front of the church and the main street. He was indicating the space in which the church's Evangelicals were safe. "You walk like this, with your Bible under your arm, and they know you are Evangelical," he said, and took his Bible and firmly placed it under his arm as a demonstration of how to carry it.

This idea was something that I had heard before but only vaguely understood. In fact, my strategy up to that point had been the opposite. I had generally hid my Bible in my bag, thinking that it would be viewed as a sign of weakness, and had concentrated instead on cultivating a distant, preoccupied look and a determined, heavy stride. Afterward I took Augusto's suggestion and carried my Bible under my arm. I do not know if this was the reason I never had a problem in my months of fieldwork there, but it certainly made me feel more confident as I moved through the area.

Agustín, a member of the church and resident of Petare, explained his experience in the following terms. When I asked him about his experience with danger he told a long story about how his brother-in-law had been killed in the neighborhood where they lived and how they had to leave because they were members of the victim's network. This changed, he explained, a couple of years later when he became Evangelical: "After I embraced the Lord, I no longer had that fear. I would walk with my Bible over there [their old neighborhood] and I wasn't afraid of the malandros. Because the malandros respect hermanos. I wasn't afraid anymore. But before I was afraid. I would always hope that I wouldn't run into one of them."

Perhaps the most important tool that being Evangelical provides for navigating a dangerous environment is a prestructured response to attackers that permits them to avoid humiliation and reduce losses while not drawing violence: "reprehending" an attacker or preaching to him. One of the most anguish-producing aspects of living in an environment in which being approached by beggars is a constant reality, and being assaulted is a constant possibility, is thinking about how to react. On the one hand, there is great variation in the persistence of a beggar's request, and frequently begging turns into an assault. On the other hand, giving scarce resources to every beggar is not an option for anybody. And when an approach turns into an assault, the victim usually maintains this attitude and wants to minimize losses by, for example, giving up the petty cash in her billfold while concealing the wad of bills or watch in her pocket. Thus rather than the stereotype of a quick hit, an assault usually has the character of a negotiation extending over thirty seconds or even a few minutes. In the best case the assailant is convinced not to assault. Midlevel success is to get the assailant to take money but leave personal documents, or take something of less value than what the victim actually has. But anything other than silent compliance comes at the risk of violence from an angry, scared, frequently drugged assailant. Most Caraqueños of the popular sectors have been robbed numerous times, and their victim narratives are told in terms of how they engaged the assailant, as well as how much they lost compared to how much they could have lost. Evangelicalism provides a means for such engagement. In everyday conversation, as well as in my interviews, I heard innumerable stories about confronting assailants by preaching to them or invoking "God's authority."

Alberto told me the following story about being assaulted when he was leaving a vigil at 5:30 in the morning.

> I start walking and from a dark corner three guys come out. And I reprehended them. I mean I was in saintliness because I had been praising God all night. They said, "This is a robbery," and I said, "I'm an Evangelical, what do you want? Christ loves you. What are you doing out robbing at five in the morning?" "I want money" [one of them responded]. I saw that he was getting a little nervous and one of them said to the other, "No. He's Evangelical. My mom's Evangelical." . . . And the other one said, "Rob him. Take his wallet, or I'll shoot you." So I don't know, I reacted by giving him my wallet and saying, "Be patient, be calm, Christ loves you." So they took the wallet and looked through it. And I usually only have with me 300 or 500 bolivars. They took it from me, and I said, "Do me a favor and give me my wallet with my ID card and my papers. They're expensive." "Okay, sorry, I just need to buy another *pitillo* [vial of crack]," [he said]. "Okay, but that'll kill you," I said.

Alberto got robbed, but his faith in God and his ability to make meaning of the situation helped him to confront the threat and minimize the damages. He held on to his wallet and identification papers.

Inerio described a more successful confrontation with an assailant:

> I was sitting with my girlfriend and this guy comes up and says, "Give me money, I don't want jewelry, I want money." I was sitting there and I didn't feel afraid like [I used to]. When I used to see a delinquent sometimes I myself would take my watch off and give it to him. At that moment I said, "I am an Evangelical Christian and you're not going to rob me," perfectly. He

> wanted to leave, and I called out to him and said, "Come here." I started to explain to him about the Gospel and preach to him, and I think I even blessed him because he broke down and [repeated] the prayer of faith.

When I first started my fieldwork and began to hear these stories, I was extremely incredulous. I thought these stories were ex post facto heroic reconceptualizations of actual behavior. Certainly, there is embellishment and reconstruction to make the facts serve a purpose, but I found they had an important element of truth. The first such story I heard was Eduardo's recollection of being held up as he and Ramiro walked home through their barrio. Eduardo said that Ramiro had stood up to the assailant and preached to him, but, disappointed and embarrassed, Eduardo said that he, in contrast, had not used "God's authority." I doubted this story; by that time I knew Ramiro well and he had not mentioned it to me. I was somewhat surprised when Ramiro corroborated most of the details and treated it nonchalantly, as something he simply had forgotten to mention.

Spending time with Evangelicals in dangerous situations, I had several opportunities to witness such confrontations firsthand. The following happened with Ramiro himself. I often gave Ramiro and whoever else was going his direction a ride home. It was on my way and saved him a considerable walk and wait at a bus stop in the dangerous Caracas night. One evening I was giving Ramiro and two other hermanos who were staying with him a ride home. At the end of the Avenida Fuerzas Armadas we stopped at a bakery. Venezuelans tend to have a light, late dinner. Among these Evangelicals, this often means some fresh bread with slices of white cheese. That block is a turnaround for one line of urban buses and has an all-night gas station and two late-night bakeries. That night, as was usually the case, there were no streetlights, meaning the only light was provided by storefronts and passing vehicles. The area at that time of night was usually crowded with buses and taxis queuing to buy gas, men chatting and drinking beer, and drug dealers, homeless people, and various other street urchins crisscrossing the six-lane street.

These stops always worried me, and that night was no different. I was tense sitting in the driver's seat as Ramiro and I discussed the survey I was planning to conduct in the church the next day. He was looking over the most recent version of the questionnaire, and I was looking at him and listening to his comments. At one point I saw his eyes widen as he looked past me. I turned to see a man walking rapidly across the street directly toward us. He was drug-addict skinny, with several small scars on his face, and shabbily dressed, his pant leg rolled up to reveal a bandage. As he traversed the last ten feet to my car door he said, "Look, they shot me in the leg and I can't work. Give me some money. I'll get on my knees if you want." As he ended his phrase he facetiously collapsed to his knees in the street with both hands on my car door—over the open window so that I could not roll it up. I was paralyzed, expecting him to whisper that he was armed. But before I had a chance to think about how to react and almost immediately after the potential assailant had finished his sentence, Ramiro responded, shaking his finger, "Get on your knees and seek God!" To this the beggar-cum-assailant immediately turned away, said "Thank you" in English, and ran off across the street with a hyena-like cackle. My heart was pounding. I asked Ramiro, "Did you know him?" He had responded so quickly that I thought perhaps it was a local character from his barrio. Ramiro had already returned to looking at the instrument—obviously not sharing my need to debrief. He looked at me and said, by way of explanation, "No. I'm not scared of what a drug addict can do to me. I have Christ on my side." He turned back to the instrument again, saying, "*Conchale* [Shoot], the Devil interrupted us, what were we talking about?"

Evangelicalism also provides a means for overcoming the humiliation and pain when such confrontations are not carried off skillfully or simply fail. Gregorio told me this story:

> A couple of guys came up to me and I had a jacket on, and a watch. They said, "Give me your money, give me the jacket, give me your watch." I had the peace of God in me at the time, and I said to him, "Jesus loves you. Jesus loves you and wants to change your life." But they kept on: "Give me your money. Give me your jacket. Take it off." And I would say, "Christ loves you," and would keep talking to them about the Lord. Since they kept on, the Word of God came to me, the verse that says: "If someone asks for your coat, give them your tunic as well." Those words came to my mind. [I thought,] "I can't love my jacket or my watch more than the Lord. This is vanity. Praise the Lord because it is he who gives us [things]." So I take off my jacket. "Go ahead, take it," with serenity and peace in God. "Take it." What else [could I do]? And you know what? They took off running like they were scared. *They* were the ones who were scared! And I got home and I was a little—not furious or mad—but yeah, bothered. "But God, I am your child, why did this happen to me?" I said. And there is a verse in the Bible in which Jehovah says, "God will pay back in kind." I thought: "Yes, God. Unleash your anger." And when I said, "Lord, give me revenge," the Lord said to me, "I am large in mercy." "Lord have mercy!" I cried. And I began to cry for those guys that had assaulted me. They are with the Enemy and don't know God, right? I went and asked God to have mercy. "Lord

> please do not let anything happen to them. Let them come to know you." Then I remembered that the jacket had a Bible study guide in it, and I put [the situation] in God's hands. I said, "God, have mercy [on them]."

Evangelicalism gave Gregorio a means to confront his attackers—dragging his feet by preaching to them. In this case it was unsuccessful. But it also provided him with a means to work through his emotions regarding the experience. With Evangelical concepts he turned anger into feelings of benevolence, defeat into victory. He came to see them as the true victims—victims that might be led to God through the Bible study guide he left in his jacket pocket.

CONCLUSION

As the teleological promise of Venezuelan modernity wanes, Caracas's lower-class majority has become ever more marginalized and atomized. They have tended to respond with individual or household-level survival strategies. Most of these strategies are tolerable if uncomfortable. However, the strategies most common among men, such as drinking, drug use, gambling, and crime and violence can seriously worsen the situation. Although these "works of the flesh" can provide a short-term sense of agency, in the medium and longer term they can become a new burden for men and their wives and families. And they aggregate into a larger social context of crime and violence that affects everyone. Evangelicalism can, in effect, provide a man with an "alternative masculinity" (Connell 1987) that can help him overcome and find substitutes for these strategies when they become self-destructive.

CHAPTER 4

Imagining Social Life II

Addressing Personal and Social Issues

The complex of substance abuse, gambling, crime, and violence described in the previous chapter constitutes the most common reason the men I studied gave for conversion to Evangelicalism. Leaving the analysis there would amount to a serious distortion. Often the problems leading to conversion are simply acute versions of the issues of personal development and social connection that most people experience at some point in their lives. The men I discuss in this chapter reported enduring periods of dis-ease that they found difficult to shake. In Evangelicalism they found a package of meanings and practices that helped them to both conceptualize and address their problems.

PERSONAL DEVELOPMENT

Economic Problems

While most of the men I interviewed live in circumstances that would seem desperate to this author and most readers of this book, their expectations are also determined by their class situation. I was constantly surprised when respondents who seemed to me to be struggling through economic marginality said they in fact had not experienced economic problems and could always manage to find the resources they needed. Nevertheless, there were a number of men who reported going through moments in which especially acute economic circumstances broke the equilibrium of their lives. Such moments are gendered in important ways. For men in a society that still holds to increasingly elusive patriarchal ideals, economic problems are not just experienced materially; they undermine important aspects of masculine self-esteem and social status. The ideal of the efficacious patriarchal provider is embedded in social relations, and the man who cannot fulfill this role receives subtle status affronts if not outright ridicule from others (Lamont 2000).

Ismael, for example, converted when he was unemployed. He had lost his job, and because he was unable to support his wife, he faced the ultimate masculine humiliation: he had to send his wife back to her family in Venezuela's interior. "I felt small," Ismael said. "I felt—Imagine, I was thinking about sending her stuff to her house, to San Fernando de Apure, where she's from, because I didn't have any way to support her. I was getting money together to pay her mother [to bring his wife home]. I didn't have work. I had recently been laid off. It had been about a week, and my savings were almost gone."

Juan Zerpa's life started to fall apart when he went through a serious economic crisis. While it caused problems between him and his family, the most serious consequence was the deterioration of his relationship with his girlfriend. As his resources diminished, he lost her respect—culminating in her refusal to have sex with him until he found work. When I followed up on this, he offered a lucid description of the gendered humiliation of unemployed men.

So you two started to have problems when you were unemployed?

Yeah, because when you make money, you know, there is a certain freedom; you have enough to please a woman. Of course, it's not like they [women] want to be with you just for your money. But it is really nice when you treat a woman like the most beautiful thing there is. You take her here; you take her there. And you give her attention. All that costs money! So as long as you can do that, she respects you. But when you have a problem finding a job and you haven't had a job for a while, things change. She is the one who, little by little, begins to dominate you. She is the one who, little by little, starts making the decisions. Even if you want to make the decisions like before, you don't have the face [to do so]. You are embarrassed to say, "Let's go there because I want to," because you know that you're not the one who is paying. So it's like something subconscious. She says, "Let's go here, let's go there." "Okay, let's go," and you can't say anything. So things changed, and she said she was disillusioned with me because I wasn't the same man as before, that I was weak. You see? More than anything else it was that. Because when you don't have any buying power, you don't feel secure in the world.

We do not need to take at face value Juan's description of his former girlfriend's behavior—the breakup may well have had nothing to do with his unemployment—to accept as fact that his unemployment undermined his self-confidence as an efficacious patriarchal male.

Evangelicalism provides a variety of means for addressing economic difficulty. It is frequently argued that participation in Evangelicalism provides networks and contacts that are fruitful for small businessmen (Martin 1990; Roberts 1968). Indeed, after visiting the United States early in the twentieth century, Max Weber (1946) said that Baptist churches function as reputation banks that provide clients with an assurance of a member's honesty. Evangelicals themselves frequently express a version of this logic. I had the following exchange with Ramiro.

> *Do your clients generally know that you are Evangelical?*
>
> Yes, all my clients. When I first talk with them, I tell them that I am a professing believer in the Gospel of Jesus Christ and they trust me a lot. Some clients have paid me a thousand dollars or more without signing them a receipt. They have trusted me because I come recommended and they have the impression that Evangelicals are responsible.

Because most of his new clients are referrals, trust is an important factor in Ramiro's economic success. Furthermore, this reputation translates into networks among hermanos. Membership in a church means that other hermanos both feel obliged to assist an individual and have more confidence in his trustworthiness. As Juan Santiago explained the situation:

> I hadn't worked for something like two years. Doors were shutting all around me. . . . I had gone for two years without work, nothing. "Lord, what's happening?" [I thought.] . . . I met an *hermana* here [in the church after converting], and she introduced me to one of her bosses where she works. And since then doors have been opening all over through the hermana here in the church.

Although all of this certainly happens, evidence for an overall tendency is weaker than one might expect. For example, when Rafael obtains contracts he usually employs other Evangelicals from his church. However, he continually told me about the problems he had with them and once said that he hired them instead of other people who were more capable and responsible because he felt it was his duty to help them get their lives together. In other words, he did not hire them because of trust based on their being fellow Evangelicals. Fernando does work similar to Ramiro and said flatly that he no longer hired hermanos because they did not respond well when he criticized their work. Silvio, who has his own silk-screening business, said he avoids doing business with hermanos because they always want special deals for his work—something he cannot provide with his barely surviving home workshop. After participating in Emmanuel Church for a few months, I became a sort of clearinghouse for obtaining Evangelical workers for various home repair projects and services for my extended network of in-laws. Other than Ramiro, who often helped me at no charge, only in a handful of cases did these contacts pan out. Frequently unanticipated church activities prevented them from showing up when they had promised, or they did not follow up on contacts I gave them. In sum, the importance of employment networks among Venezuelan Evangelicals has more to do with their efforts at mutual support than with their reputation for honesty and hard work. In this sense Venezuelan Evangelicals seem to demonstrate a "caring self" more than a "disciplined self" (Lamont 2000).

Prayer and trust in God did seem to give my respondents the confidence that economic problems could be overcome—confidence that in turn can help them to focus on living one day at a time. When Silvio converted he had economic difficulties, but after converting they got worse before they got better. He had a series of jobs from which he was laid off for one reason or another but always managed to get by:

> God is never going to let me hit bottom. When he sees that I am getting to the point of screaming, he is going to help me. . . . When I think there is no solution, God opens a door for me. . . . One way or another, God opens a door for me. So what does this make me want to do? Keep moving ahead, keep trusting and hoping and waiting for the Lord.

Jorge and his wife eke out a living for themselves and their four children by selling soap products. He said they do not do much business with the members of their church, and when they do it is usually in small quantities. But God is the one who ensures their business's success. When I asked him the following question I was thinking in terms of networks and reputation. Jorge, however, went in his own direction with it.

> *So do you think being Evangelical helps you in your business?*
>
> Yes, I would say so because God protects your finances and your work because there are always envious people, used by the Devil, that don't want others to get ahead and want you to be just like them. But since you read the Bible—Being in Jesus Christ—the Lord sends angels that protect your

> work, that protect your things so that bad influences do not affect your work. And it's God that has opened doors for me with this job. Because before I used to try to sell things, cologne, shampoo, [isopropyl] alcohol, but things would always fall through. People wouldn't pay. Nothing worked out. But now that I'm in Christ, everything is going better.

Jorge grew up in an Afro-Venezuelan family that practiced witchcraft, and his view of "bad influences" carries over into his Evangelicalism. His remarks demonstrate that his faith in God's favor gives him confidence that permits him to live a marginal existence one day at a time.

Self-Improvement

All the conversions to Evangelicalism presented in this book can be seen, in some sense, as having been means of self-improvement. However, there were several cases in which individuals were already undergoing a relatively successful process of getting their lives together, and Evangelicalism was a means to further this progress or consolidate gains. Manuel, for example, felt responsible for his mother after his father left her. When he moved to Caracas to look for a job, he renewed his Evangelical participation to make sure that he would be someone his mother could count on. Fernando's first marriage had ended after he gradually began to spend more and more time in the street and in bars. I asked him if this had caused him problems as well in his second marriage before he and his wife had become Evangelicals. He responded, "I met this woman [his current wife], and I saw that she was a good woman. . . . I left behind the life I was living. I said to myself, 'I'm wasting my life. Where am I going? What am I doing?' So I began to organize my life, you see? . . . And then I arrived to the way of the Lord and here I am."

Enrique told the story that he had started taking life seriously when his first son was born.

> Until that year, I had a sort of sporting attitude toward life. After that year [1990] my life changed a lot. I started to look at things more seriously. I was studying at the university [postsecondary technical school] and starting to take things more seriously, first of all because I felt a lot of responsibility toward my child . . . [and] I began to be concerned about reading, about advancing in my studies, advancing in some personal areas.

Enrique started to participate in revolutionary groups in 23 de Enero where he grew up, in the hope of changing the world his son would grow up in. In a political protest in 1992 the police opened fire, and he received three gunshot wounds that almost killed him. After this, and because he became disillusioned with the greater interest his fellow activists showed in drugs and arms than in study and discussion, he slowly withdrew from political activism. With a coworker he participated in some Tadeo human development workshops and found in Bible study what he was looking for.[1] Having completed all the levels of Tadeo he tried a Seventh-day Adventist church for a few months. But he did not like it. When he went to a noon service at the Plaza El Venezolano near his downtown office, he was taken by the message and converted:

> I realized that [political activism] was not a fruitful method of struggle because we had tried to change men. We had tried to modify behavior, but I realized that many of my companions were still alcoholics. [They] were people that cheated on their wives and in their personal lives had not changed. And me neither! None of us had. I was a leader . . . and I couldn't use myself as an example because I had problems with drinking, with women. I had unstable relationships with two different women. I really did not feel that I was a good example for society. And when I came to the Lord, I saw that there was a model society and I said, "Hey, the Gospel is what I was looking for." I was searching, looking for that model society, and I've found it in the Gospel.

When I asked Enrique what he meant by a model society, he emphasized that in Evangelical churches there was a classlessness that permitted peasants and the uneducated to teach college graduates. "What we didn't get from socialism, we've been able to get from Christ, as a social leveler," he explained. Evangelicalism, then, became a way for Enrique to pursue the desire for self-improvement and involvement in social action that he had developed from the time his first son was born.

Emotional Problems

Emotion suffuses all the conversion experiences of my respondents. It is involved in both the experience of problems and the finding of solutions. However, six of the men I interviewed had emotional problems that themselves posed difficulties. Three of these had received medical attention for depression. The other three described their preconversion condition in terms of persistent emotional distress.

Gregorio told me he had suffered depression in his life, especially during one period a few years before he became Evangelical when a girl-

1. Tadeo workshops in Venezuela are (controversially) sponsored by certain sectors of the Catholic Church and are officially ecumenical.

friend he loved very much left him while he was serving in the military. However, he represented his becoming Evangelical in terms of God miraculously reaching out to him in an experience full of coincidences. He had quit his job and gone to Caracas to pursue a promising music career but instead decided to follow the Lord and dedicate his talents to spreading the Word. When we actually reconstructed the events, however, the sequence changed importantly. He actually had been laid off of his good job as a textbook salesman and was using his severance pay to go to Caracas, record demonstration songs, and submit them to a record company. He had long dreamed of launching a music career. While in Caracas he stayed with Evangelicals he had met through his Evangelical brother and learned about the Gospel from them. In the following, he tells the story of his experience with the record company.

> *So when you got to Caracas you went to the record company?*
>
> Yes.
>
> *And what happened?*
>
> I went there and submitted some demos, and then I experienced the decisive moment in the life of any Christian. I already believed in the Lord and was learning about the will of God. But I was pursuing my own personal wish, my own vanity. "This [record contract] is everything I've ever wanted" *[imitating his mind-set at the time]*. And I spent all my savings on that. And at that moment, God began to work on me, to work on me hard. And I had already submitted the cassette to the record company and I had the copy, the registration slip, where you go with your songs to copyright them. But God was working on me in that first year [in Caracas]. At one point I thought and reflected. . . . And I took the registration slip and ripped it up and threw it in the wastepaper basket and said, "Okay, Lord, I'll follow you."
>
> *And they never called you?*
>
> No. Thank God *[laughs nervously]*. Thank God.
>
> *Hadn't they said that they were going to call you?*
>
> Yes, but I asked God [for them not to call me], and I thank God because they never did.
>
> *They simply didn't call.*
>
> Thank God because—Incredible *[nervous smile]*.

I changed the subject because I had pushed too far already. Gregorio looked uncomfortable and hurt behind his nervous smile. It seems clear that he ripped up his registration after the period in which he expected the record company to get in touch with him. Broke, unemployed, his dream of a music career dashed, he likely saw a world of possibilities in the Gospel he was hearing about from the people he was staying with. During the time I knew him, several years after his conversion, Gregorio was married and had three children and was still trying to get a music career off the ground. His full-time dedication to his "music mission" meant that his family endured continual economic hardship—skinny and scraping by on his wife's meager earnings. I include Gregorio in this discussion because his pursuit of a music career seemed beyond all reason (not only to me, but to others who knew him) and likely was tied to his history of depression.

Of all the men I interviewed, Wilkenman was one who truly seemed to have suffered from serious mental illness. Intelligent, intellectual, and introverted, he fared poorly growing up in a hellish barrio on Caracas's west side—named, appropriately enough, the Asylum, after the state psychiatric ward located there. He said he was continually mocked and frequently beaten up; one of these occasions, probably a rape or another act of humiliating violence—was still so painful to him that he said he did not want to talk about it. It was but one event in a childhood that left him feeling impotent and resentful toward the world. As an adolescent, he spent his days at home without friends, watching television and violent movies and reading anything he could find. He would entertain fantasies of grandeur and develop entire scenes about being powerful, controlling large masses of people and changing the world dramatically. At different times in our three and a half hour interview he said he had wanted to be like or had admired Adolph Hitler, Benito Mussolini, Jesus Christ, Satan, Vladimir Lenin, Karl Marx, Pablo Escobar, and several U.S. presidents. He also described how he pretended to be Simon Bolívar's son, wondered whether he was an extraterrestrial, fantasized about being the president of Venezuela, or a nineteenth-century caudillo, and drew up plans to plant bombs in strategic places in Caracas like the terrorists he saw on the news. When he was exposed to Evangelical radio through his mother and grandmother, he started to listen to it day and night, frequently calling in to radio talk shows. He started going to his grandmother's church and then found his way to Emmanuel Church. In the following he explains how becoming Evangelical flowed out of all of this.

> I wanted to change the world in a radical way and had conflicting tendencies—a struggle between good things that were within me and bad things. So when I arrived to the Lord, I thought, "Hey, with Christ it is possible to

A boy stands at a window in Barrio San Agustín.

> do a lot of things, to save souls." . . . When I prayed and did vigil I came to think that everything was chaos and that Christ was coming soon—so many souls to save, to save the world. I wanted to save the world when I was little. Everything else was rebellion and Satan confusing my mind. I was in darkness, but then the light shone. Now I don't feel like I used to because I don't follow my emotions and impulsiveness like I used to. I am more mature. I know a lot I didn't before. Now I try to look to God for the guidance.

The attempt to save souls provides Wilkenman with a sense of purpose and with the ability to change the world in some way. When I met him Wilkenman was a functioning young man, if not completely stable. At the end of the biographical part of the interview I told him we were going to change the topic, and he insisted that this was because I thought his life was "disgusting rubbish." This gave rise to a sort of interpretive struggle between us over what I "really" thought of him. When I returned five years later I was told that he had quit the church over doctrinal issues and had become Jewish. But during the period I knew him, Wilkenman was active in the young people's association, had friends for the first time in his life, and had begun to study to finish high school. Extreme cases such as his show with clarity the processes that take place with many converts. They feel a deficit of control over some aspect of their lives, or over life in general, and want to gain a sense of agency. Evangelicalism can portray their issues and provide them with a project of change or supplement an existing project of change.

Health

A number of scholars have emphasized the importance of faith healing in a context in which there is inadequate health services. However, such an explanation must be carefully constructed as the notion of sickness in Latin America is much broader than the biomedical perspective typically assumed in the industrialized West. What Diane Austin-Broos (1997) writes about Jamaica is true as well in Venezuela: individual hardship is understood in terms of a bio-moral malaise resulting from negative spiritual influences of all types (see also Scheper-Hughes 1992). Thus frequently what people are referring to when they speak of bodily illness are issues that in the industrialized West would be considered nonbiological. For example, during the six years I lived in Caracas, we had a number of women work in our home to clean and take care of our small children. These employer-employee relationships never ended with the woman frankly explaining that she was unhappy with the working conditions, had received a better offer, or had personal issues to attend to. Usually the women would simply not return after a payday. But when a reason was given, it was always in terms of health; headaches, stomach problems, and dizziness were the most common complaints. When the women were concerned about doing the more arduous cleaning tasks such as ironing or washing windows, they did not demand more money or other compensation but instead insisted that such tasks would overheat them and subsequently cause a chill to enter the body, and therefore they posed too great a risk. They rejected cheap foods for lunch such as black beans or lentils by saying they were hard on their stomachs. I saw this expansive notion of sickness in my interviews as well. Respondents frequently described how their problems with delinquency and drugs would affect family member's health. Alberto, for example, told me that his mother's osteoporosis got better or worse depending on his behavior and church attendance. Rather than insincere manipulation, all these manifestations of sickness should be seen on their own terms: as normal meaning making within a culture that does not naturalize mind-body dualism and therefore does not actively deny bodily manifestations of emotional distress.

"Faith healing," then, is commonly a means of addressing crises of personal and social dis-ease that are inscribed on bodies (Chesnut 1997). None of this denies the importance of issues that would be recognized as "sickness" from a biomedical perspective. Two of my respondents, for example, converted after their relationships ended because of impotence. Orlando and his wife converted after their child's respiratory problems apparently led him to faint. As he told it, their child had "died" but was revived when they called in to an Evangelical radio station to receive prayers. When the child fully recovered they became Evangelicals in an attempt to maintain their health and well-being. They explained, "We have continued to seek him [God] more and more, get closer and closer to him so that he continues to sustain our lives." Some of those who are most likely to see out faith healing are elderly people with arthritis and other incurable illnesses, parents with sick babies, and people with handicaps. Thomas Csordas (1994) has shown that such faith healing can actually work to the degree that sickness is affected by mind-body links.

The Afterlife

An undergirding motivation for this book is to break down rigorous distinctions between sacred and secular, ideal and material, or this-worldly and otherworldly needs. Here religion is presented as a type of action through which needs and goals of all types are pursued. Even the term *salvation* frequently refers to salvation from concrete ills and pressing problems. However, there is one need that is fulfilled only by religion that should be mentioned: the need for assurance of one's existence after death. As Bronislaw Malinowski (1954) argued classically and Andrew Greeley (1995) argued recently, the prospect of an individual ceasing to exist is a disconcerting personal and social phenomenon, and most humans need an interpretive strategy for taking an attitude toward it. Of course, this does not take place tabula rasa. Venezuelans of the popular classes have Catholic notions of heaven, hell, and purgatory, and these frame their attitudes toward death. But a few respondents told of how the clear meanings provided by Evangelical preaching and discussion regarding the afterlife had engaged them.

Renlón converted a few years after his wife had done so, going through a slow process of listening to sermons and participating in Bible studies and vigils. I asked him at one point what messages had stuck with him. He answered:

> One day, the hermano was preaching in our house . . . and what got my attention was that he gave a message. It was so simple what he said: "Liars will not enter into the Kingdom of God." That was it. That was the message that hit me here [puts hand to chest] in the heart. So I started to think, "So is it true what Evangelicals say? *[Pause]* Is it true what my mother-in-law says?" Because my mother-in-law would preach the Word to me, and she would say that, that there is a Hell, that if you die without Christ you go to Hell and everything. She preached all of that to me, the Christ would come again, that he was looking for a people. . . . And that message was what got to me. That hammered at me. That message hammered at my mind.

Orent had originally converted with his mother during an Evangelical campaign. But after being baptized and going to a church with his mother for a year or so, he slowly drifted away. After moving to Caracas and living with a friend, they both converted together at a campaign. In several different places in the interview he described his motivation as thinking that the end of the world was near and that it was time, therefore, to reconcile with the Lord. When I asked about his mother he said that she had continued as an active Evangelical since the time they each had converted and that she would encourage him to become Evangelical again. I asked him what types of things his mother would say to him. He answered, "Well, you know, a mother always gives advice and keeps an eye on you, praying, and fasting. She is always concerned that her children believe in God and gives advice: 'Look, the Lord is coming soon. How is it possible that you are separated from him?'"

For many of those struggling with existence on the margins, shoring up goods in the afterlife is about as abstract and distant a concern as purchasing life insurance. But it has some attributes that explain its high profile in Evangelical preaching and evangelizing: no one can say it does not affect him or her, the stakes are high, and you never know when it will become relevant. For this reason it is frequently used in evangelization as a sort of ace in the hole to which there is no possible response.

SOCIAL LIFE

The second most important group of problems precipitating conversion among Evangelical men is social. By far the most important of these are problems surrounding male-female conjugal relations. Following this are problems with peer social life, one's family of origin, and the unmet desire for social activism. I should note that my discussion here has to do not with social issues per se but with the personal experience of social issues. In each case Evangelical religious practice does not necessarily address the social issue. Rather it helps the individual confront the social issue in a way that he finds satisfying.

Relationship Problems

In Venezuela, as in most places, male-female relationships are among the most problematic areas of social life. Couples who want to be together do not get along as they would like to. One person is unsatisfied with the behavior of the other and wants to modify it. One person wants to end the relationship but cannot find a way to do so. Or a breakup occurs and is difficult to deal with. These problems are common everywhere, but in contemporary Venezuela the attempt to live together in an intimate relationship and share socioeconomic fortunes has been complicated by la crisis.

It would be inaccurate to attribute the matrifocal character of lower-class households in Venezuela to la crisis as it has a long history here as well as elsewhere in Latin American and the Caribbean (Fonseca 1991; Hurtado 1999; Smith 1973). Scholars have attempted to debunk assumptions that matrifocal household are deviant and anomalous by portraying them as rational adaptations to contexts in which men's and women's economic contributions to the household are relatively equal or tilt toward the woman (Smith 1973; Stack 1974; Tanner 1974). A matrifocal household is one in which men as fathers are only sporadically present and power and provision are based on kinship networks that run through mothers and other females. However, scholarly description is a different issue from cultural legitimacy. It should be uncontroversial to suggest that both men and women of Venezuela's lower classes hold on to an ideal in which an efficacious and powerful pater familias, through his work *en la calle* (in the street), provides for his wife and children and exercises dominion over and receives respect *en la casa* (in the home).

That this model never described many Venezuelan families and does so even less now does little to abate its character as a valued cultural model.

One of the main effects of la crisis has been the intensification of labor force participation among household members. Given the rarity of a family wage for working men, women and children increasingly work to supplement family income (Cariola et al. 1989; Cartaya and D'Elía 1991; Tramontin Querales 1999). Indeed, women are frequently more economically viable than men, given their greater readiness to take on cleaning jobs and navigate the continual adaptation that is required of the informal labor market. These processes have accentuated the de facto matrifocality of lower-class families. Both men and women resist formal union when it is clear that men will not be able to consistently contribute to the household; men shy away from the prospect of institutionalized humiliation, and women resist marrying men who present an unattractive risk. When a man commits to a wife and family, the wife is often the de facto head of the household and rebels if her husband makes traditional patriarchal demands for female subservience. To complicate matters, in contemporary Venezuela the idea of getting married and renting or buying a home is elusive for the majority. Usually a new couple and their children stay with one of their parents for several years, bringing along all the normal baggage of in-law relationships. Unable to fulfill the traditional patriarchal role of "hegemonic masculinity," men frequently seek to escape the household in favor of the more satisfying domain of status consumption in the street or bar and extramarital sexual conquest (Bourgois 2001). Such escapes generate further conflict as women, not without reason, suspect infidelity and resent lost resources (Brusco 1995). Marital conflict often takes the form of gendered insults as the woman questions her partner's masculinity and the man engages in misogynist humiliation. Verbal standoffs can turn into physical mismatches when a man begins to batter his wife. The dynamic underlying physical abuse is generally a man's attempt to dominate his wife and/or children (Bourgois 2001; Ptacek [1988] 1998).

The most common way that Evangelicalism addresses a conjugal problem is by providing an interpretive frame through which two people can communicate, negotiate, and come to terms (Smilde 1997). Jorge explained that he and his wife loved each other but would inexplicably fight over nothing. "There was no communication between us until we came to Christ," he said. Martín and his wife were about to separate when they converted, after which their relationship improved on many fronts. But he pointed out in particular how they grew closer when they started waking up every morning to pray together. Eric and his wife had serious problems that culminated when her pregnancy ended in a stillbirth. As Eric told the story, his wife blamed him for this, but becoming Evangelical permitted them to overcome the problem:

> She said it was my fault that the child had died because I didn't take her to see a witch. Somebody had told her that another woman had cast a spell on the child. I mean, I had a girlfriend near where we lived. We had a sort of romance going. And they had told her [his wife] that I had an affair going on with that woman and that she had done some witchcraft so that the child would die. . . . The witch told us he could do a counter-spell that would cost something like 12,000 bolivars [about U.S.$200], which was a lot of money, compared to today. "You can find the money," she would say. "You can find the money." I could, but I wasn't about to give 12,000 bolivars to a witch. . . . When the child was born dead, man, that was hard.
>
> *It affected you a lot?*
>
> Yeah, of course, because you know what it's like to have a child die because you didn't want to spend 12,000 bolivars on a witch? But I stopped feeling guilty when I accepted Christ. And she [his wife] also realized that.

Eric's story seems less incredible when one is aware of the generalized belief in witchcraft among Venezuela's popular sectors. And it probably had a lot to do with his wife's wanting to draw attention to the problems his affair was causing the family. Becoming Evangelical corresponded with Eric's vision of the invalidity of witches. For her, the changes in his drinking and infidelity probably more than made up for her interpretive defeat on this point.

Renlón told me that he and his wife had had serious marital problems. She converted to Evangelicalism first, and he eventually did as well. I followed up on this point.

> *You said that before you became Evangelical you, as a couple, had a lot of problems. What type of problems did you have?*
>
> Well, I would come home drunk, almost every day. I would come home drunk every night at ten, eleven, twelve at night, or at two [in the morning]. So when I would get home she would be mad. She would get mad at anything. We would fight about nothing. I always blamed her. I knew that I was at fault, because I was drinking every day and that tires and bugs you [his wife] after a while.
>
> *And since you became Evangelical how have things gone?*
>
> Good. Thanks to the Lord we've been *[hand motion like smooth sailing]*. We've fought, but it's different now. Everything is calmer, I mean it's not like before when we would throw things at each other and slam doors. Now we don't do that.

How is it different now? When you fight, how is it different?

When I see that she is really mad, I let God take care of it. When I see that she is really mad, I say "Let's talk later" or something. And meanwhile, I look for a way for us to agree on the rules. We always try to not fall [into that]. I mean there are always going to be fights. But not like before because before we used to throw things and yell. . . . But not anymore. I thank God that that has ended because we argue but not like before, now we have more wisdom. I say to her, "No, give a good example. Let's leave it at that, look the neighbors are watching."

These examples show how Evangelicalism can provide a language with which couples can work through their marital problems. As several researchers have argued, this language presents a form of neopatriarchalism that shores up men's authority at the same time that it supports women's autonomy (Brusco 1995; Smilde 1997; Wilcox 2004). While these data only provide the perspective of men, other research has shown that this type of "patriarchal bargain" is attractive to some women (Brusco 1995). Nevertheless, one partner's Evangelical conversion should not be seen as inevitably leading to harmony and consensus. In some cases Evangelicalism gives one of the members of a conflictive relationship a means to understand what he or she is going through and provides a new tool with which to assert power and control in the relationship. This leads to dissolution as often as rejuvenation. Both Ramiro and Enrique, for example, converted in the midst of acute relationship problems despite their wives' lack of interest in Evangelicalism. In both cases the decline of the relationship had much to do with their substance abuse. Becoming Evangelical helped them overcome that problem and gain moral authority vis-à-vis their wives. In both cases their wives left them shortly thereafter. It appears that in each case the damage had already been done; their wives interpreted conversion as the latest in a long string of attempts at self-reform. Furthermore, the Evangelical lifestyle is singularly unattractive for many women who bristle at the idea of not using makeup; not wearing pants, short hair, jewelry; and having to profess subjugation to their husbands.

Juan Zerpa also converted in the midst of serious problems with his longtime girlfriend. With little choice, he consented to abstain from sexual relations with her until he found work. Becoming Evangelical coincided with this difficult moment for him and gave him a sense of legitimacy and power vis-à-vis his partner. The following is an excerpt from one of our interview conversations.

> *So when you started attending there [a church by his house] had you already broken up?*
>
> Yes, I mean I was still with her, but I no longer had [sexual] relations with her.
>
> *Once you arrived to the Gospel, or already beforehand?*
>
> She told me that she was not going to have sex with me until I found a job and I said, "Okay," and she swore she wouldn't. "Okay," [I said], "I'll fulfill your promise." *[Juan facetiously bowed his head.]* But that was right when I started to go to that church and so it was immediate. Right when I started, none of that [sex].

Juan's conversion provides him with the strength to fulfill his girlfriend's demands and also a sense of self-legitimacy as her spiritual superior. Juan tried to convince his girlfriend to convert, but, he said, "she is very hardheaded and doesn't like to be told what to do." In the end, her attempt to manipulate him seems to have gotten away from her as he found a way to turn it back on her. And his attempt to change her did not work either: she eventually decided to end their relationship. In any case his religious belief permitted him to see this as God's will and continue with his life.

The strict norms of Evangelicalism can also provide a means for individuals to act to break off a dysfunctional relationship. Inerio had a long-term affair with his uncle's wife, with whom he had a child that the uncle unknowingly assumed was his own. They tried to break off the relationship several times but failed. When Inerio converted one of the first things he did was go to the house of his lover and say that they could not continue their relationship since he was now an Evangelical Christian. Inerio explained, "When I became a Christian, I said to her that we couldn't keep doing this because I am in the Gospel now, I surrendered to Christ. And she accepted that."

Among the several problems that Luis had when he converted was that, in addition to his wife, he had a woman on the side. He had tried to end the second relationship several times but could not. When he became Evangelical he was finally able to break it off:

> There was another woman. But with the will of God, I was able to leave her, escape from her. Because alone—I would go home alone and ten days later I would be back at her house. I couldn't stop seeing her. I would say to myself, "I'm not going to go over there anymore." And a little while later I would be back there crying, "Look, forgive me, I want to be with you again." And she would let me in again. And now I've been in the Gospel for a year, and if she comes looking for me, I try to get rid of her. I preach Christ to her.

Conversion to Evangelicalism appears to have helped some of the men overcome the grief of breaking up. Andrés was seething when his "main" girlfriend left him for another man. He plotted to seek revenge on her and her new companion and feared what he might do. This, along with other problems, led him to become Evangelical. Ricardo went through two painful breakups within a couple of years. In each case it was the woman who left him; and both caused him a lot of pain—in the first case because he had a child with the woman, in the second because the breakup occurred when his girlfriend had an affair with his cousin who lived in the same house. This second breakup immediately preceded his conversion.

Family Problems

Family relationships are dealt with extensively in chapters 6 and 7. Here I want to point out that all the family problems common in the industrialized West—lack of communication between parents and their offspring, differences in opinion regarding acceptable behavior—are equally present in Venezuela. In addition, the declining resources families have at their disposal reduce the centripetal forces of belonging; less than ever before do children see their own life prospects tied up with those of their family. As with the case of male-female relationships, conversion to Evangelicalism can provide a vocabulary for more effective communication, or it can simply provide a basis of legitimacy for one of the aggrieved parties. In the latter case it is not uncommon for family problems to become worse. But for the convert, an increase in problems can be outweighed by the benefits of a new interpretive framework for conceptualizing them.

Peer Social Life

For six of my respondents, loneliness resulting from a lack of peer fellowship was instrumental in turning to Evangelicalism. Each of these persons was in some sense different, awkward, lacked confidence, or found himself in a social situation that did not provide satisfying interpersonal contact.

José María came to Caracas from the isolated Pacific Coast bay he grew up on in Colombia's remote Chocó province. He has no family in Caracas and has, for all practical purposes, lost contact with his family in Colombia. He is functionally illiterate, although he says he can read the Bible and write his name. A poor man's skinny, he wears out-of-style, ill-fitting clothes, and his manner reflects his peasant roots. In our interview he told me that he has never spoken well:

> Before I came to the Gospel, I didn't talk. I was, how should I say, I wasn't an expressive person that would just sit down and talk to someone else. I would go up and sit down next to a person and wouldn't say anything. I was shy and nervous. But when I arrived to the Way of the Lord, the Lord has helped me, has given me freedom. I treat people with the love of the Lord. I treat people the way God wants you to treat them, with the respect they deserve but always with the exhortation that they have to repent because Christ is the only way to salvation.

José María now preaches at a service one day a week in a plaza in downtown Caracas. He has a confident if not socially dominant manner. He clearly was not a high-status member of the church. In social groups in the church his opinion was rarely solicited and usually not heeded when he voiced it. Despite having a nice tenor voice, he was cut after the first round of auditions for the new church choir. But he was always welcome in church activities and was treated with the friendly respect accorded any hermano. Whenever I talked to him at the back door of the church, he never missed the opportunity to hand out pamphlets to passersby while we talked or, if no pamphlets were available, say "Seek God" or "There's power in Jesus." The attractiveness of José María's social existence can only be understood by comparing what it would be like without his religious participation. In a social environment in which men are valued for economic and physical power and in which verbal and mental quickness are the key assets on which manhood is built, Evangelicalism provides José María with an attractive alternative masculinity.

Wilkenman grew up as a loner, spending most of his time at home being resentful about the abuse and mockery he was subjected to. In describing his first visits to Emmanuel, he said it was the most beautiful place he had ever been. He clearly was not referring to the physical infrastructure of *el ranchón*:

> I saw people. I saw the love that I was looking for in "the world" but couldn't find. I thought that here [in Emmanuel Church] I would be able to live in peace. And from what I had heard about the Gospel on the radio, what I wanted was peace. . . . There wasn't [so much] malice—So [I thought] this is where I belong.

For those men who fare poorly in the highly aggressive atmosphere of the popular classes in Caracas, the basic respect with which Evangelicals treat each other provides new, more satisfying social relationships.

Social Activism

While la crisis has seen growth in new social movements and non-governmental organizations, it is precisely in the sectors that need it most where the decline of state services and party patronage has left people without the social capital to address community needs. This does not mean, however, that there is no desire among members of the popular sectors to participate in social activism. The "great commission" of Christianity—to go out and bring the "good news" to others—provides a ready-made logic of social activism—what Evangelicals call *obra social*—aimed at improving the world. Evangelical obra social is generally abstract enough to adapt easily to the skills and resources of members of the lower working classes and is less likely to lead to frustrating failures and defeats that highlight educational and economic deficits (Burdick 1993).

About two years into my fieldwork at Emmanuel, Enrique and several other church leaders asked me to develop a plan for a program that could attend to community social needs; because I was an educated sociólogo they assumed I would come up with something really impressive. After a week or so I presented them with the outline of a project whereby they would use a space in the church for an abasto and a café. I pointed out that large sums of money were spent by Emmanuel's hermanos on coffee, soft drinks, and snacks at the nearby bakery and that if that money were kept in the church, any number of activities could be financed. I suggested subsidizing a low-cost child care facility in the church during the day. This could both help single parents from the community and provide jobs for members of the church. The project was received with great praise and enthusiasm. But it never received any concrete efforts to implement it by church leaders, Enrique, or anybody else.

Such projects are not unknown in Caracas's Evangelical churches—in fact, I had adapted the project from something I had seen in another church—but neither are they common. The *obras sociales* that Evangelicals developed themselves were usually quite different. They would go out with a megaphone to preach on a street corner, organize daily services in a plaza, stage a weeklong revival in a barrio, organize a workshop or conference in a school on a Saturday, speak on radio shows, do Christian theater, visit the sick in hospitals, bring bags of food to needy neighbors, or any other activity they could think of. Sometimes these were onetime events, sometimes recurring. Sometimes they were carried out by an organized group referring to itself as a "ministry," sometimes by an ad hoc collection of individuals. Below I look at two formal "ministries" and one individual initiative.

A "ministry" begins when an idea occurs to a few friends in the church. They might speak to the pastor about it, and he would give his blessing—perhaps mention their activities in the Sunday morning announcements before the congregation. They would put tremendous effort into coming up with a name, a logo, T-shirts, a charter, a detailed division of labor, and perhaps an organizational hierarchy for a group that might only consist of five or ten members. The God with Us Theater Group, for example, performed dramas they had written in plazas, schools, churches, or anywhere else that would have them. Most of these dramas were oriented toward the problems of drug use and delinquency that afflict this social context. They inevitably ended with one person dying a violent death and another becoming Evangelical. In one play I saw several times, the malandro protagonist converts and ends up going to a Bible college in the United States. The productions end with an altar call and respondents repeating the "prayer of faith." All the members of this theater group are young people and constitute a tight-knit group of friends. The group gives them experience with organization, singing, dancing, acting, and recording, as well as a feeling of contributing to their community.

From my first experiences with them, Enrique and Ramiro told me of their All Things in Common Ministry. The title reflects Enrique's previous experience in leftist activism, and indeed they tried to focus on social problems. I participated with them in a number of workshops they held in schools and churches in Caracas and outlying areas. They presented talks or showed movies on drugs, sexuality, marriage, and the Christian life. For each of these events, Enrique printed diplomas for those who attended. For the more important events, he had T-shirts made for those who were giving the workshop in order to give the appearance of being a team. He also wrote and distributed a schedule of activities down to five-minute intervals that were never actually referred to once the event started. The individual activities were often an hour or two behind schedule, and entire parts of the planned list were dropped or improvised according to unforeseen limitations or opportunities arising during the event.

Andrés had no organization or group with which he worked. Rather he organized events himself, usually in the ultra-poor upper barrios of Caracas's south central valley. When he was a member of Emmanuel Church he told me he did not like being a "pew Christian." He preferred to go out to preach the word and do obra social. I had to opportunity to see several of his projects. One of the projects, organized by Andrés and Enrique, was a weeklong campaign. Every night they plugged in sound equipment on the back patio of a rancho that looked out over several large neighborhoods in El Valle. They held a full service on the patio: Bible reading, sermon, singing, and prayer. At various points they yelled through the microphone for everyone listening to turn the lights of their ranchos off and on—usually with quite impressive results. Another time I spent an afternoon with Andrés on house visitations. We visited a number of homes that were dealing with maladies all too common in the community—a suicide, a sick baby, a disappeared husband. In each case Andrés talked with the person, read a few verses from the Bible, and ended with a prayer. One Saturday evening he organized a party for neighborhood children at an Evangelical's house. This included a few talks about aspects of Evangelicalism, a giant pot of chicken and rice, and two piñatas that the children broke open.

I am not arguing here that Evangelicalism is a viable resource for addressing social issues—interesting points could be made for and against such a position, but that is not the goal here. Rather I am attempting to show that for men who desire involvement in social activism but have few opportunities in which to pursue it, Evangelical forms of social activism have some attractive characteristics. First, they tend to rely on episodic bursts of energy. In an uncertain atmosphere in which few things can be planned, this type of obra social can be set aside for a month or two when other demands absorb one's attention. Second, anyone with a basic knowledge of the Evangelical message can engage in it. John Burdick (1993), in contrast, has provided a sensitive portrayal of the way traditional community activism can highlight embarrassing differences in human capital and social status among members of the popular classes. Third, whereas in this context of intransigent structural inequality social activism of any type generally has unimpressive if not paradoxical results and thereby leads to disillusionment, Evangelical obra social always imparts a feeling of achievement and success. Whether five people or five hundred attend a workshop, drama, or party, success is declared and a feeling of achievement is earned. Compare this to the coffee shop–child care cooperative I had suggested. This not only would have required some start-up capital; it also would have required constant attention as well as organizational skills that these Evangelicals might not have been confident they had. It also would have had a clear bottom line by which success and failure could be measured.

CHAPTER 5

Imagining Evangelical Practice

> Our intelligence, like our activity, presents two very different forms: on the one hand, are sensations and sensory tendencies; on the other, conceptual thought and moral activity. Each of these two parts of ourselves represents a separate pole of our being, and these two poles are not only distinct from one another but are opposed to one another. Our sensory appetites are necessarily egoistic: they have our individuality and it alone as their object. When we satisfy our hunger, our thirst, and so on, without bring any other tendency into play, it is ourselves, and ourselves alone, that we satisfy. [Conceptual thought] and moral activity are, on the contrary, distinguished by the fact that the rules of conduct to which they conform can be universalized. Therefore, by definition, they pursue impersonal ends. Morality begins with disinterest, with attachment to something other than ourselves.
>
> Émile Durkheim, "The Dualism of Human Nature and Its Social Conditions"

In the preceding chapters I showed that Evangelical religious practice can fit into projects of self-reform among poor Caracas men. But I am yet to address the most difficult question: how can people intentionally adopt a set of religious beliefs and practices in order to confront life problems? The tradition of thought that defines religion and culture in contradistinction to individual rationalistic action can be traced to Durkheim if not earlier. But despite this long-term conceptual trend, the incompatibility of intention and belief has been built on as a presupposition, not established through argument. One exception is the political philosopher Jon Elster. Although he is committed to a rationalist paradigm of social scientific explanation, Elster has spent his career identifying and circumscribing human phenomena not susceptible to rationalistic explanation. Reviewing his examination of intention and belief prepares us for the empirical analysis of the next two chapters. Elster (1983: 43) argues that there are certain mental states that are "by-products," meaning they "have the property that they can only come about as the by-product of actions undertaken for other ends. They can never, that is, be brought about intelligently and intentionally, because the very attempt to do so precludes the state one is trying to bring about." Beliefs are one of these mental states. Many beliefs would undoubtedly be useful for a given individual, yet cannot be intentionally achieved by her. Elster puts it as follows: "Belief, like courage, can be instrumentally useful, and yet be out of reach for instrumental rationality. It is part of the notion of a belief that to believe something implies the belief that one holds the belief for a reason, and not merely because of the utility of holding that belief" (51). It is easy to understand why it is incompatible for one to decide to hold a belief and have reasons for holding a belief. If one already has reasons to hold a belief, then effort is not needed. Thus if one needs to make an effort to believe something, the reasons for holding that belief are insufficient. For this reason, Elster argues that even if it were possible to decide to hold a belief *p*, one would have to forget that decision for it not to undermine the belief: "If the decision to believe *p* is to be carried out successfully, it must also obliterate itself from the memory of the believer" (Elster 1979: 49–50). The attempt to believe, then, is a case of what Elster calls the "moral fallacy of by-products": the attempt to will what cannot be willed. And the attempt to explain a desirable by-product as the result of intentional action he calls the "intellectual fallacy of by-products" (Elster 1983: 43).

"By-products" can be brought about intentionally, but only by means of nonstandard causality—in other words, by fluke. Elster gives the example of his son commanding him to laugh. Since one cannot *decide* to be amused, Elster found the command so ridiculous that he did indeed laugh. Thus the attempt to bring about the by-product worked but only through nonstandard causality not intended by the actor. By-products, says Elster (1983: 56), "may come about intentionally and nonintelligently, if the agent achieves by fluke what he set out to bring about." But what does it mean to achieve something unintelligently, by fluke? Presumably this means the person, like Elster's son, "misunderstood" the causality through which the by-product was actually produced. In the conclusion to this chapter I discuss the way dualist theories of meaning reify the distinction between literal and figurative meaning making. Such reifications misconstrue the relatively stable, widely accepted concepts used in science and common sense as "literally" true representations of the world useful for acting in it at the same time that they misconstrue the less stable, less widely accepted concepts called "cultural" or "religious" as largely subjective, necessarily inaccurate representations used for abstract contemplation. What if Elster's son had a set of concepts explaining why Elster laughed when he commanded him to? What if, guided by this set of concepts, he could repeatedly produce his desired result through such commands and thereby validate these concepts? While for Elster this would be "unintelligent" because it does not correspond to a "literally true" view of the causality involved, it would be precisely the type of reflective intelligence pragmatist theorists such as Charles Sanders Peirce (1877), John Dewey (1922), and Hans Joas (1993) point to: the creation of concepts that successfully relate acts and consequences. For pragmatists, whether a concept is literally true is quite irrelevant, as logic is created and tested through successful practice in the world. The preceding chapters have shown that Evangelical meanings provide the men in my study with imaginative rationality with which they can confront problematic aspects of their social existence. The next step in the argument is to show that these problematic experiences can include religious practice itself.

The historian of religion Jonathon T. Smith writes that while human beings have imagined deities and modes of interaction with them throughout history, "second order, reflective imagination" of *religion* is a relatively recent activity confined to scholars. "Religion is solely the creation of the scholar's study. It is created for the scholar's analytic purposes by his imaginative acts of comparison and generalization. Religion has no independent existence apart from the academy" (Smith 1982: xi). While it is useful to realize that people do not practice "religion" in the abstract but a particular religion in the concrete, Smith overstates the distinction between scholarly and everyday thinkers. As the mass media attest, nonscholars speak about "religion" all the time—whether it belongs in public schools, its role in politics, its place in the family. In the case of Venezuelan Evangelicals, the term *religion* is used continually, to refer to "false" creeds created by humans—usually Catholicism. And they engage in second-order thinking about their own religious practice all the time. In fact, their conversations are not simply first-order discussions about God, the Devil, and the means of being in right relationship with them but rather second-order discussions of what are and are not the proper goals of Evangelical practice, the evidence for their religion, and how they came to practice their religion. By "second-order" is meant cultural meanings and practices that conceptualize the way cultural meanings and practices themselves work. Culture conceptualizes not just the world; culture conceptualizes culture itself. There is, of course, no hard and fast distinction between first-order and second-order meanings. The religious meanings used to conceptualize social life in the previous two chapters already imply reflection on how Evangelicalism works. And the second-order meanings reviewed in this chapter frequently speak about everyday social life. But this chapter focuses on the ways in which Evangelicals focus on their own religious practice. It is not about how Evangelicals imagine "religion"—although that comes up occasionally. Rather it is about how they imagine their own Evangelical practice. Hence the title "Imagining Evangelical Practice."

It is this second-order imaginative rationality that allows me to address Elster's account. Three basic issues can be distilled from Elster's review of intention and belief. First, the notion "instrumental" denotes a situation in which ends are "other" to the means used. An instrument is a tool that we use for a task that goes beyond that tool. When brought into the analysis of religious practice, this would mean that this-worldly benefits are not integral parts of the religious practices that generate them. Second, in Elster's portrayal, people must have reasons to believe beyond their own self-interest. Put differently, they must have intellectual reasons for believing, not just reasons for wanting what a belief can provide. Third, people must not themselves feel responsible for their belief. As mentioned above, if a person must make an effort to believe, the reasons for that belief are ipso facto inadequate. Below I address each of these issues using empirical data to demonstrate how my respondents imagine Evangelical practice. In brief, I show that

- whether a set of practices is "instrumental" or not is itself constructed through cultural concepts. In the case of Pentecostal Evangelicalism in Venezuela, while some this-worldly ends are indeed outside of the realm of the spiritual, the issues of self and the family described in chapters 3 and 4 are within it. As a result, seeing Venezuelan Evangelical religious practice as instrumental—as a means to something external to it—is false to the phenomenon.
- the Evangelical meaning system presents projects that conceptualize the way Evangelical practice affects its consequences. Projects that meet with success provide Evangelicals with good

reason to believe. The Evangelical meaning system also provides a repertoire of meanings through which Evangelicals can make sense of failed projects. Thus Evangelicals often have good reason to believe: on balance their religious projects have delivered on their promises.

- the Evangelical meaning system provides adherents with narratives that describe their own conversion processes in terms of God's agency. These narratives shape memories of the conversion process in such a way that God's role is emphasized and the convert's role is minimized. This, in effect, provides additional legitimacy for the belief as not a mere product of the individual's efforts.

LOCATING INSTRUMENTALITY

Plaza El Venezolano

Virtually every plaza in Caracas has an Evangelical service or pastor preaching at some point during the day. These events range from a self-appointed individual preaching to a captive audience at a bus stop to well-organized initiatives with sound equipment and municipal permits that dominate a plaza for several hours daily. One of the longest-running examples of the latter is the service that takes place every day at noon at Plaza El Venezolano in the heart of downtown Caracas. A block from Plaza Bolívar, and two blocks from the National Assembly, Plaza El Venezolano is swarming throughout the day with ice-cream vendors, shoeshine men, people on work breaks, and parents with small children. The plaza has cement benches and four cement pools and fountains that have not functioned in years but on which people sit. Steps leading up to the street along the north side of the plaza serve as an amphitheater for the noontime services.

Services begin to build around noon with informal singing by the regulars, who arrive early. At ten or fifteen minutes past the hour the person who is directing the event introduces the first preacher, who begins with a Bible reading and then gives a "message" for a half hour or so. There is generally a dominant theme, but the preaching is ad lib and any number of topics might be touched on. Toward the end the message works into an informal but highly structured altar call. First the pastor addresses the audience with a question likely to receive a positive response, such as "Raise your hand if you believe in Jesus." The knowing regulars let the visitors respond. After the preacher gets his audience to raise their hands, he announces that he would like them to come down so that he can pray for them. He prays over the usually ten to twenty people who comply, then asks them to repeat after him the "prayer of faith"—a prayer in which a person professes his or her faith in Jesus Christ.[1] Afterward someone from the church takes down their names on a notepad and gives them a Bible tract. Interestingly, since the names are simply for prayer, they do not take down a telephone number or address or any other information that would allow the church to contact these people later.

I have seen these plaza services, depending on the day, the weather, and the skills of the preacher, draw from thirty to two hundred onlookers. There are three basic strata of attendees. Those standing close to the people leading the service are Evangelical regulars who may have a hand in organizing the plaza services. They sit behind the preacher or other speaker, clapping and saying "Hallelujah" to points they agree with, and play instruments—guitar, bongo drums, maracas, tambourines—during the singing. They also constitute the pool of fill-in preachers on those occasions when a scheduled preacher does not show up. Then there are those who are sitting on the steps in front of the preacher. These are usually Evangelicals from different congregations and others who are interested enough to sit down to watch but do not have a hand in organizing the plaza services. Behind those sitting on the steps stand curious onlookers. The Evangelicals who frequent the plaza service are often stereotyped as people with "nothing better to do." But like the men on Tally's corner (Liebow 1967), they usually work after hours in security or cleaning jobs, are between stints of marginal employment, or work for themselves on their own schedules. Others work downtown and drop by on their lunch breaks. Ramiro, for example, works independently as a remodeling contractor. When he is between contracts he attends the plaza service every day. When he is working he makes an effort to take a long lunch on Thursdays—his day to preach.

I taped the following message in the first month of my fieldwork at Plaza El Venezolano. I was just getting to know Ramiro and other plaza regulars. As always when he preached, Ramiro was dressed in a heavy wool suit on a hot, sunny day. He is one of the truly gifted preachers at

1. There are numerous versions of the prayer of faith. In all of them the speaker asks to be cleansed of his sins, recognizes Jesus Christ as his only savior, and asks to be filled with the Holy Spirit.

the plaza, and his messages regularly draw more than one hundred onlookers. When the music died down that day, he picked up the microphone and surveyed the crowd with his infectious smile.

"To Jesus Christ!" *[he yelled.]*
"Gloria!" *[responded those Evangelicals who knew the routine.]*
"To Jesus Christ!"
"Gloria!"

"Do you know why there is peace in this plaza? Because when his people are praising him, God is present. He promised in his Word that he would be present when his people praised him. When the People of God praise him what happens?"

"Wonderful things happen!" *[responded the Evangelicals in the audience.]*

"Glory to God's name. The week before last I was talking here about the family. I'm very concerned about the family. There are lots of fathers of children here. Raise your hand if you are a father *[raises his hand]*. God bless you, fathers. How about mothers of children *[raises his hand]?* God bless you, mothers. I had a concern weighing on my heart this whole past week because last time I spoke about not wasting your money on things other than bread, and not wasting your efforts on what does not satisfy. But I've realized that in Venezuela and in the whole world, the root of the problem is the family because what did Satan come for? To steal and destroy. Steal what? Your peace. Destroy what? The family itself—Glory to God's name.

"But God came so that man could have life, and have life in abundance—Alleluia to his name. This concern of mine is not a fantasy; it's not something somebody told me about. Because in that world I left behind—Glory to God's name—I was a victim.—Praise the name of the Lord. I want you to stop for a moment—Alleluia to God's name—because I want you to share with me. In the book of Joshua, chapter 24, verse 15, the Word of God under the blessing of the Father, Son and Holy Spirit, says: 'If you do not like serving Jehovah, choose today who you serve: either the gods of your ancestors when they were on the other side of the river, or the gods of the Amorites in whose land you inhabit. But I and my house will serve Jehovah.' Did you understand Joshua's decision? 'But I and my house will serve Jehovah.'—Alleluia to his name.

[Praying:] "Father, in the name of Jesus, glorify yourself this afternoon. Look at our friends here. Lord, he who has problems in his home, perhaps he has an idol [in his house], or he has a God that has not been able to do anything for him. Holy Spirit of God, glorify yourself this afternoon. Throw off the blinders, the darkness of religion,[2] and let your Word live. Penetrate hearts and do your work. Because your Word says you never return empty handed. Glorify yourself in the name of your blessed son. Father, while I minister your word, free he who is imprisoned. While I minis-

2. "Religion" here refers to Catholicism. Evangelicals consider "religion" man-made, whereas Evangelicalism is "salvation."

ter your word, free them of sin, free them of uncleanliness and vices. Glorify yourself this afternoon. May your son Jesus Christ illuminate this place. I thank you my teacher. Amen.

"Do you know why I chose this passage? Because I am continually concerned about the Venezuelan family; because I am Venezuelan. I am concerned about Venezuela because I am Venezuelan. I have been to other places and have been able to see that they also need Christ—Blessed is the Lord's name. The root of the problem is the home. When you look around you today, sons and daughters rise up against their parents. But the Bible itself says this. I always say that this *[raising the Bible]* is tomorrow's newspaper. Whatever comes out tomorrow in the newspaper, my Christ has already announced—war and rumors of war. But sons and daughters are rising up against their parents. Why have sons and daughters risen up against their parents? I am going to tell you: the Devil has told them a lie. I am going to unmask the Devil as many times as God gives me the opportunity—Alleluia to his name. The Devil has passed off a lie to society, to the family: 'He who reads the Bible is going to go crazy.' And with that lie, he's fooled you. Because the Devil knows that the Bible is the revealed truth. Christ said, 'Know the truth and the truth will make you free' *[applause and shouts]*. That is why when man discovers that the revealed truth is here, he separates himself from religion; he separates himself from gods, and chooses to serve the God that made the heavens and the earth—Alleluia to his name.

"You might be saying, 'Do you really think the problem in my home is happening because I don't read the Bible?' Well, perhaps you do not have the God who made the heavens and the Earth but rather an idol. You worship [José] Gregorio, you venerate Maria Lionza, Felipe the Negro, Guaicaipuro, Chiquinquirá, the Caridad del Cobre.[3] But do you know what Joshua did? The people of Israel had thrown out God and had turned back to idolatry. The spirit of the Lord came over Joshua and spoke to the people [through him]. And God has asked me to tell you this. Do you want to continue serving the Gods that have ruined our nation; that have ruined our country? Well, here [in this plaza] is a people that are going to serve Jehovah. We are going to follow the path of Christ because only Christ saves the sinner.

[Applause and shouts]

"Men don't care about their behavior in their homes. I'm going to tell you something—because I was a victim of a divorce. I was victim of a divorce. When I was thinking all of this through, the Lord told me "testify to them about where I rescued you from"—Alleluia to his name. Because it is necessary that I tell you the great and wonderful things Christ has done in my life—Alleluia to his name. Perhaps you are one of those who are like

3. The first of these is a folk hero worshiped as a saint in Venezuela but yet to be beatified by the Vatican. The next three are figures from indigenous or Afro-Venezuelan traditions. The last two are local names for the Virgin Mary. Grouping them together highlights Evangelicals' rejection of Catholicism as not Christian.

me. In my house, I cooked on Sundays for the woman who was my wife, who was my companion. I would cook at home; I would serve her breakfast in bed. Listen to this! *[Cupping hands around mouth as if telling a secret]* I served her breakfast in bed!

"But what I did with my hands, I undid with my feet—Glory to the name of the Lord. Because afterwards I would go out and spend the whole night away from my home because I didn't have the God who made the heavens and the earth—glory to the name of the Lord. Perhaps you are saying, "But I don't do this, I don't do that. So why am I a victim in my home?" Perhaps you take a day off for your wife's birthday. You give her a rose. But the next day you come home drunk—Glory to God's name. What you did with your hands, you undid with your feet. Why is this? What's behind all this? I'm going to tell you who is behind all of this: Satan! The Devil that came to kill, steal, and destroy. But my Christ came to undo the work of the Devil."

[Shouts of "Alleluia!"]

Ramiro went on to enjoin those in attendance to accept the God that Joshua accepted rather than the "dolls" and "idols" that Catholics try to peddle. He went on to criticize a Charles Bronson movie for usurping God's justice, as well as television programs that glorify sex and violence. He contrasted what Catholicism and the mass media provide with what truly accepting the Lord can provide.

"When you permit God to come into your life, blessings come to your home. But if you worship and venerate idols, do you think your home is going to be blessed? Never. You won't be [blessed] because God doesn't make mistakes—Alleluia to his name."

"Gloria!" *[the Evangelicals responded.]*

"Christ, in his mercy and his love, came to find and save those who have lost their way. 'But,' you might say, 'most of the people I know who have become Evangelical, it's because they've gone through problems, they've had problems.' Well, they're people who have recognized that they can do nothing without Christ. They are people who recognize that without Christ, man is lost, doing bad things, doing things that do not please God—Glory to the name of Jesus."

Ramiro returned to the theme of Catholicism, urging people not to simply follow a religion because their ancestors did.

We don't preach about tradition. We preach about Christ—Alleluia—He who came to free captives; he who came to give life to man—life in abundance, [he who came] to spill his love over us. . . . Do you think that we [the Evangelicals present] are here just to get attention, or because we want to put a suit on, or to show that we can speak, that we can talk pretty? No! We are here because God has put his love in our hearts so that we can bring you his transforming Word, that Word that can change the drunkard, that

> Word that can change the young man who is unfaithful to his wife—glory to the name of Jesus—that man who is idolatrous, drowned by what his ancestors said. Now they *[pointing at the Evangelicals present]* know that's wrong, that the only savior, the only escape route for men is Christ.

Ramiro continued, speaking about the loss of morals in the family and how those who accept Jesus Christ and teach their children Christianity will see blessings in their family. He spoke about how some try to seek God's protection through witchcraft, without success, of course. He then continued to speak about problems of the family and solutions.

> There are many people whose homes are chaos and who suffer the consequences of their sins. They prefer to throw themselves on the Metro tracks to end their lives. Many give in to alcoholism. Many give in to drugs. And it turns out that neither drugs, nor alcoholism, nor death can solve the problem, because the chaos continues. But when you decide that "I and my house will serve the Lord," the Lord comes to bring blessings to your home. And just so that you know, this isn't something that someone told me. Nor is it a fairly tale. No. I came to Jesus in anguish. The Bible says, "In anguish, many will seek me," and I was the victim of a divorce. I was abandoned with a little boy like this *[puts hand down to middle of thigh to show how small his child was]*. And where is that little boy now? Look where he is *[points to his son in the audience]*. There he is, growing up with me and with Christ, because Christ helps you . . . he's studying and brings home good grades for the Glory of God.

Ramiro went on to tell how he truly has to follow what he preaches in his home, for otherwise he would be setting a bad example for his son.

> But he [Ramiro's son] can testify—Blessed be His name—that since Christ came to my life, he helped me and has continued to help me and will continue to help me, because I decided that my house and I will serve the God that made the heavens and the Earth. This God has changed many lives. . . . I used to be an alcoholic. I used to consume drugs. But now I don't do it anymore. We discovered—Glory to the name of Jesus—that we were victimizing ourselves, that we victimized ourselves and our families—Glory to the name of Jesus. But now we realized that Christ is the only escape route. Christ is the only mediator between God and men. There are no other Gods. There are no dolls that can give you salvation. Only Christ saves. Only Christ saves the sinner—Alleluia to his name. . . . The family is the fundamental base of society. But if the fundamental base of society is itself based on drugs, alcoholism, and promiscuous sex, what will our society be like tomorrow?

Ramiro promised the audience that if they say, " 'Christ, I am a sinner. I recognize that until now my family has had their backs turned to you—my family that does not want to read the Bible. But now Christ, we want to serve you,' I am sure that Christ is going to bless you. He is going to hear what you ask for. He knows what your problems are and he is going to solve them—Alleluia to his name."

Ramiro then went through a series of Bible verses having to do with God in the home. He had another Evangelical read through the verses as he analyzed them. Genesis 18:19 speaks of Jehovah protecting the house of Abraham. Ramiro spoke about God being the only way.

> "Jesus Christ said: 'I am the way, I am the truth and I am life . . . So why, then, do we venerate José Gregorio? Can somebody tell me why? Somebody who loves Gregorio, show me [why] in the Bible. Somebody who loves Chiquinquirá, somebody who loves the Virgin of the Caridad del Cobre, or María de San José, the most recent one [to appear]. What have they done for Venezuela? The most recent idolatry that was planted in our country was when the supposed sumo pontifice, John Paul II, did this *[Catholic hand motion of blessing]* for Venezuela's future. And look how Johnny left us: sunken in idolatry. They spent billions of bolívares on that temple, on the highway to get there and on the trip they made to Guanare. But what's happened? Have they paid the doctors? Look at the Pérez Carreño hospital—the last one that belongs to [the] Social Security [Administration]. They're going to close it."
>
> "They already closed it" *[someone from the audience yelled.]*
>
> "They already closed it—Alleluia to the name of the Lord. You know how much they need to pay the doctors or to pay substitutes for the Pérez Carreño Hospital? Bs. 400 million. And they spent Bs. 1–2 billion on that idolatry that didn't bring any change to our country. Well some say it did bring change to our country, but for the worse. . . . Can you see that we've grown accustomed to what our ancestors handed down to us? They have us mired in misery. For how long? People of Venezuela, City of Caracas, wake up and react, Jesus Christ is calling you. Jesus Christ is calling you. It's not the pope that's with you. This is the moment. Wake up and react. Jesus Christ loves you and wants to change you."[4]

By the end of his message Ramiro was sweating profusely, no longer smiling, and had the intense, penetrating gaze he always had by the end of his messages. He worked into the altar call and prayed over those who responded.

4. These last few sentences are a parody of the themes of the two papal visits to Venezuela. In his first visit the pope used a rhyme that became very popular: *Venezuela amigo, el Papa está contigo* (Venezuela, my friend, the pope is with you). The Venezuelan hierarchy's official theme for the second visit, widely transmitted on billboards and in television advertisements was, "Venezuela. Wake up and react. This is the moment."

Daily downtown Caracas plaza services begin with singing. In preparation for his sermon, the preacher kneels in prayer behind the musical equipment.

After the music, a Bible reading precedes the sermon.

The preacher begins with a testimony of his own troubled past.

The sermon leads to an altar call.

An Evangelical regular helps in the laying-on of hands. He prays over the visitor and pushes back on his forehead, in a gesture that implies spirit possession.

From Instrumental to Spiritual Projects

Durkheim writes that religion is not a guide to action (Durkheim and Mauss 1963: 81–82) but rather a contemplative behavior engaged in by people who feel an external power that demands their worship. Elster writes that a belief might be instrumentally useful but not within reach of our intention. How, then, can we make sense of Ramiro's presentation of "the Gospel" as precisely a guide to action and his injunction for people to believe so that God will bless their homes? There is nothing unique about Ramiro's "message." The only thing exceptional about this service was the fact that I taped it. Messages similar to these happen twice a day, every weekday in Plaza El Venezolano and are echoed in Evangelical churches throughout Caracas. Ramiro openly tells how he accepted Jesus Christ as a way to improve his life. Far from being ashamed of his "project" of self-reform, he repeatedly draws attention to it. Why does this not undermine or even challenge the sincerity of his belief? Why does this not appear to him or anyone else as evidence that he had ulterior motives? A clue comes when he says: "The Bible says 'In anguish, many will seek me.'" Ramiro, in effect, finds a description of his action in the sacred text itself.

My interest here is not whether Venezuelan Evangelicalism is or is not biblical but the way religious meaning systems, as contained in sacred texts, sermons, and everyday religious discussions, portray religious practice itself. The symbols and constructs contained in religious meaning systems actually make reference to human life-in-the-world, not just to each other as classic structuralism would have it. Thus social scientists who want to understand the impact of religious meanings on action cannot simply see them as faceless, abstract "values" that motivate or as norms that restrain. Meanings portray the world. And the subjects or "situations" they portray inevitably include religious practice itself. Thus if we want to understand what are and are not tenable motives for a concrete form of religious practice we must actually look at the content of the meanings religious practitioners use to describe that concrete religious practice. This chapter examines the meanings Venezuelan Evangelicals use to construct what are, for them, the proper motivations of religious practice. Put differently, it examines how and where these Evangelicals locate the dualism between sacred and secular, religious and nonreligious.

Prosperity Theology

Judging from Ramiro's sermon as well as the presented in the previous two chapters, it would seem safe to say that Evangelicals see their relationship to the supernatural as a sort of script for action, as a special secret to success in attaining their goals, whatever they may be. But the terrain is more complex than that. Not every need or desire is considered the legitimate object of Evangelical practice. Indeed, one of the religions that Pentecostal Evangelicals criticize most—with an urgency equal to that they have for Catholicism and traditional Afro-Venezuelan religions—is another variant of Evangelicalism they refer to as "prosperity theology." The men I interviewed (whom, for clarity, I refer to in this chapter as Pentecostal Evangelicals) criticize the instrumentality of prosperity theology in terms quite similar to those used by Durkheim. Digging into this criticism will provide a fuller understanding of what, for them, are and are not proper motivations for religious practice. Put differently, looking at the way these men construct their own religious practice vis-à-vis "prosperity theology" will help us to locate Pentecostal Evangelicals' own dualism.

When Venezuela's Pentecostal Evangelicals speak of prosperity theology, they have in mind several churches that have a largely middle-class social base, emphasize "health and wealth," and belong neither to the CEV nor the CEPV umbrella organizations. Scholars have referred to churches of this type as "neo-Pentecostal" (see Cleary 1997). There are, indeed, visible differences when one attends neo-Pentecostal churches. The female members of these churches use makeup, have stylish haircuts, and dress according to contemporary fashion, unlike Pentecostal Evangelical women, who wear long dresses, wear their hair long, and have unadorned faces. The discourse is optimistic, emphasizing triumph, blessings, and salvation more than condemnations of "the world" or predictions of Armageddon. The pastor of Iglesia Renacer (Rebirth Church), a large neo-Pentecostal church in downtown Caracas, ends each of his services by saying, in unison with the congregation, "May the Lord bless you richly and powerfully." There are occasionally crass promises of well being. But for the most part the discourse differs only in emphasis from the Pentecostal Evangelical churches I observed. What is important for this analysis, however, is not the truth of my respondents' perceptions but how they use prosperity theology as a symbolic foil against which to define their own beliefs. During my fieldwork, they frequently described prosperity theology as the single most important threat to their mission. Pastors of Emmanuel Church conducted workshops and delivered sermons about "false doctrines," with special emphasis on the "errors" they see in prosperity theology. One Sunday they brought in a pastor from an Emmanuel Federation church in the interior, introducing him as a "world authority" on new age religions. He went through a detailed description, not inaccurate to my mind, of the connection between prosperity theology and new age philosophies. He ended with the exhortation, "The appearance of prosperity theology is the beginning of the apostasy."

To pursue Pentecostal Evangelicals' views of prosperity theology, I asked my respondents a two-question sequence. First I simply asked them what prosperity theology was. Then I followed up by asking how it differed from the Evangelical idea that God blesses his followers. The 70 percent of respondents (34 of 49) who were familiar with it commented on it in clear negative terms as false doctrine. Half of those who commented (16 of 34) said it represents a distortion of priorities. Eric said, "There's an error there. They don't bother talking about spiritual prosperity, just material prosperity." Juan Miguel argued, "Well, you know, there *are* blessings. But blessings aren't just material. Blessings can be spiritual as well." Others argued that prosperity theology missed the fundamental message of the beatitudes. Miguel Vicente explained, "They say that if you don't have money, you're condemned. In other words you are damned because you are poor and that is outside of biblical parameters. I mean, that throws out everything that the Lord says about 'blessed are the poor because that's where the kingdom of heaven is.' They don't accept that, and that's why they misinterpret God's word."

It would be a mistake to see these answers as simple rejections of wealth. Only six of thirty-four men included in their answers a negative opinion of wealth—usually seeing it as a distraction that draws attention away from God. Rather, prosperity theology appears to violate the subtle logic of my respondents' religious exchange with God. In his classic exploration, Marcel Mauss (1990) portrayed the logic of gift exchange in the following way: A gives × to B, knowing that it may lead B to return y, but without any assurance of the matter. It is precisely the indeterminate, "nonreversible" character of the exchange that underlines its moral character. And in my respondents' views, this is exactly what prosperity theology violates. God indeed blesses his followers materially when they focus on their spirituality. But prosperity theology sees this sequence as determinate and therefore reversible. This undermines God's autonomy and the moral basis of the relationship. Indeed, close to half of the respondents took exception to the determinate terms prosperity theology uses to portray God's blessings. Key verb phrases they used to express their disagreement were *have to be* or *must be* prosperous and *cannot be* poor. In the following exchange, Victor explains the difference between prosperity theology and the doctrine they follow.

> The foundation of [prosperity theology] doctrine is that Christians shouldn't be poor because we are the King's children and we should live in complete prosperity and they—it's like they measure your spiritual capacity or your relationship with God, according to your economic earnings. And, in fact it seems like they talk about money a lot. In services they speak directly about quantities of money. So there's a contradiction with the Word.
>
> *But what's the contradiction? In the [Emmanuel] Church you also hear that God blesses his followers.*
>
> Sure that's true: that God blesses his children. [But] we can't pass over the fact that a person who is economically well off or who has improved economically might not be a Christian. We can't forget that. Of course, God

> blesses. But we can't be determinant, like he who is poor isn't right with God. That's what they [followers of prosperity theology] focus on.

Davits said, "God blesses us, no? But he blesses us economically as well as spiritually. [Prosperity theology] has a measuring stick for each thing."

Others objected to prosperity theology's reversal of the causal sequence. Enrique explained the basics of prosperity theology, and I asked him whether this was different from the theology of his church. He responded, "It's different, totally different, because the Bible itself says that we should seek God and his justice first, and everything else will come as an addition. . . . You seek him and afterward he will give you your blessing as the celestial Father. But prosperity theology inverts the order. It's not God that's first, but money that's first." When I asked him how prosperity theology was different from his church's beliefs, Henrique explained, "Okay, for example. If God is going to bless me, he's going to first bless me spiritually. The economic part is secondary. Okay, so if I first worry about my spiritual life, I'm going to grow in everything else because God is going to bless me, because he is seeing my devotion to him."

Another aspect of the logic of gift giving is that, since the sequence is indefinite, not determined simply by its structure, successful exchange requires the autonomy of both actors. Prosperity theology is seen as trying to oblige God and appropriate his agency. The logic is nicely displayed in the following exchange with Ramiro.

> *Do you know what prosperity theology is?*
>
> I know what it is. They call it "super-faith" because it rests on men. . . . They think of God as the one who gives to them because they want him to. And I think that God is the one who knows human hearts. God knows who to give to and who not to give to. When I do this, I'm being an extremist. I'm trying to mold God to my will. But I believe that as a creature and creation of God, I should mold myself to my Father. If he loves me, he will give to me.
>
> *So how is this different from prosperity theology, from the Evangelical belief that God blesses his followers?*
>
> God blesses you by his grace, by his will. [Prosperity theology teaches] that I have to oblige God that he has to give me something. I believe that God is God and God is the one who gives according to his criteria.

All thirty-four respondents who knew something about prosperity theology mentioned the determinate terms in which prosperity theology seeks exchange with God, prosperity theology's reversal of causal sequence, or the way prosperity theology undermines the autonomy of

God. They speak in terms very similar to those used by Elster: people practice their religion because of sincere belief in God and desire for eternal life, and any benefits that accrue to believers arrive only as byproducts. Reversing the sequence as prosperity theology does, crudely gets priorities wrong and could well be self-defeating. This is consistent with Mauss's intent as he sought to show that there is a precontractual, moral base to all forms of exchange without which it would be impossible. How, then, can we reconcile this with Ramiro's message in which Evangelical practice is portrayed as an effective form of action in the world? I think we can conceptually reconcile this apparent contradiction by looking at Max Weber's historicization of dualism. Then we can work through it empirically with a series of more concrete questions.

From Universal to Historicized Dualism

Weber's distinction between "instrumentally rational" and "value-rational" action has long been seen as synonymous with the dualism of Durkheim, Parsons, Alexander, and others who portray it as a timeless, universal element of human culture (see Durkheim 1973: 150; Parsons 1937). However, this similarity is misleading insofar as Weber saw such dualism as a particular historical development characteristic of "rationalized" Western modernity (Weber 1946). In his sociology of religion he argued that there was no fundamental distinction between magic and religion. The most basic orientation toward the supernatural, that is, the most fundamental reason for religious practice, is this-worldly salvation from concrete ills (Weber 1968: 399–400). Such practice, wrote Weber, is a relatively rational form of action that follows rules of experience and is distinguished from other "pragmatic" scientific views only in the modern perspective. Weber portrayed the movement from magical to religious forms of action as a process of systematization of religious ideas pushed along by religious leaders and followers as they confront failure (437–39). When acts oriented toward influencing the supernatural in such a way as to bring benefits in this world succeed, they validate the religious belief system and legitimate the religious leader (427). When these acts fail to bring about the intended results, followers might assume that that god is ineffective or that the means of addressing him are unknown and therefore forget him. Sustained religious practice, as opposed to episodic magical interventions, begins when leaders and followers develop systematic interpretations for dealing with failure. There are a number of possibilities and directions that this can go. However, the stablest form of religion develops when the religious ethic comes to include a notion of "sin" that burdens the conscience beyond any concrete results. In other words, a religious ethic develops that rises above the vicissitudes of everyday social life insofar as any given success or failure is not enough to challenge faith in it. When taken to its logical conclusion, this process reaches a point of abstraction in which religion becomes permanently present in the believer's mind and has few if any concrete referents in this world. While this process represents a systematization of doctrine, Weber sees it as an "irrationalization" of the goals of religious practice away from this-worldly aspirations and toward an otherworldly yearning to be good for good sake (424).

The postcolonial anthropologist Talal Asad likewise puts the distinction between religious meaning and this-worldly practice in historical context. He sees the entire movement toward conceiving of religion as an autonomous structure of meaning with an essence that must be kept distinguished from politics or science as a historical product of the medieval Catholic Church's attempt to clearly demarcate the terrain of discourses and practices over which it was sovereign (1993: 38). And it did this not simply through cultural logic but through far-reaching social powers (35). "Thus what appears to anthropologists today to be self-evident, namely that religion is essentially a matter of symbolic meanings linked to ideas of general order (expressed through either or both rite and doctrine) . . . is in fact a view that has a specific Christian history. From being a concrete set of practical rules attached to specific processes of power and knowledge, religion has come to be abstracted and universalized" (42).

Both Weber and Asad would see the dualism between utilitarian and moral motivations as the outcome of a particular historical process with no teleological necessity. The degree of systematization of any given set of religious practices and the direction it takes depend on myriad historical factors. Dualism and the concomitant issue of instrumentality, then, become empirical issues. Whether a given system of religious meanings is dualistic, the extent of that dualism, and its character need to be uncovered through empirical research.

Legitimate Motivations for Accepting the Lord

Dualism is generated by certain social and cultural conditions rather than universal principles of mind, and it is normal, therefore, that there will be diversity in the character of dualism not only between religions but also between individuals of the same religion. Thus we must look for tendencies rather than clear rules that are followed. The questions regarding prosperity theology above were abstract and elicited general dispositions and attitudes toward instrumentality. But in order to more closely locate the dualism of my respondents, I used more fine-grained tools. In this section I present data from a sequence of concrete questions I worked through with my respondents. The text and rates of acceptance are presented below.

> *Please tell me which of the following ideas would be legitimate Christian doctrine and which of them would be false ideas from prosperity theology.*
>
> 1. *"Accept the Lord so that he will change your life."*
> 2. *"Accept the Lord so that things go well in your house [family]."*
> 3. *"Accept the Lord so that things will go well in your business."*

An examination of the answers to each of the preestablished responses helps locate Pentecostal Evangelical dualism.

1. "Accept the Lord so that he will change your life" (45/52, 86.5%) Fully 86 percent of the respondents said this was legitimate Christian doctrine. Indeed, so intuitive was the answer that only a few of the men responded with more than a word or so. Ramiro said, "That's logical. When someone accepts the Lord in his life, he changes." As usual the most interesting data came from misunderstandings. When I asked Gregorio, a traveling evangelist and Christian musician, the first question, he thought I was stating a belief from prosperity theology and asking whether he agreed with it. He looked uncomfortable and responded in a way that reveals the categories Pentecostal Evangelicals use to conceptualize their religious practice:

> To change your life? Well, you know what? I have frequently used that phrase, but, but, without basing it in that theology, or that doctrine. I mean I base what I say on what the Lord says in Revelations, "I renew all things." So he who accepts Christ is a new creature. I've used those texts. . . . But not because it's from them [followers of prosperity theology]. If it's from them, I didn't realize it.
>
> *So when you hear that idea, is it a legitimate Christian idea, or false doctrine?*
>
> Well, I mean Christ—He changes lives!

Only seven of fifty-two respondents disagreed with the idea. Five argued that one should accept Christ in order to be "saved," in other words, to gain eternal life. Three argued that you should accept God because you simply felt that he was real. Most of these disagreements followed the logic of gift exchange. You can reasonably expect God to change your life, but that should not be the primary motivation. I say more on this below. In sum, while 15 percent of respondents thought that eternal life and truth were the only legitimate motivations for religious practice, for the others, changing one's life was clearly legitimate.

2. *"Accept the Lord so that things go well in your house [family]" (37/52, 71.1%)* In Venezuelan Spanish, the term *house* refers not just to the physical structure that provides shelter but to the family as well. It is used in much the same way in the Old Testament of the Bible—indeed, Ramiro's message centers on the example provided by "Joshua and his house." The patriarchal family has been under serious stress during la crisis, and presiding as the pater familias of a productive and peaceful household is an elusive yet powerful dream for most of the men I interviewed. This phrase also received majority assent but now only 71 percent. There are similar numbers of dissenters on the basis of the idea that the quests for eternal life or truth are the only legitimate motivations (7 of 52). But the difference that makes the difference comes from ten negative responses based on the greater uncertainty of the impact of conversion on family life. For these respondents, the idea of converting in order to improve family life was not illegitimate. It was simply impractical and misguided. Several respondents pointed to the vicissitudes of life in poverty to a degree that they did not with the previous question. Henry, an elevator operator, said that even when you are in the Gospel, "there are tough times and there are joyful times. . . . There are moments in which you go through tribulations, and moments that are good. . . . There are times you have enough and times you don't." Several respondents pointed out that the fact that you become a Christian does not mean that your family is going to be Christian. Eric said:

> Well, that's sort of borderline because my accepting the Lord doesn't guarantee that things are going to immediately get better in my home. There could be problems, because if I am Christian, but the others in my household are Catholic, or witches, or whatever, they could rebel. I mean things aren't going to go well. There's going to be conflict.

José Gregorio told me he did not think improving one's family life was a good reason for accepting the Lord. When I asked him why not, he said, "Because when God comes into your life, you are going to develop a witness for others to see. But if God doesn't change the others *[shrugs his shoulders]*—I can be a witness. I can change, but if they don't want to I can't force them."

Several respondents told personal stories that supported José Gregorio's comments. Henry said that living with his Catholic family was tense after he converted. For example, when his father's auto repair service was broken into, he inflated the insurance report and got angry when Henry refused to lie to the police to corroborate his story. Silvio expressed doubts about any immediate effect. He related that he and his sister had been at odds most of their lives—including after he became an Evangelical. However, Silvio said, as he slowly became "more humble in the Lord," he was able to make amends with his sister and they now live in the same household in peace. "But," he continued, "I've heard of other cases in which the person accepts the Lord and [the family] starts to try to trip him up, mock him. But I think that's just for a while, because later they learn to respect each other. I mean, that's what happened with my sister." In other words, these respondents argue that converting to the Gospel could change your family life in the long term, but you certainly cannot count on it in the short term. This makes sense given that the individual cannot generally control the religious behavior of family members and given the unpredictable environment of Caracas.

3. "Accept the Lord so that things will go well in your business" (26/49, 53.1%)

Responses to the statement about converting in order to improve family life were interesting in that while the overall rate of assent dropped with respect to the previous question on individual change, this does not appear to result from a rejection of the object of intentionality. Rather it reflected reservations regarding the increased uncertainty of family-level change. However, with the question regarding business, assent does decline because respondents rejected the idea that success in business is a legitimate object of religious practice. Here material goods are much more likely to be seen as inappropriate reasons for conversion. Looking closely at this brings us to the main point of this chapter: the basic well-being of the individual as well as the life of the family are themselves considered "spiritual" issues. Thus working on them through religious practice is not instrumental.

Ramiro argued that God helps the Christian prosper but that the Christian cannot make the mistake of thinking he is controlling God: "Is God committed to your business? No. He is committed by the Word to help you and bless you. But it's not like I'm going to use the Bible or God and impose that it's going to be like this and this." Pedro said that this is not acceptable: "We're obliging, or I mean we're trying to direct

God [if we say that]." Fredy argued, "The Lord doesn't promise that he is going to give us riches here on earth. However, we accept the Lord, and by his mercy, in some cases, he can help us in our business. But it's not like the Lord promises that he is going to multiply us in our business."

Why would asking God to make your business prosper be any more of an attempt to control him than asking for eternal life, personal change, or an improved family life? The question is phrased exactly the same. Presumably God would be entitled the same liberty in each case. These Evangelicals respond this way because they do not consider business success a spiritual goal. Since it is not spiritual it is an instrumental use of religious practice and a manipulation of God. It is acceptable to ask for it, or desire it, but not to expect it. George said, "When you preach to a soul, to a person, you have to preach that he [surrenders] to Christ so that he will save you, because all that other stuff is business, the material world. The Lord adds it after the person is saved and is seeking Him with constancy." Agustín agreed with the idea of converting in order to change your own life or your family life but balked at the idea of converting to change your business: "No. That's too—when you accept the Lord you're not thinking about material things." Victor pointed to the disjuncture between accepting the Lord and business success, saying the latter is not a necessary condition for the former, so there should be other reasons: "I don't agree with that [reason]. Because I believe that accepting the Lord is something much bigger. Not out of economic interest, because there are many people who have not accepted Christ and do have stability, economic stability in business."

A few respondents explicitly made the contrast in a way that reveals what "spiritual" means for them. César Miguel argued, "When a person prefers Christ, what's secular gets set aside. So a Christian wouldn't say 'surrender to Christ so that the Lord makes your business prosper.' A secular person might say that. The best question you've asked me so far is the first, "come to Christ so that Christ will change your life," because that's what God does." Even more telling was the following exchange with Vincenzo, beginning with his initial response to the statement:

> That's getting into prosperity theology. The idea is that you accept Jesus Christ for his mercy, not because you're thinking about monetary gain.
>
> *Okay, so what's the difference between accepting the Lord so that things go well in your home and accepting the Lord so that things go well in your business?*

> When we talk about the home we're talking about living together peacefully, spiritual things, living harmoniously, without thinking of prosperity. That would be the true motivation, thinking about spiritual life, harmony, and the integrity of our home life. That's what we would think about first.

Vincenzo clearly associates spirituality with home life—a tendency that is even clearer in Ramiro's message at the beginning of this chapter.

Understanding Variety

Pentecostal Evangelicals in Venezuela do distinguish between sacred and secular, spiritual and material. However, this does not correspond to the distinction between contemplative and intentional, moral and technical, or even collective and individual. To the contrary, for the Pentecostal Evangelicals studied here, the life of the individual and the family are spiritual concerns. Conflict, disorder, sorrow, and unfulfilled basic necessities in the life of an individual or his family are symptoms of the presence of evil. Accepting Jesus Christ, therefore, is seen as a legitimate means of straightening out the life of an individual and bringing peace and prosperity into the household. Durkheim (1995: 34–35) understood that different religions could divide the sacred and the profane in different ways. But because he saw religious concepts as figurative if not substantially arbitrary, it was impossible for him to imagine how a particular division of the sacred and the profane in a particular religion might affect the very function of that religion. While there certainly are religions in which religious meanings are simply contemplative and represent the collectivity, in many others religious meanings provide guides to action and can represent the life of the individual. Pentecostal Evangelicals see family and the individual as legitimate intentional objects of religious practice but express doubts about pursuing business success through religious practice. Caracas's neo-Pentecostal churches, in contrast, openly aim at material success through religious practice. The Christ for All Nations Center (CCN), for example, has frequent workshops and events oriented toward entrepreneurship. All of them speak of spirituality as part and parcel of business success. They can do this, quite simply, because it is incorporated into their theology and portrayed as sacred. In 2003 the founder of the CCN, Apostle Raul Ávila, preached a series of twelve sermons titled "Connect with Your Money." He began each sermon with a paraphrase of 1 Timothy 6:10: "Wrong relationship with your money is the root of all evil." Ávila's messages said that the problem is not money in itself but when people see money as the ultimate goal rather than their servant. While to an external observer this may seem like a laughable embellishment of the Bible, Ávila's exegesis, speaking ability, and personal charisma make it plausible enough to sustain the belief of his hundreds of congregants.

Not only do religions differ in terms of how they locate instrumentality, *individuals* from the same church can differ from each other. In the data presented here, even when speaking of projects of the self, about 15 percent of respondents do not agree that it is acceptable to convert in order to improve your life. For them, only the quest for eternal life and the search for truth were legitimate reasons for converting. How can we make sense of such differing opinions? One possibility is that some Evangelicals—perhaps through seminary training or extensive Bible study—have worked through the issues with more analytic rigor, systematizing their personal religious meaning system to the point that the only truly legitimate motivations for religious practice are otherworldly. However, looking at the complete interviews of these "otherworldly" individuals points in a different direction. For example, Martín disagreed with the first statement regarding conversion as a project of self-reform:

> The idea is legitimate, but at the moment that you surrender, you seek God not so that he will change your life but because you feel an emptiness and God fits in that empty space. You don't change so that God changes your life but because you feel a calling. Afterward, he changes everything. Everything comes afterward.

But, paradoxically, he uttered this statement approximately half an hour after telling me, in the same interview, that he had converted to overcome substance abuse and save his marriage (see pp. 128–31).

We can make sense of such seeming contradiction if we remember to think of a meaning *system* not as a rigorous structure but as a loosely integrated *repertoire* of meanings that are often multiple and contradictory (Sewell 1992; Smilde 2004).[5] Focusing on their contradiction pri-

5. This is the source of my discomfort with neo-Durkheimian theorizations of cultural meanings in terms of "moral order" (Alexander 2004; Smith 2003). I understand "order" to mean a logical or methodical arrangement of elements. Following Weber, I think the rationalization of a repertoire of religious meanings to the degree that calling it an *order* would make sense, is a contextually localized, historically unusual phenomenon. In general, such constructions of order are confined to religious intellectuals. In some specific circumstances such religious intellectualism becomes part of the religious practice of the laity (Weber 1968: 507). However, in most contexts the religious laity have a repertoire of meanings that are marshaled for specific situations. This repertoire will not normally be rationalized but rather will contain numerous mutually incompatible meanings that are inconsistently used. I frequently use the term *system* to refer to this repertoire. It denotes a

oritizes the spectator's view over the social actor's. What is relevant to the latter is the way specific meanings work for specific ends in specific situations. As would be suggested by Weber's portrayal of religious systematization arising through confrontation with failure, the religious concept that regards salvation as the most important motivation for practice provides a constancy of commitment that is not provided by an emphasis on concrete rewards. The concept of a God who delivers concrete blessings in the here and now provides a concrete motivation for conversion that is not provided by emphasis on eternal life. Ramiro, whose message to non-Evangelicals at the Plaza El Venezolano did not mention the afterlife, frequently made statements about eternal life in his Sunday school classes at Emmanuel Church. In the latter context, working with baptized converts rather than potential converts, the focus was more on sustaining commitment than on initiating it. Here again Ramiro would never consider this cynical manipulation but rather a tailoring of his message to his audience, a marshaling of premises for a specific argument.

In sum, apart from a handful of individuals who, at least on the occasion of my interview with them, argued that only the afterlife is a legitimate motivation for religious practice, for the Pentecostal Evangelicals interviewed here, the self and family life are *themselves* considered spiritual. Thus religious practice seen as a project of self or family reform is not an instrumental use of religion; it is an integral practice of it.

ADOPTING PROJECTS, PORTRAYING OUTCOMES

The second reason Elster doubts people can decide to believe is that people must have reasons for believing beyond simple self-interest. More precisely, they must have intellectual reasons, not simply self-interested ones. But what happens when intellect and self-interest point in the same direction? As Ramiro's message demonstrates, becoming Evangelical is openly presented by evangelizers as a golden opportunity for those with problems to straighten out their lives. It is presented as a project through which certain desired ends can be obtained. This project consists of a bundle of concepts that portray the social world, how it works, and how Evangelical practice affects its consequences. This

group of interacting, interrelated elements without an assumption of logical arrangement or coherence.

project can be adopted and tried on by adherents. This is the first-order imaginative rationality we saw in chapters 3 and 4. When this project meets with success it is powerfully validated. However, success and failure are not always easy to discern, and the Evangelical meaning system contains a repertoire of second-order concepts that can portray them in ways that support, or at least do not invalidate, the religious meaning system.[6]

Projecting Success

The concept of imaginative rationality rests on an image of human beings as agents who confront problems by making meaning. However, they do not do this wholly anew in every case. Dipesh Chakrabarty (2000: 177–78) says imagination can be "subjectless" when it consists of "practices sedimented into language" rather than voluntaristic elaborations. Evangelicals often do create complex meanings through acts of bricolage—by combining and recombining existing elements from the cultural context. More often, however, preexisting projects are communicated to them by members of their social environment, and they adapt and fit them to their own life circumstances in anticipation of future benefits. Consider the experience of Guille. Guille is tall and imposing, the son of Italian immigrants. He does low-level factory jobs to support his young family. In the period of his conversion he found himself in the midst of a situation in which he had threats on his life from two independent sources: he had run afoul of former coworkers when they were fired for theft and he was not and of malandros in his barrio because of an apparent dirty look. In the midst of his predicament, he went to a service at the Evangelical church he grew up in but had abandoned many years before. The sermon preached that day made clear to him that God was the solution to his problem. Guille explained:

> And he [the preacher] spoke about Isaiah, chapter 41, that says that those who fight you will be shamed and confused and you will not see them anymore. That was a Sunday, the day I converted. And those words hit me and I began to cry in front of everyone. I didn't care who was watching.

The message hit home with Guille. It provided him with a project for dealing with his problem. If he would return to Evangelical participation, perhaps God would rid him of his enemies.

6. This corresponds, then, with Emirbayer and Mische's (1998) portrayal of "projectivity" and "evaluation" as two essential elements of agency.

Martín related a similar story. He and his wife had been arguing for a week straight and were about to separate. Although he had a serious drug problem that he would not recognize and his wife was not fully aware of, a flash point with her was his smoking, since he did that at home. Martín told me:

> We were going to separate, we were having problems. And then we heard on the radio an hermano saying that Christ could transform my life, that he could rid me of the vice of cigarettes, that he could pull me out of the world in which I was living—which for me was impossible.

This led Martín and his wife to seek out an Evangelical service that afternoon to see if it could provide them with a solution to their marital difficulties.

Communication of conversion as a project of self-reform comes not only from preaching and evangelization. It also comes from exposure to living, breathing Evangelicals. Indeed, this is the idea behind Evangelical "testimonies," the demonstration of God's work in you—either through storytelling or by example—in order to bring others to the faith. Ugeth discussed his thoughts on seeing that his former accomplices had converted to Evangelicalism:

> And when I got there, I saw all of these childhood friends, and wow, I saw the miracles that the Lord had done in them, and I said, "Hey, if the Lord was able to rescue this guy, then what they say about the Gospel—that it is the power of God—is true, because I see that it has changed a lot of people." "So what would it hurt to try? It can't hurt to try," I said.

In chapter 6 I examine more closely the logic of testimony as it works through networks. The point I want to make here is that an Evangelical's biographical profile can provide others with the notion of cause and effect through time that they can generalize and imaginatively accommodate to their own lives.

A religious meaning system does not have to be adopted in an overwhelming rush of conviction. Elster (1979: 177–78) suggests that people can "try on" beliefs to see if they work: "It *is* possible to overcome fear by repeating to oneself 'I am not afraid,' even though initially the statement was false. . . . One can in this sense intentionally adopt new beliefs and attitudes, trying them on, as it were, to see whether they are compatible with the boundary conditions of one's life. . . . There is a 'zone of indeterminacy' within which saying makes it so, and the borders of this zone are themselves indeterminate, i.e., incompletely known."[7] Indeed, many of my respondents spoke in terms of trying on Evangelicalism. Ugeth described the day he actually "accepted Christ": "I surrendered in Plaza El Venezolano one day that I was there and I said, 'Okay, today is the day, I'm going to become Evangelical and see whether there is a change in my life.'" Juan Betancourt had been having problems with his new wife because he was spending more time in bars than at home with her. Together they tried different forms of spirituality in order to obtain peace in their home and stuck with Evangelicalism. "And the spiritists couldn't do it," Juan explained. "I wanted a change in my life, and some hermanos told me, 'Look, if you receive the Lord in your life, there is a change.' And that is how I entered into the way of the Lord."

Some of the men described this trying-on period as a deal with God: If God would solve their problem; they would believe and begin to follow him. Jhony explained how he asked God to help him kick his drug habit: "I spoke to God and I told him that if he would rid me of this, I would believe in the Gospel, I would make an effort, I would look for a way of getting to know him." (Also see the deal with God made by Henrique below).

Explaining Success

It is quite easy to understand how common problems experienced by men of Caracas's popular sectors can be resolved by adopting the Evangelical meaning system and its norms of behavior. In most cases my respondents reported resolution of their major problems in the short term. Table 4 lists the ninety-seven instances of eleven conversion-precipitating problems reported by my Evangelical respondents and whether their life histories show that these problems were resolved. Of course, such a remarkable success rate needs to be put in context. First, since this sample only includes men who continued in their Evangelical project to the point of baptism, there is undoubtedly a strong overselection of those who had a modicum of success with their Evangelical project. Those who experienced quick defeats, such as a drinking binge

7. This may seem like a strange position for Elster to hold, given my portrayal of his theory. But he immediately follows this by saying the scope of such processes is, in his view, extremely limited. A goal of this book is to argue that this process is not as limited as Elster thinks precisely because of the way religious and cultural meanings can conceptualize it.

the next day, likely dropped the project altogether. Furthermore, "resolution" of some of these problems is synonymous with being Evangelical. This is the case for substance abuse, gambling, social problems, concern about the afterlife, and, for the most part, violence. Being Evangelical to a large extent *is equivalent to* being sober, not gambling, not doing physical harm to others, and assurance of eternal life. Also, adequate peer social life and emotional well-being are largely coterminous with being Evangelical because it implies participating in a religious identity that says you are special, important, and valuable as God's child. It would be difficult if not impossible to both admit to emotional or social problems and continue to participate. Those areas in which the Evangelical meaning system seems to have had less success—problems with conjugal relations, the family, economic stability—are clearly those in which the beneficial consequence is outside the scope of the self and not directly provided by participation. Only a longitudinal study that follows converts from the moment of their conversion through a reasonable period could adequately answer how successful the meaning system really is in providing what it says it will provide. However, it should be uncontroversial to argue that it is indeed successful in most of the cases of continued participation. In what follows I look at cases ranging from clear resolution to partial resolution to no resolution at all to analyze how such results affect a believer's appropriation of the meaning system.

Clear successes, of course, are experienced as direct confirmation of the validity of the meaning system. In Martín's testimony he conceptualizes the fruits of his new dedication to the household as the work of God:

> I changed from one day to the next, I began to dress differently, I started coming here to the Gospel, and started feeling differently. I stopped smoking and, wow, I saw the power of God. And then, my wife and I, we used to get up in the morning and pray together before going to work. I would be sleeping and she would wake me up. We would get up and pray together and everything we asked for, God would provide. At the beginning we had problems because my mom had thrown us out of her house because of the fighting—we used to have really ugly fights. So we lived in a rented place with just a couple of bedrolls. We slept on the floor on the bedrolls, and we had one single pot and a little electric stove. So we asked God, first, for a gas stove. And then we would pray and God would give us everything. Then we prayed for a stereo and God gave it to us, a bedroom set, and God gave it to us. We saw the work of God. And we started to get along well, because the spirit of God was moving there in our household. . . . Before I used to spend all my money on things that didn't have any purpose.

Table 4. Resolution of Conversion-Precipitating Problems

Life Problem	Number of Occurrences	Number Resolved
Substance abuse	24	23
Gambling	2	2
Violence	18	18
Economic difficulty	8	5
Self-improvement	8	7
Emotional difficulty	8	8
Conjugal conflict	11	6
Family problems	7	5
Peer social life	7	7
Health	2	2
Concern about the afterlife	2	2

From a social psychological perspective, it is easy to understand how Martín could overcome his substance abuse through the feeling that he had supernatural help, how praying together brought him and his wife together, and how no longer spending money on drugs and alcohol could allow him to accumulate goods. And given the elusiveness of these goals before his conversion, it is understandable that Martín would experience them as the work of God and clear evidence of the truth of the Evangelical meaning system.

Those who committed from problems of substance abuse frequently describe how their cravings and desire for their substance of choice disappeared with their conversion. Bartolo had a familiarity with Evangelicalism from his days in prison and from observing his Evangelical brother. He had recently had a "personal encounter" with God but had not begun participating in a church yet. On his way to the beach one weekend he met a neighbor who was with a group of Evangelicals also going to the beach. The neighbor invited him to join them, and his experience that day convinced him God was working on him:

> So they invited me along, and I got in with them, I went to the beach with Evangelicals. And when I went to the beach I was used to consuming marijuana on the pier, drinking beer, smoking cigarettes—always. But this time I didn't even remember to smoke a cigarette, or marijuana, or beer. All we did was swim, talk, eat fish, and have fun. But I didn't even remember any of that perverse stuff. I hadn't realized that the Lord had completely cleansed me, from the inside out. So in the afternoon when I went to my

> house, I had a pack of cigarettes in my sweatshirt, and when I tied it around my waist, the pack fell out. I didn't remember that I smoked until I saw the pack of cigarettes.

Bartolo's description is consistent with the intersubjectivity of drug and alcohol consumption. As discussed in chapter 3, alcohol and drug use is an eminently social phenomenon whereby others' consumption provokes desire in the individual. The inverse seems equally true: being in an environment of abstainers can result in diminishing desire for consumption. For Bartolo, this understandably could have been experienced as miraculous evidence that his encounter with the Lord days earlier was real.

Guille likewise interpreted the resolution of the threats on his life as God answering his call:

> Within a couple of days, I saw that the guys who were looking for trouble with me didn't care about me anymore. One of them was thrown out of his house. They even threw his wife out. They had to sell the house. One of the men was fired from his job [where Guille worked]. In other words, God was beginning to solve my problem—to the point that they were obliged to leave the area where we lived. God made them go away in a big way, and the guy who, this is a shame, but the guy who wanted to kill me ended up getting killed himself. And so I saw how God cleared everything up for me.

Henrique converted in a moment of economic scarcity. He had had a difficult year in which he could not even cover basic necessities when he was accepted into a training course to become a bank teller. The course functioned as a sort of selection process determining who would end up with the jobs. In the first weeks of the training course, an Evangelical classmate took him at lunchtime to a nearby plaza where Evangelicals held daily services. There he converted. As he describes his conversion experience, "The moment when I converted I said, 'Lord, if you give me this job, I am going to serve you, I am going to remain faithful.' That's what I said to the Lord, and that's what the Lord did. I mean, the Lord gave me that job, because doing the course didn't guarantee that I was going to get the job."

I have arranged these four stories from more to less plausible. In the case of Martín, it is plausible that when he and his wife became Evangelical their relationship improved and that they experienced a new prosperity when he was no longer drinking and doing drugs. The case of Bartolo is also largely plausible, even if now it is told in clearer, crisper terms than those in which it was actually experienced. The case of Guille is less probable. This causal sequence could happen—a person caught in the middle of a vendetta becomes a nonthreatening "worthless" enemy by becoming Evangelical—but when I asked Guille he said that the men who were threatening him did not know that he had converted. It is more likely that the conflict never reached the point of direct confrontation and petered out. Becoming Evangelical gave him confidence that God was on his side and would help him through the difficult situation. When he did get through it, regardless of how the causality actually worked, it was powerful confirmation of his recently adopted meaning system. Henrique's case is similar. He was going through a very difficult situation. From my understanding of such training courses, only a small minority of individuals who demonstrate genuine inability are let go. Henrique's situation was desperate, however, and he likely could not tolerate the anguish of not knowing. His "deal with God" served as a source of power for confronting his incertitude. It is unlikely that becoming Evangelical had anything to do with getting the job (although it is conceivable that through his work partner his superiors came to know that he also was Evangelical and therefore perhaps trusted him more). But regardless of whether it did or not, getting the job was powerful confirmation for him of the Evangelical project he had undertaken.[8] In each of the above cases a social scientist can distinguish whether the causal link between "being Evangelical" and the consequence is objectively discernible, unclear, or clearly nonexistent. But for those involved, each of these cases is experienced in the same way, as clear evidence of the truth of the Evangelical meaning system.

Explaining Failure

Because my participant observation centered on practicing Evangelicals, clearly unsuccessful religious projects were difficult for me to observe. But frequently converts experienced only partial resolution of problems they had had when they began their Evangelical practice. Ramiro, for example, resolved his problems with substance abuse and violence, but his relationship problem continued as his wife was unimpressed by his Evangelical project. Within a year, she left Ramiro without explanation while

8. Weber (1968: 427) makes the point as follows: "The historical accident that Isaiah's steadfast prophecy actually came to fulfillment—God would not permit Jerusalem to fall into the hands of the Assyrian hordes, if only the Judean king remained firm—provided the subsequently unshakeable foundation for the position of this god and his prophets."

he was out with his son buying a bicycle pump. Enrique experienced something similar. It appears that the damage to his relationship was already done at the time he converted. His wife began an affair with another man, and when Enrique discovered it he forced her to leave. Both Ramiro and Enrique interpret these relationship failures as having been God's will.

On one occasion, I did have the opportunity to witness a roundly unsuccessful Evangelical project. I first met Ángel when he had just gotten out of jail and was brought by an hermano to Plaza El Venezolano to give his testimony of deliverance from drugs and violence. He told of his "life in the street," of having robbed and killed and done time in prison, and how through Jesus Christ he was now putting his life back together. After a few months Ángel disappeared. Sometime later Ramiro and Enrique came across him in a downtown park dirty and homeless. They cleaned him up, gave him clothes, and brought him to church with them. Ramiro had Ángel stay at his house for a few weeks and even paid him to work with him on his remodeling projects. After a couple of weeks he disappeared again. I had not noticed his absence until I happened upon him on a downtown sidewalk. He was sitting in a security guard's chair at the entrance to a parking garage, nonchalantly spinning in circles, pausing occasionally to ask passersby for change. He was dirty and obviously using drugs again.[9] When I later asked Ramiro what had happened, he said that Ángel had frequently expressed fear regarding some enemies to whom he owed drug money and who had found out where he lived. Ramiro did not know if it was true or if he was making it up because of cravings for drugs. Whichever was the case, Ángel's problems with drugs and violence were not solved, and he dropped his Evangelical project.

Other cases similarly indicated that unsuccessful projects led to discontinuation. One respondent from my control sample of non-Evangelical men had been Evangelical three years before our interview. Melvin reported that after three months he backslid and resumed his crack habit with even more force. He never went back to an Evangelical church but finally overcame his addiction through Tadeo human development workshops sponsored by the Catholic Church. Similarly, in the Venezuelan sociologist Anabel Castillo's (1997) book on juvenile delinquents in Caracas, one of her interviewees said he had tried to reform himself while in prison: "I was behaving. I had become Evangelical because I wanted to

9. When he asked me for money to buy bread I offered to go with him to buy a hamburger at a stand about ten yards away. He refused, insisting on money instead; he said he knew where he could buy bread cheaply and did not want to eat until later.

change my life. . . . But my friends in La Planta [a prison in Caracas] said, 'What? You're going to become Evangelical here?' . . . They stabbed me, and I left the Gospel. So, as they say, I grabbed my gloves and got back in the ring" (71). In both the case of Melvin and the young man Castillo interviewed, the religious project's failure to make good on delivering the sought-after benefits undermined their commitment.

A single failure does not necessarily lead to discontinuation. When we think about action in terms of "projects" rather than "moves," it is clear that immediate resolution of problems is not required for individuals to continue participation. In most projects the end point at which the desired outcome should occur is not fixed and hope for a successful payoff can always be postponed. There must, of course, be some important successes in the individual's life or in the lives of those around him; otherwise, commitment will most likely wane. Weber (1968: 427) states the point thus: "Should the effort to influence a god prove permanently inefficacious, then it is concluded that either the god is impotent or the correct procedure of influencing him is unknown, and he is abandoned."

However, a successful meaning system, whether religious, political, or scientific, usually has interpretive tools for coping with setbacks, for making sense of failure. Indeed, Weber saw engagement with failure as one of the main motors of the systematization of religious doctrine, as it is precisely in the moments of failure that some of the most active culture work takes place. Digging into the Evangelical meaning system as it is used by the men I interviewed shows that it not only helps them to imagine the way religious practice affects its consequences; it also helps them conceptualize what went wrong when benefits do not materialize.

To get at these subtleties, I took respondents through a two-question sequence I developed after considerable participant observation. I asked the second question after the respondent finished answering the first.

Q1. How would you explain the following? There is an Evangelical family that is very prosperous. Things are going well for the father in his job, the mother keeps the house clean, and the children get good grades in school. Next door there is a worldly family, and everything is going wrong. The father is always unemployed, the house is dirty, and the kids aren't doing well in school.

Q2. How would you explain the following? There is a worldly family that is very prosperous. Things are going well for the father in his job, the mother keeps the house clean, and the children get good grades in school. Next door there is an Evangelical family, and everything is going wrong. The father is always unemployed, the house is dirty, and the children aren't doing well in school.

Not surprisingly, in most responses to the first question there was a straightforward relationship to correct religious practice. Luis used terms that appeared in most of the other responses:

> How do you explain this? Well, because the wages of sin is death. Things turn out well for those who have God in them. God protects them. God helps them. They cry out to God and God listens. The Bible says God doesn't listen to sinners and things are always going to go badly for the sinner. Everything goes wrong and he has no peace. The Devil robs his peace. The Devil gives him anguish, he bothers him, in order to finish him off, to kill him and take him away. In contrast, he who is with God, God gives him peace, gives him patience, gives him wisdom. He gives him everything good, gets rid of the bad and protects him.

Several respondents suggested that God frequently tries to get through to unbelievers by rewarding observant Christians. For example:

> Sometimes God does things so that the unemployed and unconverted person sees the Christian family for whom everything is going well, and understands that that family has Christ. And since he doesn't have Christ, everything is falling apart. So he is going to wonder and go over to that Christian and ask him how it is that everything goes well for him, that his children are behaving. . . . And so he's going to want to get to know that same God that is protecting the other guy so that he too can change his life and so that his household will be the same as the neighbor's household with kids getting good grades and everything going well.

The answers to the second question, of course, are more complex. If becoming a Christian is supposed to improve your life, if the Holy Spirit guides you and protects you from the satanic influences non-Christians are subject to, how can you explain failure? This situation is not foreign to these respondents as every Evangelical at some point or another confronts this everyday version of the problem of theodicy: how can bad things happen to believers? The most common answer is that the person is making some sort of error in religious practice. Even when one is Christian, one can be subject to misunderstandings and be misguided, and this is the subject of frequent injunctions for Evangelicals to *revisarse*—examine themselves. Henrique said, "Something is going on in that Christian family. Either they forgot about God or they aren't leading a life that conforms to what God demands." Juan Miguel had a similar view:

> They have to examine themselves to see if they really are living the Word. Because you can't explain that. There can be disagreements between chil-

> dren and parents, or at certain times there can be dark clouds over a household, but not all the time. Understand? Because if they've really been born again, and are [living] with the Word, they have to sit down and figure out how to fix what's going wrong. Something's going on in that home.

However, assuming an error in religious practice is not the only way to respond to the problem of theodicy. There are a number of other conceptual possibilities. Among these Evangelicals there are two primary directions. The first is what Weber referred to as "providence": the assumption of an insurmountable chasm between an all-powerful creator and puny human beings who have a hard time understanding God's mysterious ways. God, in this view, is beyond human ethical judgment. The men I interviewed frequently emphasized God's mystery when confronted with the paradoxical situation. Josue, for example, simply shrugged his shoulders and said, "God's plan. That's God's plan." José María answered in similar fashion. Functionally illiterate and usually unemployed, he lives the everyday problem of theodicy more than most: he is confronted daily by the fact that most non-Evangelicals have an easier, more prosperous life than his. He thinks about it in a way that emphasizes he is in no position to judge God:

> I wait in the Lord. If God has prospered them [the non-Christian family], then Glory to God because he has made them prosperous. I'm not going to take that to say to God, "Okay Lord, why have you made this worldly person prosper while I live in decadence?" That's not a fight I can pick with the Lord. Rather, I say, "Thank you Lord for being with me, for helping me to live, for giving me what's necessary. Because if you make me rich, I could lose sight of you."

But the most common way of using the chasm between God and humans to answer the everyday problem of theodicy is through the notion that God tests and educates human beings through difficulty. In Evangelicals' view, God frequently puts believers through "trials of fire" to purify them like "fine gold." Inerio said:

> There are times in which we Evangelical Christians have to be tested in everything. The Word teaches us that we have to go and be tested like fine gold. Today we see how God's people are suffering, are needy. But that doesn't mean that that Evangelical is necessarily wrong with God, that his spiritual life or family doesn't please God. Rather [it means] that God tests, God permits struggle, he permits trials so that we become firm in his Way, in his Word.

Frequently the two logics of incorrect religious practice and the chasm between humans and God can be freely combined. In fact, the logic of self-examination is precisely to figure out if the troubles you are having are the result of incorrect religious practice or simply trials from God that must be endured. Pablo combined them thus:

> Perhaps that family, that father isn't right with God, or isn't doing something that God is asking him to do. There must be some reason that they are in that situation. Or maybe they are going through a trial—the Lord teaching them that he is the only one who sustains them.

The second direction in which everyday theodicy can be interpreted is dualism: the idea that God does not control all that happens in the universe and is not the only supernatural being that is active. Aspects of the world may be simply outside his control or under the control of "autonomous powers of darkness" (Weber 1968: 524). In dualistic views this world is devalued and debased when compared to those things that are saintly. Evangelicals frequently use dualistic images to reinterpret defeat in this world as a premonition of rewards in a better, future world. In his response Miguel Vicente devalued worldly success: "In material terms they might have it all, but in spiritual terms they have nothing. I mean, when they die, they lose because they don't have salvation." Renlón used the same combination of trials and dualistic devaluation of worldly success to explain the situation: "Well, he has to examine himself. It could be that he's going through a trial. God is testing him and the worldly guy. As I said before, the Devil makes people prosper too, in order to make the Gospel look bad or the Christian family [look bad]."

There is also a dualistic construction that, building on an image of a world not fully controlled by God, argues that humans have to maintain themselves as human beings rather than wait for God to take care of everything. Orent pointed this out:

> [Can I say] for example, "I'm not going to clean the house because I'm just going to pray, pray, and pray all day long," or "I'm not going to eat anymore, I'm just going to read the Bible?" No! I should take some time to read the Bible, and some time to clean my house, time for my work. . . . Just because I want to become saintly doesn't mean I can ignore everything else.

In this view the problems Evangelicals have are not the result of incorrect practice, trials from God, or Satan's mischief. Rather they are the result of irresponsibility. Pedro said, "You see a lot of Christians who blame their mistakes on God and that's wrong. Some say, 'Oh,

God's punishing me.' [I say,] 'No. Get that out of your head. It's *your* irresponsibility.'"

I have sought to show that the opposition Elster sets up between deciding to believe because believing will benefit you and having reasons to believe is a false one. The Evangelical meaning system provides a comprehensive set of metaphors that portray the world in such a way that the this-worldly effects of religious belief are understandable through religious ideas. Positive consequences serve as validation of these religious ideas. Defeats and setbacks are considered symptoms of wrong practice, last-ditch efforts by Satan, or God's attempt to "process" the believer. In other words, among the features of the lived world conceptualized by religious meanings is the way religious practice itself works or does not work.

NARRATIVES OF HIS AGENCY

Enrique and Juan Carlos

The Thursday night movie for new converts was showing inside the sanctuary of Emmanuel Church and Enrique and I slipped out to talk. We chatted in the street just outside the church doorway—occasionally pausing for the deafening roar of the buses—until Enrique invited me to his car to show me a book. We sat in the car in the dark vacant lot across the street from Emmanuel Church. As was my custom at that time in my research with this informant—we had worked together for over two years—I had my tape recorder on. While I was sitting in the passenger seat, talking, Enrique was sitting in the driver's seat looking over his right shoulder. He interrupted me, "Look, that kid is smoking drugs." In addition to being a place for church members and visitors to park, the vacant lot served as a sort of way station for transients: a place for a homeless person to sleep off a day's drunk, a place for a man and a woman to argue away from their in-laws, or, frequently, a place to inject or smoke drugs tucked away behind a car or a pile of boxes. Enrique jumped out of the car as I fumbled to keep up with him with my tape recorder in hand. Formerly a gas station, the vacant lot still has cement islands where the gas pumps once were—the only remnants of the latter being the twisted, flattened metal tubes sticking out dangerously. Sitting on one of these islands was Juan Carlos, a chubby, pimple-faced young man, wearing purposefully messy and baggy clothes and long hair, stylishly cut but unwashed and greasy. He was taking crystals of crack cocaine from aluminum foil and carefully placing them in a small pipe. Enrique started to talk to Juan Carlos while he continued to pack his pipe.

Enrique: What are you doing smoking that, man? Can't you see that that does bad things to you, to your body, to your life? *[Pause]* Eh, varón?[10] *[Pause]* Varón, look me in the eye. *[Pause]* Why are you smoking drugs? *[Pause]* Where do you live? Do you live alone? (5)

Juan Carlos: No, I live with my mom, my little sister, and my brother—

Enrique: *[Interrupting]* Do your mom and your brother know you're doing drugs?

Juan Carlos: Marijuana, not crack, like I'm doing right now.

(10) *Enrique:* Why are you smoking crack? You have to quit. You're going to destroy your life man. *[Pause]* That's bread for today, hunger for tomorrow. Right now you're going to feel good. But tomorrow you're going to be in bad shape.

Juan Carlos: It's a curse, hermano.

(15) *Enrique:* It's a curse and you know it. So why don't you look to Jesus Christ then? *[Pause. Juan Carlos finishes packing his pipe and puts it up to his mouth.]* Varón, respect me when I'm talking to you and don't smoke that right now. Don't light that right now. Listen to me a minute. Can't you see that you're going to destroy yourself with that, man? Look at (20) you, you're tense. Look how your eyes are all over the place. And if you smoke that you're going to feel good but tomorrow you're going to need it again, and then you're going to need it again until the Devil finishes you off. Is that what you want? Is that what you want for your mother and brother (25) and sister? Is that what you want?

Juan Carlos: What's the question?

Enrique: Whether you want to continue this lifestyle destroying yourself little by little.

(30) *Juan Carlos:* I haven't destroyed my life yet.

Enrique: Whatta ya mean you haven't destroyed your life yet? How are you going to get over your drug dependence? Have you always had to use drugs to feel good?

Juan Carlos: No.

10. *Varón* is a way of saying "man" in Spanish that accentuates masculinity. It is not usually used in common Spanish parlance other than to refer to the sex of a baby or a small child, but Evangelicals use it continually instead of the more common *hombre*.

35 *Enrique:* Uh huh. *[Pause]* Did you used to depend on drugs to feel good? Were you dependent? No. So why do you depend on drugs now in order to feel good?

Juan Carlos: Because I fell, into using drugs—

Enrique: *[Interrupting]* At what age did you fall?

40 *Juan Carlos:* Age fifteen.

Enrique: Oh, c'mon. How old are you now?

Juan Carlos: Twenty-two.

Enrique: You can't keep on like this, man! You're going to destroy yourself. Satan wants to destroy you. And there's a way to
45 escape it. You don't think there is a way to escape it?

Juan Carlos: *[Pause]* Escape, *[pause]* yeah I think so.

Enrique: Why don't you come to the church and toss that [the crack].

Juan Carlos: You got a Bible there?

Enrique: Yes I do.

50 *Juan Carlos:* Let me see it a second to show you a verse.

Enrique passed him the Bible, and Juan Carlos paged through it until he found what he was looking for: 1 Corinthians 13, the verse in which Paul speaks about the preeminence of Love. He read it out loud.

51 *Enrique:* Uh huh. That's about the preeminence of Love. And when are you going to put that in practice?

Juan Carlos: I put it in practice with others.

Enrique: With what others?

Two other Evangelicals who had seen us as they were entering the church came by and, in typical fashion, abruptly interrupted the conversation. Enrique impatiently answered their questions while Juan Carlos took a drag from his pipe. When they left he turned back to Juan Carlos.

55 *Enrique:* Christ loves you, man. *[Pause]* Christ loves you. *[Pause]* Christ wants to free you from your vice. You're a young man, good looking. Satan wants to possess you.

Juan Carlos: I hadn't consumed crack for four months until today.

Enrique: Look what the Bible says *[pages through the Bible until he*
60 *finds a verse]*, "the Devil came to kill you, steal your life and your peace, and destroy you." That's what Satan came for. But Jesus Christ came to destroy the work of the Devil. Get

65		up from the stupor you're in, man. You're causing your mom and kids problems. Your brothers and sisters are seeing your example. Do you want them to be tomorrow like you are today? You're not a good example for society, son. And Christ knows it, he's putting his hand out to you and saying, "Hey my son, I love you. Stop that foolishness, man." You're desperate to do drugs and Christ doesn't want to see you that
70		way.
	Juan Carlos:	Yeah, you're right. The Devil is like a roaring lion.[11]
	Enrique:	Look at your eyes. You're in bad shape. You can't deny you're in bad shape. Since you don't recognize that you have a problem, God can't do anything in your life. You don't
75		want to acknowledge that you have a problem, varón.
	Juan Carlos:	I know I'm lost.
	Enrique:	So!? You're twenty-two years old and you know you're lost and you're not valiant enough to get up? You're such a coward that you'll continue to be lost? Your not valiant enough
80		to stand up and say, "No, I can't keep going like this."
	Juan Carlos:	*[Interrupting]* Excuse me, stranger. *[Gets up to leave]*
	Enrique:	Aren't you!?
	Juan Carlos:	Yeah, I'm valiant.
	Enrique:	Okay. Let's go to the church then *[pointing to the church].*
85	*Juan Carlos:*	What's your name?
	Enrique:	Enrique. What's yours?
	Juan Carlos:	Juan Carlos.
	Enrique:	Juan Carlos, let's go to the church, man.
	Juan Carlos:	See ya around. [Walks away]

Juan Carlos quickly disappeared into the dark Caracas night. Enrique was unfazed by his lack of success. "Trapped by drugs," he said, shaking his head. We squeezed between parked cars, crossed the street, and walked into the church. The movie was about to end, and Enrique needed to give the closing comments.

Three Dimensions of Narrative

Elster argues that even if it were possible to decide to believe, this decision would have to be obliterated from memory for the belief to be sus-

11. The metaphor is from 1 Peter 5:8.

tainable. Evangelical conversion narratives do precisely this. In the previous section I showed that Evangelical concepts are bundled together into projects of change that have a narrative structure insofar as they function through "emplotment," by placing events in a sequence with a beginning, middle, and end. Evangelicals also imagine their own conversion histories through narrative. In what follows I use the Evangelistic exchange between Enrique and Juan Carlos, and other qualitative data, to suggest that understanding three aspects of narrative—the play of canonicity and particularity, the predication of intention and agency, and the narrative reconstruction of events past—can illuminate the way Evangelicals minimize their own responsibility for deciding to believe.

Canonicity and Particularity Actual narratives as told or written represent a synthesis of the "canonical" and the particular. Every cultural context has a "narrative canon," a finite set of abstract story lines through which action can be made recognizable. However, actual narrative is always instantiated through particulars (Bruner 1991: 6–7; Polletta 1998: 421–22). The act of successful narration consists precisely of taking canonical story lines and accommodating them to specific circumstances and actors. Consider how Enrique narrates the life of Juan Carlos.[12] From line 59 to line 62, he lays out the canonical by reading from and paraphrasing the biblical narrative (John 10:10). From line 63 to line 70 he accommodates this to hypothetical characteristics of Juan Carlos's life. The work of the Devil becomes Juan Carlos's role as a bad example and his desperate need to do drugs. The work of Jesus Christ becomes reaching out to Juan Carlos, presumably through this evangelistic interaction.

For the issue at hand—how people come to adopt a religious project of self-reform—both particularity and canonicity are important. First, compartmentalized views of meaning are overcome through the self-referentiality provided by particularity. Rather than an abstract meaning system that is adopted through unconstructed rational action, Evangelical narrative predicates religious significance of the evangelistic encounter itself—the interaction between Enrique and Juan Carlos. Thus assent to the belief system, had it occurred, would have been an assent to a definition of the present situation more than an abstract leap of faith. Juan Carlos would not be simply contemplating the abstract validity of

12. That Juan Carlos does not assent to the evangelization in this case is not important; it is the narrator's behavior that is relevant here.

the meaning system or what it would mean to him in the future. Rather, he would be thinking about what is happening to him at that very minute. In this perspective it is not Juan Carlos who is going through a decision process, it is God reaching out to him and Satan holding on.

Second, the finitude of the stock of narratives available in a culture functions not only to *restrain* potential paths of action (Polletta 1998: 424) but also to *enable* by permitting subjects to identify an external source for their potential path of action. Juan Carlos does not see himself as the source of the package of beliefs he is being presented with. He might not even see Enrique as the source since he apparently had some knowledge of biblical themes: he himself found a relevant verse (lines 50–51) and even correctly, if somewhat sarcastically, used a biblical metaphor for Satan (line 71). Except in very rare cases, average Venezuelans do not experience the Evangelical message as entirely novel. Almost all believe in the Christian God and regard the Bible as a sacred book even though active religious participation is uncommon and Christian beliefs have little impact on behavior. Evangelization and conversion, then, are less the presentation and appropriation of a new belief that individuals need to convince themselves of than the selective presentation of a meaning system they already assent to in remote abstract terms but which is not actively engaged in their thoughts or action. In the conversion process it becomes "believed-in" insofar as it is highlighted and felt more intensely (see Sarbin 1998).

The way the canonical can effectively provide an externally valid narrative portrayal of this-worldly self-interest can be seen in the following respondents' stories. Ramiro, for example, uses the biblical event sequence "In their anguish they will seek me" (Hosea 5:15) in his story about becoming more confirmed in his faith after his wife abandoned him and his son: "I didn't pay much attention to God's calling until in anguish I had to look to God. It was after she [his wife] left that I really became solid in Christ. When I most needed him, he was there for me. He was the solution. That was when I really became solid in him." Ugeth said that he converted when he realized that God wanted people exactly like him who had hurt others and whose lives were in ruins. He paraphrased 1 Corinthians 1:27: "He says in the Word that he chose the low and despised to shame the wise. And I've realized that it's true." The point for our purposes is that these respondents see the project they adopt not as their own idea but as something that comes from an external and valid source. This underlines the substantive importance of Chakrabarty's

(2000: 177–78) "subjectless imagination." Such subjectlessness is important when perceptions of the self's action can undermine the practice.

Intention and Agency Narrative analysts generally agree that the primary target domain of narrative constructs—in other words, the primary subject matter conceptualized by narrative—is human intention and its consequences (Bruner 1991; Polkinghorne 1988; Ricoeur 1984; Stromberg 1993). Narrative humanizes time by relating the flow of events to human intentions and actions and their consequences, intended and unintended. The literary theorist Kenneth Burke (1969) saw drama in terms of a "dramatic pentad," a particular construal of scene, agent, act, agency, and purpose. A given drama presents a particular relationship between the parts of the pentad (see also Bruner 1991; Farrer 2003). This special vocation makes narrative constructs well suited to the situations in which potential converts experience a sense of dis-ease caused by akrasia (see chapter 3).

The Evangelical narrative reorganizes the internal bargaining between the potential convert's selves by portraying the problems he is experiencing, as well as their origin, in the relationship between his action and the agency of supernatural beings. This dramatic "ratio," to use Burke's term, explains what happened in the past, what is happening in the present, and projects potential futures that depend on whether the person does or does not assent to the narrative. Where a situation of akrasia exists, the Evangelical narrative works to highlight it. Where this situation is not preexisting, Evangelical narrative often works to create it by actively "dividing" the self (Harding 2000: 35). Throughout the evangelistic exchange between Enrique and Juan Carlos (see lines 1–2, 10–13, 19–45, 63–80), Enrique provides Juan Carlos with negative images of his own life, in effect trying to maximize his discomfort (At one point [lines 30–45] they even seem to have a brief debate over whether Juan Carlos's life is destroyed.) And he provides a supernatural explanation for these would-be problems by saying the Devil is behind them (lines 24, 44, 57–62). Finally, he tells Juan Carlos that the solution is simultaneously God reaching out to him (lines 55–70) and Juan Carlos's recognition of the problem and submission to God's reaching out (lines 72–88). Thus Juan Carlos's action is necessary, but it is not the primary agency through which the sequence of events is taking or will take place.

This is key to understanding how a person can intentionally believe. The Evangelical narrative constructs the act of believing in such a way that the individual is not the only, or even the most important, agent in this act. It is God who is reaching out to him, and he simply needs to let God carry out his business. Indeed, among Caracas's Evangelicals the act of assent is most commonly referred to as "surrendering to," "receiving," or "accepting" the Lord. All three verb phrases suggest an image of God working on the individual to get him to convert, with the individual simply lowering the barriers and opening himself up. Other common images are those of being "called," "chosen," and—especially among those overcoming drug problems or dangerous situations—"saved" or "rescued." Bringing down these barriers and "surrendering," then, is constructed as interaction—rather than action—in which God is the primary agent.

Temporality: Remembering God's Agency The central feature distinguishing narrative from other linguistic devices is temporality; narrative is, in Jerome Bruner's (1991) words, "irreducibly durative." Whereas metaphor creates a new portrait of a "timeless" feature of the world, narrative brings about "a new congruence in the organization of the events" through emplotment (Ricoeur 1984: ix). When emplotment is applied to the biographies of living people, it necessarily reaches into the past to cast events in a new light. Of course, I say nothing new in asserting that rather than a point of time along the model of Paul on the road to Damascus, Evangelical conversion is a process extending long after "accepting the Lord." Below I focus on one central aspect of this process, the reworking of memories of the events leading up to the original conversion. After conversion has taken place, as the Evangelical works through his or her memories (see also Csordas 1994), aspects of the circumstances surrounding the conversion are highlighted and stylized to emphasize God's agency in the process. Narrative, as a portrayal of temporal structures, is the primary linguistic form through which this process is carried out. Evangelicals tell each other stories, or testimonies, about the work of God in their lives. By emphasizing God's agency, the individual minimizes his own responsibility for the belief and thereby increases its external validity. Respondents frequently point to hard-to-explain aspects[13]

13. In effect, these hard to explain facts function similarly to Thomas Schelling's (1960) "focal points." A focal point is an obvious and salient feature of the environment that permits intersubjective understanding. If *A* knows *X*, knows that *B* knows *X*, and knows that *B* knows that *A* knows *X*, then certain suboptimal outcomes can be avoided. Among Evangelicals, facts and events for which there is no generally accepted explanation function similarly. If *A* knows of no generally accepted explanation for *X*, knows that *B* does not know one, and knows that *B* knows that *A* does not know one, then he can be reasonably confident that using it as evidence for the supernatural will be accepted. See Amelie Rorty, cited in Elster 1986: 115–32, on the idea of "trading on ambiguity."

of their biographies to support the idea that God has chosen them, has protected them, has tried to communicate with them, or otherwise has tried to bring them to convert. These, in effect, are what Dorothy Smith (1990: 62) would call practices through which meanings are disassociated with the interests and actions of the self. There are multitudes of ways this can be done, and I will review some of the most common ones.

Caracas Evangelicals frequently tell stories of close calls occurring in the period before their conversion, in which a God with plans for them spared them from danger. Ugeth said that in the period leading to his conversion, he tried several times, in the depth of his depression, to commit suicide. "But God had a plan for me," he explained, "and I didn't try it with things that could actually hurt me but with detergent and things like that. But it wasn't me, it was the Lord who had a plan for me." Bartolo told this story of the events leading up to his conversion:

> They shot me in the leg and the bullet passed through my pant leg in the center of my thigh and exited the backside of my pant leg, but it didn't even touch my skin. It's a miracle of God because there is no explanation. The bullet curved from that close? The only explanation is that the Lord opened my leg in two, the bullet passed through, and he closed my leg in a second. I still have the pants. I remember because I was really impressed. It was a pair of pants with holes in both sides right in the center and it didn't even hit my skin. Once also they pointed [a gun] at my ear and I didn't know it. I saw him and the shot sounded. If I don't do this *[turns and ducks]* my head gets shot off. And in all this, I always heard the voice of God: "It was me. I liberated you."

The concrete events that lead one to commit to God are frequently portrayed as God's work to get his attention. Guille converted in the midst of a crisis in which his life was being threatened by two independent sources. He told me, "It was through that problem that I saw, that in part it was God who was reaching out to me." Ernestillo converted after he was implicated in a murder that occurred in his neighborhood and he feared what both the police and the deceased's family and friends would do to him. Here he shows how he has come to interpret the police interrogation he was subjected to: "They beat me a lot, and I came down with pneumonia. They gave me a bath at two in the morning and shocked me with electricity. But I still didn't understand that it was God who was processing me through all that."

Evangelicals frequently point to dreams as the mechanism through which God worked on them and brought them to commit. It should be noted that the belief that dreams have a supernatural derivation or are a form of extrasensory perception is not peculiar to Evangelicals but widespread in Venezuelan culture. Even among educated individuals, a dream that something bad has happened to a loved one, for example, will provoke an early-morning telephone call to make sure everything is all right. Here we can simply regard them as difficult-to-verify forms of experience[14] that have no generally accepted explanation and can plausibly be portrayed by a Evangelical as God reaching out. Ramiro described this process after he attended an evangelistic campaign: "And from that night on, I started having dreams from God; that in Caracas the buildings would sink. There were earthquakes. I would be there crying out for them to save me. From that point on [God] began to work on me through dreams and I began to look for him." Teodoro converted before he arrived in Caracas:

> I arrived to the Gospel by means of dreams from the Lord, two dreams that he sent me in Caja de Agua [in the Andes], in the town where I was born. He touched me through dreams that I was on a cloud in the air and in front of me was a sort of cloud that moved and I would say in the dream for him to take me, to not leave me. And then I would hear him say, "Seek me and you will find me"—And I would insist for him to take me. But he insisted also that I had to look for him: "Seek me and you will find me. Seek me and you will find me."

Respondents frequently portrayed the new emotional states, needs, and desires that brought them to convert as God reaching out to them. Because they did not have them before, their origin is available for conceptualization. Vincenzo explained why he persisted in the Gospel despite several bad experiences in the first few churches he attended: "God had given me a spiritual necessity. . . . [It wasn't until] I got here [Emmanuel Church] that I was able to make it a reality and accept Jesus Christ." Carlos Gómez told how an Evangelical had witnessed to him and invited him to church on Sunday: "The hermano said to me, 'Come to church with me on Sunday.' I said, 'All right.' And the hermano even stood me up. He probably thought, 'Naw, this guy's not going to go.' But I was already touched by the word. The Holy Spirit was already working on me, and wham! That's when he [the Holy Spirit] came to me and brought me [to the church] and I'm still [here]." Jorge explained that he

14. By this I mean difficult not only for others to verify but also for the person himself to verify. Dreams that are difficult to remember can be, through time, interpreted and reinterpreted in small increments until they fit with the Evangelical narrative in such a way that they are convincing even to oneself.

would commit street robberies but then feel guilty about it: "I would do it, but afterward, within me, I would repent and think, 'I'm getting in trouble here.' And I was seeing that I wasn't giving a good example to my kids. *[Pause]* God was working on me."

Finally, the ability of preachers and evangelists to describe in religious terms the situations commonly confronted by members of Caracas's popular sectors is frequently portrayed as evidence that God is speaking through them. In Venezuela the lives and problems of the popular classes are rarely covered in the mass media or reflected in popular culture, so their common situations and predicaments are usually experienced as particular and unique. Thus when a stranger describes these experiences in detail and ascribes religious meaning to them, they are understandably regarded as supernatural—as clear evidence that God is speaking through the person.[15] Enrique had previously been a member of a popular Catholic group and then an Adventist group but had stopped attending. A couple of months later he converted when a coworker invited him to an Evangelical plaza service near their downtown office building. "They were preaching the Word, Enemesio Bolívar was preaching, and God really spoke to my life," Enrique said. Juan had started to participate in an Evangelical church in the midst of a struggle with depression and dependency on prescription medications. He told a story about going to an evangelistic campaign at a baseball stadium:

> God spoke to me through him [the Evangelist]. It made me very happy because the hermano touched on the topic of depression. Even though I was attending church, I was not very solid. I had a lot of spiritual weaknesses. And the Lord spoke to me through hermano José Sapico. And he said in his sermon that depression is a spiritual emptiness, a spiritual emptiness that needs to be filled with Jesus. Wow. That message hit me head-on.

Ramiro attended an outdoor service held by Evangelicals in his barrio: "[The preacher] spoke and the sermon hit me directly. And I said to myself, 'Hey, this guy knows what is happening in my life. Why does he know what is going on in my life? How does he know that all of this is happening to me?' I didn't know that God was using him." In all these cases the person is reworking—usually through the act of telling his testimony to others—the events that led to his conversion in a way that minimizes his own role and maximizes God's agency. As a result, his be-

15. In his study of North American Catholic Pentacostals, Csordas (1994) observed the same phenomenon (see esp. 146).

lief gains credibility as the product of something other than his efforts at self-improvement.

CONCLUSION

I have examined Venezuelan Evangelicalism as a case of cultural agency through the concept of imaginative rationality. Evangelical men use Evangelical concepts to imagine aspects of their social context and social lives in ways that make them more amenable to their agency. They use these concepts consciously in projects of self- or family reform. In this chapter I went one step further to address the question of whether people can decide to believe. I analyzed how Evangelicals imagine their own religious practice—in other words, how they construct second-order beliefs about the way their belief and practice work. I focused on three main issues: the nature of instrumentality, the reasons for belief, and the location of agency in conversion. First, the instrumentality of a given religious practice is defined by the religious meaning system itself. The Pentecostal Evangelicals studied here think some forms of religious practice are instrumental; indeed, they actively construct their own identities vis-à-vis the "prosperity" churches that are growing in Caracas. They disagree and disparage the latter's crass focus on money and entrepreneurial success, seeing them as signs of insincerity. However, they themselves consider issues of the self and family, as well as their basic social and material reproduction, spiritual issues and legitimate goals of religious practice. Second, Evangelicals have good reason to believe. They comprehend, adopt, and construct Evangelical projects of reform that are inevitably followed by consequences. When these consequences are those predicted by the Evangelical project, the latter is validated. When the predicted consequences do not materialize, a project may be dropped, or it might be extended through a number of different interpretive strategies. Third, practicing Evangelicals imagine their own biographies using Evangelical narratives that in effect minimize their own agency in that process while maximizing the agency of God. This reduces their own responsibility and increases the plausibility of their Evangelical belief.

It is worth asking why all three of these ways of imagining Evangelical practice coexist. Logically any one of them should be enough to adequately support Evangelical belief. If self- or family reform is spiritual, then there is no threat that it will appear to be an instrumental use of religion. If Evangelical metaphors of God's power provide a plausible theory of the way religious practice effects its consequences, the believer has sufficient reasons to believe. And if the conversion narrative erases the believer's role in adopting belief, there is no reason to try to make those beliefs appear reasonable or religious. Holding all three is a little like a lawyer defending her client from murder charges by saying he was not at the scene of the crime, saw someone else do it, and did not intend for the victim to die.

I think the issue is nicely addressed by Bourdieu's (1977) "economy of logic," the idea that "no more logic is mobilized than is required by the needs of practice" (110). Internal coherence between one element of a culture and another is not as important as how they can be used individually in practice. To play them off each other in order to determine if they are consistent would be to fall into the objectivist error that assumes the spectator's role. Rather, these three elements of the Evangelical meaning system are mobilized for different tasks in different contexts. So, for example, Martín speaks of converting to save his marriage and then about salvation as the only legitimate reason for conversion. Ramiro says he converted during a seven-death vendetta in which he sought God "in his anguish." Yet he also says that he converted after God spoke to him through an evangelist and began to work on him through dreams. These different schemas are marshaled depending on the interpretive context, as "strategies for dealing with situations" (Burke 1957: 256).

Before moving on, there is one other issue that needs to be addressed. How would this imaginative rationality look different if my data came primarily from women instead of men? Feminist scholars have long argued that women use symbols differently than men. Carolyn Walker Bynum (1987), for example, has shown that religious women in the Middle Ages experienced dichotomous Christian symbols such as "blessed are the meek" not through symbolic reversal, as did men, but as a profound deepening of their everyday experience. Carole Gilligan's (1982) classic study shows that women are more likely to engage in relational reasoning when confronted with moral dilemmas. The women in her study worked through the impact of decisions on concrete others rather than reasoning from abstract moral codes (see also Elshtain 1981; Wallach Bologh 1990). And Dorothy Smith (1990) argues that there are two ways of making meaning. The "governing mode" lifts meaning makers out of concrete context and presents the meanings they create as abstract, objective, and disinterested. The other mode of meaning making is centered on bodily experience that takes place in concrete location. It creates concepts in pursuit of specific purposes.

> Men have functioned as subjects in the mode of governing; women have been anchored in the local and particular phase of the bifurcated world. It has been a condition of a man's being able to enter and become absorbed in the conceptual mode, and to forget the dependence of his being in that mode upon his bodily existence, that he does not have to focus his activities and interests upon his bodily existence. Full participation in the abstract mode of action requires liberation from attending to needs in the concrete and particular. (Smith 1990: 18)

According to Smith, the governing mode misrepresents its own knowledge by "objectifying" it, abstracting it from the concrete interests and conditions that produced it. It misrepresents the knowledge created out of concrete, bodily experience in the world by invalidating it as interested, subjective, and nonobjective. She argues that a feminist perspective does not seek to delegitimize knowledge by showing that it is actually self-interested. Rather, it seeks to look at the ways interested knowers existing in concrete social relationships create knowledge, as well as the "concerted ways [knowers] obliterate their presence as subjects" from the knowledge we consider "objective."

The close reader will have recognized a remarkable similarity between the argument developed in this chapter based on research with Evangelical men in Caracas and the theory of gendered meaning making developed by Dorothy Smith. Indeed, Smith and other feminist writers are quite clear that they are not trying to essentialize gender perspectives but rather seeking to portray alternative ways of making meaning. The men in my study come from Caracas's informal city. They, like their mothers, wives, sisters, and daughters, make meaning from outside the governing mode, in pursuit of "needs in the concrete and particular." Certainly the character of these needs will differ. Women are less likely to have problems with akrasia and involvement in violence and are probably more likely to suffer issues of family conflict. Undoubtedly, they more frequently experience these issues through bodily sickness. But I think the second-order cultural dynamics examined in this chapter are likely to be quite similar among women. Women in Caracas's informal city have more in common with men from the same context than with women in Caracas's global city, much less women from advanced industrialized counties (Barrios de Chungara and Viezzer 1978). Nevertheless, this is clearly an empirical issue that will only be illuminated through further empirical research.

PART THREE

Relational Imagination

An adequate theory of cultural agency needs both a nonreductionist concept of culture as something that can have an independent impact and a concept of human agency in which people can adopt cultural meanings because they understand these impacts. I have argued that such a theory can be built on the concept of imaginative rationality. In some situations people may certainly create meanings in order to avoid or escape from their problematic experiences, as neo-Marxists would have it. However, the Evangelical men studied here seem to create meanings in order to confront problematic experiences. These decisions to believe are made possible because the problematic experiences include not only social life but also religious practice itself. Now I want to address the second question I posed at the outset: If people can decide to believe, why doesn't everyone? If people are capable of bettering their circumstances by adopting a set of beliefs and practices that will help them confront problems, keep them optimistic, and provide them with a network of solidarity, why doesn't everybody do so? More specifically, why doesn't everyone who could benefit from Evangelical "fruits of the spirit" convert?

Chapter 5 adumbrated the answer. Not all culture is available in all contexts, as neoconservatives would have it. In most cases people adopt preexisting packages of meanings that circulate in their social context and then adapt them to their lives. This canonicity is a key way that conversion can be seen as "subjectless" by respondents. But it also means that the repertoire of meanings available for them to imagine and build their own projects is limited (Polletta 1998). I refer to this as the relationality of imagination. Imagination is relational not only at the relatively abstract level of sociocultural context as captured by the idea of canonicity. It is also relational at the more concrete level of interpersonal networks. Such a significant cultural innovation as religious conversion is not simply a personal decision; rather, it is structured to an important degree by the individual's social relationships.

Conversion through network ties is, of course, one of the most established findings in the sociology of religion.[1] But what are networks, and what do they do? Networks are simply concrete social relationships that provide the basic units of social structure. And the most basic view of the way networks influence individuals comes from the theory of social psychological conformity (Festinger 1962; Marsden and Friedkin 1994). In this view all humans have a fundamental need for social relationships and cultivate and conserve them. Individuals adopt new cultural meanings and practices such as those provided by new religious movements, therefore, not because of any inherent characteristics of the latter but rather to the degree that they reduce dissonance in these relationships. Network analysis tends to see network explanations as alternatives to "deprivation-congruence" explanations. The latter explain conversion by looking at a religious ideology and inferring what deprivations it addresses and then giving causal status to these deprivations (Stark and Finke 2000). From the perspective of network analysis, in contrast, "conversion is not about seeking or embracing an ideology; it is about bringing one's religious behavior into alignment with that of one's friends and family members" (Stark 1996: 16–17). Networks are the real causes of conversion, and any reported "deprivations" addressed by the religious beliefs and practices are better seen as emergent, ex post rationalizations, or, at best, as general limiting conditions and not primary causes (see Stark and Finke 2000).

Theorists such as Christian Smith (2003: 126) and Jeffrey Alexander (2003: 16), in turn, tend to see network explanations of religious or cultural innovation as contradicting their explanations based on meaning and morality. But as criticism of the traditional approach to networks has mounted, networks research has been the subject of considerable re-

1. The literature is large. Good sources to begin with are Lofland and Stark 1965; Stark and Bainbridge 1980; Stark 1996; Stark and Iannaccone 1997; Snow, Zurcher, and Eckland-Olson 1980; Snow and Phillips 1980; Sherkat and Wilson 1995; Hoge, Johnson, and Luidens 1995; Mears and Ellison 2000; Nepstad and Smith 2001; Becker and Dhingra 2001.

formulation. The most fundamental criticism is that the conformity model of network influence is undertheorized. For example, in any given case there is no reason to think a network tie between a participant and a nonparticipant would lead to participation by the latter rather than nonparticipation by the former (Gould 2003). Unless we have information to the contrary, we need to assume that relationships are bilateral monopolies such that any threat to the relationship would be felt equally by both parties and therefore be neutral in effect. We need to know more before assuming a network tie leads toward and not away from participation in the movement we are studying (Gould 2003: 244). Critics have also charged that the very idea that network explanations of religious conversion present alternatives to cultural explanations based on meaning depends on an unnecessarily reified distinction between social structure and culture (Emirbayer and Goodwin 1994: 1427). Social networks are not simple conveyor belts for meaning; they are themselves constructed through meaningful discourse, which in turn has an important impact on how they work to diffuse meaning innovations or reinforce traditional meanings. Finally, critics argue that traditional network analysis relies on an "oversocialized" view of human beings in which the latter are acted upon by networks rather than act on them and through them (Emirbayer and Goodwin 1994: 1413; see also Cook and Whitmeyer 1992; Gould 2003; McAdam 2003; McAdam and Paulsen 1993).

The network analysis provided in chapter 6 relies on new directions in relational sociology (Emirbayer 1997; Emirbayer and Mische 1998; Somers 1993; Steinberg 1999). I show that meaning is important for understanding why networks influence in one direction rather than another, as well as for how they influence in absence of desire for social conformity. I show that networks do not replace agency. Rather, they frame the settings in which agency takes place. And in a small number of cases we can even see agency in the purposeful construction of networks. Conversion to Evangelicalism depends largely on interpersonal contexts that facilitate exposure to the meaning system or at least do not hinder cultural innovation. People are often spurred to imagine alternatives through contact in their households with people embodying those alternatives. Alternatively, they are often prevented from imagining alternatives by contact with people in their households who maintain traditional meanings. In a small number of cases they consciously choose relational contexts that will facilitate their project of reform.

In chapter 7 I push further into relational imagination through extended attention to two men who find themselves at the intersection of competing networks that provide alternative strategies. The cases of these men, whom I reinterviewed five years after my initial interview with them, extend the analysis further into the way family and friends, as well as particular meanings, facilitate or impede the ability of individuals to imagine alternative futures.

CHAPTER 6

The Social Structure of Conversion

Gabriel has suffered from epileptic seizures for most of his life. When he was a boy he worked for seven years in a shoe-repair factory. In his context it was a decent job that provided resources for his poor family; and his cousin would fill in for him when his health made it impossible to work. However, at fifteen he was in one of Caracas's nightmarish bus accidents—in this case the bus plunged into the Guaire River that runs along most of the main highway. The injuries he suffered made his seizures more frequent and eventually obliged him to quit this job. He has not worked regularly for the past fifteen years, other than occasionally helping out a family member or neighbor on construction and remodeling projects. Although he is taking medication, he still suffers from frequent seizures, and as a consequence of the resulting falls most of his front teeth are cracked or missing. Just the day before our interview he suffered a seizure, and he showed me a split in his tongue from his fall. Gabriel has lived in the same house all his life, in the upper reaches of El Valle in Caracas's south central valley. It is a violent context: his older brother was recently killed just a few meters from their doorstep. Gabriel's three sisters and mother take care of him, and his retired father gives him money from his small social security pension. Gabriel was baptized Catholic but never took first communion. Nevertheless, he makes sure to go to the Catholic church during Holy Week every year with his sisters and mother.

If Gabriel were Evangelical it would be easy to explain his Evangelicalism as a form of imaginative rationality through which he addresses his persisting medical condition as well as economic difficulties, gains the opportunity for social activity outside of his household, and works through his grief over the loss of his brother, killed by malandros. Furthermore, he has opportunity. Gabriel lives right next door to an Evangelical church and a house where Andrés and other hermanos live. In this context that means he is about ten to fifteen feet from the sanctuary and can hear everything that goes on there. He occasionally talks over the fence with the hermanos, and they try to convince him to become Evangelical. He demurs but likes to listen to the services from his living room or from the patio. He spends most of his days watching television or listening to music but turns them off when there is a service.

What keeps Gabriel from becoming Evangelical or at least attending services? In the introduction I asked the same question about Aurelio. Forty years old and living with his mother and sister, Aurelio has persisting problems with gambling, with a lost love, and with his fear of violence. Here I show that religious conversion is a significant cultural innovation and depends not simply on need, desire, or "deprivation." It is largely precluded when a man lives with members of his family of origin and none of them are Evangelical. Members of the family of origin provide social and cultural support in times of need and exercise a conservative influence, leading away from cultural innovation.

COUNTERVAILING INFLUENCE: LIVING WITH FAMILY OF ORIGIN

Sociologists assert that the most relevant network ties for determining who does or does not become a social movement participant are those that an individual uses to sustain his or her identity (see McAdam and Paulsen 1993). In Venezuela these ties are usually family ties. In the often fatherless Venezuelan family, members communicate, associate, collaborate, and simply spend time together to a degree that citizens of the industrialized West would find difficult to imagine. Children usually live with their parents until they form their own families or need to move for work or study. If none of these occurs, it is common for individuals to live with their parents well into their thirties or forties. Furthermore, housing costs lead many to stay at home well after they have their own families. Because a parent's home is often considered the main inheritance for offspring, it is common after the parent has died for several brothers and sisters to live together in the home with their own families. Individuals are expected to support and defend their family of origin

Men bring home a new washbasin.

above and beyond any other social group or ideology (Hurtado 1999). In sum, family ties in Venezuela provide identity, belonging, and a web of social support. To the degree that they are embedded in these ties, my respondents have "stakes in conformity" that make conversion less likely. In other words, they have valued social relationships that might be jeopardized by religious innovation (Stark 1996). Consistent with the idea of social psychological conformity, members of an individual's family of origin enforce conformity that prevents religious innovation. However, I go beyond this to see how men who live with their families of origin receive social and cultural support in moments of dis-ease.

Conformity

Venezuelans of the popular classes rarely object to Evangelicalism as a threat to their Catholicism. Rather, they object to the way it breaks with the flexible, context-dependent, personalistic morality and integral lifestyle characteristic of Venezuelan culture. Fervent religious beliefs and rigorous adherence to ethical standards are occasionally admired as manifestations of principled character. But more commonly they are distrusted, viewed as inevitably hypocritical and antisocial or as signs of personal maladjustment. When I asked Miguel for his opinion of Evangelicals he said they were "truly strange." They set such high standards and get so wrapped up in their religion that they inevitably betray it. "It's a religion that has a lot of rules that aren't logical," he said. "The fact that you can't drink, can't have any vices. I mean nobody is free of sin. . . . Didn't Adam and Eve sin? So Evangelicals with all their restrictions—you can't smoke, you can't drink, you can't dance—naaaw . . . who do they think they're fooling?"

Sometimes a family will welcome the conversion of one of its members if he has serious personal or social problems. But more often it is considered an embarrassment, a rebuke, or simply a loss. For example, one cause of the depression that preceded Pablo's conversion was the fact that his newly Evangelical brother would no longer drink and wrestle with him—a common form of male bonding in this context.

Such distancing is a powerful reason not to convert if there is valued and frequent rapport with non-Evangelical family members. Nevertheless, such pressures generally work silently by preventing innovation and therefore are only dimly revealed in interviews. They are most evident in the exceptional cases in which they break to the surface through conflict. Of the sixty cases in which my respondents lived with their non-Evangelical families, there were only five conversions. In four of these cases the respondent reported that their conversion caused considerable conflict in their families. I had the following exchange with Henry.

> *Since you became Evangelical, has your relationship with your family changed?*
>
> Yeah, it's changed, but for the worse. I mean there are more differences now as there is conflict because they want to separate me from my ideals.
>
> *For example, what do they do?*
>
> Yeah, they always talk to me and say that the Gospel is for people with problems, who are crazy or whatever, who feel unsatisfied with themselves.

Ernesto converted after both his mother and his father died and he was living with his older brothers and sisters. He said, "[They would tell me] that I was going to go crazy, that they were going to call the police and have them put me in the military. They would pressure me a lot to stop [participating]. One time they burned my Bible." Juan Zerpa's conversion coincided with a family economic crisis. When his father lost his taxi because of a forged-check scam, the family's only income came from Juan's low-paying job as an appliance repairman's assistant. When he quit because it required him to work on Sundays and therefore miss church services, his family was understandably displeased. He said it was not easy to keep his faith: "They were all against me because they thought I was lying [about having become Evangelical]. They treated me like I was crazy because they thought I was lying."

Returning to the case of Gabriel, I think his dependency on his family makes it unlikely that he would risk coming into conflict with them over religion. We had the following exchange.

> I spend my time listening to music or watching television and when the hermanos are there, I listen to the Word right there *[points to a metal chair on the patio, positioned next to the fence separating his house from the church sanctuary]*.
>
> *So have you ever thought about becoming Evangelical?*
>
> Well, no, since my family isn't Evangelical. I could perhaps become Evangelical. But I'm Catholic. My whole family is Catholic.

Given that Gabriel is completely dependent on his family, and probably will be for the rest of his life, it is understandable that such a step outside of the dominant family meaning system would appear to him as an unattractive risk.

In sum, a spatially present family of origin has a strong conservative effect that works against cultural innovation. In other words, the free play of an individual's imaginative rationality is reduced when living with family of origin. Men who live with non-Evangelical families of origin rarely convert even when they experience life problems, unless those problems are with the family or they lack rapport with family members.

Social and Cultural Support

Spatially present members of the family of origin not only prevent Evangelical conversion by enforcing cultural conformity; they largely preempt it by providing social and cultural support when life problems of the type described in chapters 3 and 4 arise. This support does not prevent problems as much as help young men to navigate the problem situations they encounter. Consider the case of José Luis, who, two years before our interview, was shot by neighborhood thugs. He was taking a spin on a friend's new motorcycle and rode past a group of young men gathered by the side of the road. One young man, someone he had met before, called him over. He stopped but, perceiving that their intentions were not good, took off again on the motorcycle. The one who called out to him pulled out a gun and opened fire. One bullet entered his thigh, another his buttock. He managed to stay on the motorcycle and get back home and then to a hospital. Though he recovered from his wounds, he was not out of danger: having been shot by someone meant that others, including the perpetrator, expected José Luis to seek revenge. And this meant that José Luis was a prime target for a preemptive strike (Hardin 1995; Nisbett and Cohen 1996). This was the situation in which several of my Evangelical respondents had converted (see Ramiro's explanation of cadena in chapter 3). José Luis, however, was able to resist involvement in a vendetta. In the following exchange, we can get a sense of the role played by his strong family life.

> After I was shot, I was afraid that he [his assailant] would—I thought he was going to think that I was going to do something bad to him, I mean seek revenge. And I never at any time thought about revenge because I'm not part of that malicious environment.
>
> *So you thought that he thought that?*
>
> Yeah, I mean the day after I was shot, I was sitting in the door [of my house] and he walked by and had his gun on him.
>
> *How did you know he had his gun on him?*
>
> Because he had it hanging out of his back pocket and he stared at me. My dad was there next to me.
>
> *And you were in your house?*
>
> Yeah, I was right in the door. We had the door open.
>
> *Oh, okay, and nobody said to you that you had to fix things, that you had to seek revenge or anything like that?*
>
> Well, my brother thought about doing something to the guy. The [brother] who is away.
>
> *The one who is Mormon now?*
>
> Yeah, exactly. With Frank, you know Frank [a neighbor I had previously interviewed]. They thought about doing something, and I said no, to leave it at that, that people would think it was me since the only one who had problems with him in that sector was me.

And what about people in the barrio. Didn't they laugh at you? I mean saying that you didn't make him pay?

Yeah, a lot of people said, "Man, you're a loser. You should have done something to him. You should have done something." But I thought no, that that would just put more wood on the fire.

And what did your family say?

No, my moth— . . . what they did was advise me to leave it at that, let it die out.

The avenues open to José Luis in his sociocultural context were (1) to seek revenge at the risk of continuing the vendetta; (2) to opt out of the logic by becoming Evangelical, as Ramiro did; or (3) to let it peter out at the risk of becoming the victim of a preemptive strike and with the assurance of a loss of esteem among others in the barrio. As José Luis tells the story, he took the last option. If this is true, it is clear that the influence of his family encouraged this solution. But it is interesting that he mentions that his brother wanted to seek revenge. Previously in the interview he mentioned both that his victimizer was no longer around and that his brother had become a Mormon and moved to Utah. It could well be that his brother sought revenge and then converted to Mormonism in the aftermath of guilt and fear. But in either case José Luis's story provides a nice example of how the material and cultural support of a spatially present family of origin helps individuals navigate problem situations and precludes the need for innovation. Had José Luis not lived with his family of origin, he most likely would have taken a more open role in the vendetta or become Evangelical.

As described in the introduction, Aurelio had some tense situations after he led the movement to install a gate in his neighborhood. His story about what happened reveals the strength of familial versus extrafamilial ties: "They brought a malandro to fuck me up, and I ended up letting *him* have it because I have a lot of family too! Who defended me? My family. Everyone else washed their hands [of the problem]. Everyone ran into their houses to hide and watch the fight."

There are a number of less dramatic cases in which family support simply prevents problem situations from getting out of control. Deiby grew up with a supportive mother and father and nine brothers and sisters. The same year he graduated from high school his family had to leave the apartment they had lived in for years when the owner wanted to sell. They moved back to their town of origin on Venezuela's eastern coast. Deiby moved in with his sister and soon got a job at the bank where his brother-in-law worked. He also began playing basketball in the Venezuelan professional league. However, he was forced to leave the basketball team because of injuries, and he also quit his bank job because he needed a schedule that would allow him to go back to school. Getting another job to finance his studies was not as easy as he thought it would be. Formerly with two jobs, he now had none, and the money from his severance package was quickly used up. "I found myself sort of adrift, without anything," he said. "But my sister helped me out and encouraged me." She lent him money until his father helped him get a job in the Ministry of Health through an old friend of his who worked in the human resources department. Deiby secured a job in the statistics department whose schedule permitted him to go to technical school in the evenings. Living with a family member smoothed the bump in Deiby's road toward independence, prevented it from becoming a personal crisis, and thereby prevented consideration of a dramatic life change such as religious conversion.

In the data presented here "stakes in conformity" work against religious innovation not only because of an individual's desire to maintain solidarity with significant others and their good opinion. These significant others also provide important social support as well as help make meaning of a problem situation. In other words, one's family of origin often prevents a problem from becoming a persisting state of dis-ease that might lead to a desire for cultural innovation. Of course, it is never clear whether a family's help in the short term facilitates or hinders personal growth in the longer term. Even evaluating this is largely a matter of perspective. In the cases of Aurelio and Gabriel, for example, we can clearly see that their family support provides them with enough of a cushion to avoid innovation that could well facilitate their overcoming persisting sources of dis-ease.

STRUCTURAL AVAILABILITY: NOT LIVING WITH FAMILY OF ORIGIN

My review of countervailing networks underlines the way spatially present members of one's family of origin effectively serve to prevent Evangelical conversion. This frames the importance of their absence—a situation network analysts call "structural availability." In their seminal study of networks and religious conversion, Snow, Zurcher, and Ekland-Olson (1980: 794) argue that individuals who are structurally available "can follow their interests and/or engage in exploratory behavior to a greater extent than individuals who are bound to existing lines of action" by their network obligations. In essence, this concept of structural availability itself rests on the conformity model of network influence. But here as well, we find important substantive aspects of structural availability that move us beyond the conformity model. First I look at negative examples—cases in which network influence did not work as it normally does. Then I look at cases in which people converted when they lacked social and cultural support. This leads back to a discussion of the roles of problems and agency in Evangelical conversion.

Nonconformity

When the men I interviewed were free from the influence of their families, it was usually a simple artifact of the life course. Because they married or got reasonable paying jobs, they moved out of the family home, often in the interior, to start their own households. When they convert, the ramifications for their relationship with family of origin does not weigh heavily on them. Often it is when they go home for holidays that discomfort or outright confrontation develops. Juan Betancourt, for example, migrated from the Andean state of Trujillo to make his life in Caracas. When his drinking started to cause marital problems he began looking for solutions in different forms of popular religion. He finally became Evangelical as a way to bring about the change he desired. However, when he returned to his hometown soon after, his family did not at first believe that he had become Evangelical. When they finally realized he had, his father broke down and cried because Juan would no longer drink with him.

But the character of nonconformity is most evident in those cases in which my respondents had been at odds with their families or felt the need to separate themselves from its influence. Several of the men I interviewed became "structurally available" precisely because they did not conform to the dominant meanings embodied in their families of origin. Indeed, in several cases, living apart from the family was part of an attempt to gain distance from them and conduct their lives differently. As an adolescent, Nelson suffered problems with depression that included a period of hospitalization. He has lived with depressive tendencies since and has largely experienced them through conflict with his family. He has a heavy, serious, and reflective manner combined with meticulous organizational skills. When he married and had children, his concern for *fundamentos* (fundamentals) was expressed in a religious quest. Before becoming an Evangelical, he had studied the Jehovah's Witnesses and had taken an interest in the heritage of the Jewish owners of the imitation jewelry store he managed. When an Evangelical started working for him at the store, he listened to his evangelization and ended up visiting an Evangelical church. His story about bringing his wife on his second visit reveals the way his psychic distance from his family is tied to his religious quest:

> So on Sunday we went to church because if they showed me this part that I wanted to have in my life, then I wanted her to see it too. Because, basically, we were looking for [something specific]. . . . I mean, it was for the girls [his two daughters]. I was very worried about the way things were going [in Venezuela]. The principles with which I had been raised and with which the majority of people are raised were not solid. There were beliefs that were dogmatic[1] and had nothing to do with reality. So I was really worried when my first daughter was born. I was researching Kibbutz and things like that.

For Nelson, living apart from family of origin and conversion to Evangelicalism are effects of inconformity with them. He was actively searching for alternative forms of meaning and practice that could give him the "fundamentals" he was looking for.

The case of Lenin, who converted during a two-month stint away from his family, is even clearer. Lenin speaks, dresses, and carries himself with moderation and care. But his manner and appearance belie his humble origins and tough upbringing. Whereas he has always been close to his mother, he has had serious problems with his two younger brothers. When Lenin and I discussed the nature of this conflict, he emphasized that (like his father) his brothers would drink at home, did not respect him or his mother, and behaved violently. He finally moved out in August 1995 because of his frustration over not being able to deal with them effectively: "The situation got so bad that I decided to just leave and not have to see it. My anger would consume me." During the two months he was away from his mother's house he lived in three different

1. His use of the term *dogmatic* appears to contradict the tenor of his quote, unless one understands the specific meaning of this term among Venezuelan Evangelicals. The latter refer to Catholicism as a "religion," and religions have "dogmas," defined by Evangelicals as beliefs created by humans rather than God. Evangelicalism, on the other hand, is not a religion but "salvation" and does not contain dogmas but rather belief in the "truth" revealed by God. This interpretation would be confirmed by the fact that Nelson describes his family as only nominally Catholic and his problem with them their lack of moral principles.

locations. At the end of the first month, Lenin "surrendered" to the Lord and began indoctrination classes at Emmanuel Church. As he studied the Bible he focused on verses that said he should not harbor anger toward others. This led him to visit home in September and converse with his brothers to resolve his issues with them. In October he returned to his mother's house as an Evangelical, continuing his participation until he was baptized in December. In Lenin's case acute family conflict and the ire it produced in him led him to leave home. Being away from home gave him the opportunity to reflect and innovate to address this issue, among others. By the time he returned home he had been able to gain a familiarity with and confidence in the new meaning system and use it to confront his problem.

In twenty-five of thirty cases in which my respondents experienced problems while living with their families of origin, they did not convert. However, there are five conversions that are most revealing. In four of these five cases, either one of the young man's major problems was *with* family authority figures or the respondent was in some sense alienated from his family. Henry, for example, lived with his family and became Evangelical after the rock-and-roll band he led and had invested in financially broke up and after he met an Evangelical woman he found attractive. The context of all this was long-term family problems.

> *And how was your relationship with your family from the time you finished high school [the starting point for our interview]. I mean, did you get along well with them? Did you have conflicts with them?*
>
> Yeah, the same conflicts continued.
>
> *Yeah? Why? I mean, what were the "same conflicts"?*
>
> I mean it was a sort of—I was sealed off in everything. I stayed in my shell and didn't give my family any space to enter. What I would do outside of the house my family knew nothing about. I was completely closed off.
>
> *Was that when you were in high school?*
>
> Yes, I mean it was always that way.

The conflict with his family stemmed not only from his late-night gigs at clubs but also, as he put it, from his mother's continual "enmity" toward his girlfriends. He described his usual reaction to his mother's rejection as greater attraction to the girl in question. We can assume, then, that Henry's coexistence with his family was not an impediment to becoming Evangelical when his new romantic relationship presented the opportunity.

Juan Zerpa's life began to fall apart when he quit his good job as a waiter in the hope of using his severance pay to go into business for himself. He never got around to launching his new endeavor, and before he knew it he was broke and unable to find another good job. These economic problems undermined his personality as an efficacious male, on which his relationship with his girlfriend seemed to have been based, as well as his economic contribution to his impoverished family. I followed up on his mention of conflict with his family.

> *So did you already have family problems before you surrendered to the Gospel?*
>
> I did, but they didn't really come out since I would close myself off. They hadn't come out. I would come home, go to my room and shut the door, leave, come back and do the same. I don't have my own room, I share it with my brothers. But they didn't spend much time there. So I would come home and shut myself in my room. At that time I wasn't a Christian. I was unemployed, but I had the Bible that the Lord had given me, and from the beginning when all this began, from the beginning of my being unemployed, I began to read it.

What is clear is that both Henry and Juan did not have the type of rapport with their families that could have prevented their conversions.

This lack of rapport works the same way in Evangelical households. Several of my respondents had grown up in Evangelical households, yet discontinued their religious participation during their teen years. Each said they had rebelled against something that had been forced on them. Pablo, for example, grew up in an Evangelical household and was forced to attend church with his mother:

> It got to the point that I couldn't stand church anymore and the small part that I did like about it—the prayers—started to disgust me. So when I started high school it was like a liberation. The girls would say things like "that's nerdy," "that's for adults, for old people," "that's boring." So they put those ideas in my head when I was already disliking it because of my mom's pressure. So I decided not to go anymore.

Among those who grow up in Evangelical families, it is extremely common to stop participating as young adults as a form of rebellion against their parents. Besides Manuel and Pablo, three more of the Evangelical respondents in the sample were socialized in Evangelical families, rejected it during adolescence or young adulthood, and then came back when confronting life problems. Certainly many such individuals never return to Evangelical practice. But some do, especially when they confront life problems and recall meanings imparted to them in their religious socialization. The fundamental point here is that men who do not live with their families of origin or for some reason do not have significant rapport with them are freer to try new meanings and innovate.

Self-Reliance

Men who face problem situations without spatially present family of origin do so largely on their own. They do not enjoy the timely social support families give to members who reside in the household, or interactions through which they can make meaning regarding their problems. For these reasons, religious innovation becomes a relatively more attractive strategy. In most cases the absence of family support is a background condition that is not widely recognized by men who live on their own. However, a couple of times in my interviews it was readily apparent.

Whether a young man separates from his family of origin out of desire or necessity, being autonomous and self-sufficient can be an important aspect of self-esteem. After Henrique finished his military service he did not return to the family home in the interior but stayed in Caracas working and living on his own. After tiring of his job because of the low salary and demanding working conditions, he quit, hoping to use his severance pay to import and resell goods from Miami. After losing his capital in business deals gone wrong, he spent a year unemployed, slowly selling his possessions to get by. He converted to Evangelicalism at the tail end of his economic crisis when he was going through a training program for a job at a bank. When I asked him if he had any friends or family members who would lend him money, he responded:

> Well, family. I had one uncle here, but I never went to him and told him about the situation because he lives in a place here in Caracas that is hard to get to. I didn't go frequently. But sometimes I did go to, say, spend a weekend. But I didn't tell him about the problem openly. I would just sort of swallow it and try to solve my problem some other way so that they wouldn't see that I was in such a critical situation.

What is especially interesting about Henrique's case is that he does not feel it is appropriate to ask extended family for help. And he does not even mention the possibility of asking friends or his spatially distant family of origin.

Willian is an example of one of those who lives apart from his family of origin out of economic necessity. He lucidly described the impact in terms surely experienced by others as well. He had explained to me that when he converted, he was "loaded with problems," and I asked him what type. He responded:

> I had personal afflictions, moments of loneliness. Those were tough times. Being here [in Caracas] without your family is tough. You tend to have economic problems. I also had problems with sickness, moments of loneliness. And sometimes you feel that there isn't anyone who can talk to you to raise your spirits. Because when you look at them [people you don't know very well], they have more problems than you do. So I couldn't trust them, their advice. I was always taught that my family was God, that my family would solve my problems. And I got close to some people where I would have lunch. I would eat lunch at an Evangelical kiosk and was able to place my trust in them.

Of course, it is unlikely that Willian thought his "family was God" before he converted. This is clearly an Evangelical reconstruction of what he did think before he converted: that his family was his main resource for solving his problems, and he no longer had them present. What is interesting in Willian's case is not just that he experienced the normal problems of a young man living on his own for the first time but also the emphasis he puts on not having anyone to talk to. In effect, Willian did not have trusted interlocutors who could, through dialogue, help him to make meaning regarding the situations he was going through. When he came across some people he felt he could trust at an Evangelical kiosk where he would eat lunch, he cultivated this network.

Thus those young men who do not live with their family of origin are not only freer to innovate; they are more likely to want to since they are left to their own devices when confronting a problem situation.[2]

THE MECHANICS OF NETWORK INFLUENCE: LIVING WITH AN EVANGELICAL

Conformity Effects

As mentioned above, the simple conformity model of network influence has been increasingly criticized. Clearly network influence happens. But

2. None of this should be surprising as a large part of the literature on the positive effects of religious practice on psychological and physical health focuses on social support networks (Bankston and Zhou 1996; Ebaugh and Pipes 2001; Ellison 1997; Foley, McCarthy, and Chaves 2001; Fraser 2002; Haines, Hulbert, and Beggs 1996), as does an important tradition in community studies (Saegert, Thompson, and Warren 2001; Silveira and Allebeck 2001; Walker, Wasserman, and Wellman 1994; Wellman 1982).

we need more information to establish why it works in one direction rather than another (Gould 2003). We can begin by viewing network ties not as conveyor belts directly transmitting influence but rather as culturally constituted, frequently contested, sites of interaction (McAdam 2003: 290; Mische 2003; see also Sherkat and Wilson 1995). Within these sites of interaction, there are situations in which network influence leads in the direction of Evangelical participation because there is a clear asymmetry of power or number or because aspects of the Evangelical meaning system interact with features of the interactions that take place.

In a number of cases of conversion, network influence clearly occurred in an asymmetric social context—a microsocial context in which the non-Evangelical had less social power or status than the Evangelical(s). Often this situation resulted from a move into a new household. Teodoro returned to his family from military service to find that the majority of them had converted to Evangelicalism and attended the Evangelical church across the road from their home. He soon discovered that they no longer were able to go to parties and social occasions with him. So when they invited him to attend a young adults' program at their church, he gladly went, and he ended up converting as well. When Gregorio moved to Caracas after losing his job in the interior, he moved in with four Evangelicals he had met previously. They brought him to church, and his conversion process began. While specific aspects of Evangelical meanings or practices may have been important in any of these cases, the asymmetric social context was probably more important. In most of these cases one could imagine not just Evangelicalism but almost any subcultural meaning system functioning in a largely similar way.

A number of cases of network influence, however, present precisely the situation of bilateral monopoly that Gould problematizes. In other words, there seems to be a relatively equal balance of power between the non-Evangelical and the Evangelical. In five cases a respondent converted as a result of spatial ties to a romantic interest. Juan Miguel came to Caracas after his life had fallen apart in his hometown in the interior. He soon met an Evangelical woman, whom he married. He explained, "I was unconverted when I married her, and the Lord, through her, ministered to me. He 'tamed the lamb' as they say." Henry converted the very same day that he began to live with the woman he would eventually marry. They had developed a friendship at the lunch counter where she worked. When she invited him to rent a room from her in her house—a common practice given the lack of affordable housing in Caracas—he immediately took her up on it. He described what happened next:

Two Evangelical men from Emmanuel Church.

> And that same Saturday there was a revival in the Metro [subway station plaza] and she invited me: "Come on, let's go so that you can see how beautiful it is." So I went and that's where she also invited me . . . to go up [to the altar call]. She said, "Let's go up front so that you can see how beautiful it is, let's go see!" She was the one who invited me to go up when they made the altar call.

Here we can ask Gould's question: why did the network tie lead the man to convert instead of the woman to discontinue her participation? Gould argues that frequently participation in a movement can itself add value to the relationship. As a result, participation comes to outweigh the alternative of nonparticipation. In each of these five cases either the relationship was new or the couple was experiencing relationship problems. Given Evangelicalism's strong association with family and conjugal relationship among adherents (Brusco 1995; Smilde 1997), participation likely added value to these new or troubled relationships. It is like a young dating couple going to Disneyland. It is something neither would probably do by themselves or with their own friends, but it is a forum for demonstrating a sensitive, family-oriented side that adds value to a romantic relationship. As such, it can become a reasonable thing to do together.

There is another possibility for understanding how network influence occurs in cases of equal power. Lived events can revalue existing discourses, determining the symbolic elements that dominate as well as the direction they take (Ellingson 1995; Sahlins 1985). When an Evangelical and a non-Evangelical share living space, there is continual potential for what the Russian literary theorist Mikhail Bakhtin (1991) called "interanimation," the forced recognition of alternative, competing discourses (see also Mische and White 1998; Steinberg 1991).[3] Interanimations should not necessarily be seen as intense "moments." They can just as well be time-extensive engagements ranging from cordial sharing to repeated conflict. In these data the most common form of interanimation is for Evangelicals to engage non-Evangelicals in a low-intensity but persistent way by continually providing Evangelical conceptualizations of the situations and dilemmas the non-Evangelical confronts. This requires response from the non-Evangelical, who develops a repertoire of ways to deflect the confrontation. The equilibrium is often broken when a moment of sickness, mishap, or misfortune arises that tips the interpretive balance of power toward the evangelizer, who inevitably provides an Evangelical analysis of the non-Evangelical's misfortune. The meaning system gains life for the evangelized, and he assents to it.[4]

Seven years after Juan Santiago and his wife married they began attending one of the churches I studied. But while his wife went through indoctrination classes and baptism, Juan's interest flagged. "She would say to me, 'C'mon let's take this more seriously!' You can't take God lightly," Juan recounted. But he dragged his feet until a period in which, in the span of one month, he twice spent a couple of nights in jail for disputes with neighbors. During his second incarceration, he made a deal with God and became a participating Evangelical. Juan explained, "God calls us with love. But when we don't pay attention, he calls us in other ways. What happened was that I was implicated in a robbery and went to jail. After three days I spoke to the Lord and said, 'If you get me out of here, it will be different.' That's what it took for me to actually accept Christ. He let me out under oath." In this case Juan's going to jail broke the standoff with his wife and he decided to "take God seriously."

3. This is essentially the same process as "frame alignment" as developed by Snow (Snow et al. 1986) and others. Here I use the more general and flexible term *interanimation* as it seems more appropriate to this type of everyday interaction.

4. In her study of conversion in Colombia, Brusco (1995) presents this as one of the primary ways in which women get men to convert.

A more striking example is the case of Darton and his wife, who converted when they were living with the wife's Evangelical mother. Darton's mother-in-law continually tried to get them to convert to Evangelicalism, and they occasionally went to church with her. However, it was not until their child almost died from a respiratory problem that they began to attend regularly. They viewed their son's revival as a miracle. And Darton's mother-in-law did not miss the opportunity to interpret the occurrence as a message from God. I asked Darton what his mother-in-law had to say about the event, and he responded:

> She wasn't surprised because she knows that God truly is a God of miracles. But she recriminated us. [She said] it had happened to us because we were disobedient before God—because we knew—We would always go and ask for prayers when she was pregnant, but we didn't serve him [afterward]. So she said that God did that so that we would understand that he really is a living God and that we weren't serving him—that perhaps he was calling us through our child since we weren't going [to church] on our own accord. He started calling us through our child.

Theoretically, such contingencies can work with any cultural practice or discourse. However, the character of the meanings involved can have an important impact in two ways. First, while scholars have shown how highly general and ambiguous messages can consolidate power by deflecting the potential conflicts between nodes in a network or members of a coalition (Ansell 1997; McLean 1998; Mische 2003; Padgett and Ansell 1993), here we see the opposite. Evangelicals' emphasis on clear and unequivocal discourse has precisely the goal of ratcheting down spiritual choices and provoking confrontations that might lead to conversion. Second, Venezuelan Evangelical discourse and vocabulary specializes in conceptualizing exactly the type of misfortune that lower-class Venezuelans tend to experience. This specialization, combined with the relative inattention by the mass media and popular culture, means that when misfortune occurs it constitutes prima facie evidence for the validity of Evangelical discourse.

Indirect Effects

Portraying network explanations as alternatives to cultural explanations leads to an overemphasis on conformity effects. But in many of my cases, network influence either worked through direct interaction in which conformity was irrelevant or it came through unilateral observation in which conformity was not at issue. Burke (1989) wrote that the primary attribute of symbols is precisely that they provided a vehicle in which sentiments, ideas, and discoveries could find a life beyond the experience or intentions of a single "genius." A spatially copresent Evangelical is a living bearer of symbols and practices that can be observed, considered, and tried on by a non-Evangelical, regardless of whether there is direct interaction between the Evangelical and the non-Evangelical. In my data such indirect effects fit into two general categories that I refer to as modeling and ecological influence.

Modeling In a number of cases the respondent converted not because of any apparent attempt to achieve harmony with a spatially present Evangelical but because of intimate exposure to meanings and practices that came to make sense for his life at a critical juncture. This is frequently referred to as "behavioral contagion" (Marsden and Friedken 1994). I refer to it as "modeling" because the idea of providing a good "witness" is an explicit part of Evangelical thought. Evangelicals are enjoined to evangelize not only through direct interaction but by behaving in exemplary ways and overtly "wearing their faith on their sleeves."

Bartolo, who converted in the midst of a crisis deriving from his life of violence and drugs, had one Evangelical brother. When I asked him whether his brother had talked to him about Evangelicalism before his conversion, he said he gave him Bible tracts once in a while but not much else. When I asked him why not, he said that not everybody was close with everybody else in his large family. He could count on this Evangelical brother in time of necessity. "But," he said, "in sharing and confiding with each other we weren't close. I was close with one brother, and he was with another. But we weren't close with each other like, 'hey, try this.' No, that was rare. Lack of communication, I guess that's why." Nevertheless, when Bartolo reached a crisis point in his life, he had a rudimentary knowledge of Evangelicalism that made it seem a possible solution.

An even more striking case is that of Ugeth. He converted as a result of a crack addiction that was undermining his relationship with his wife and children. During his problem period, he lived in the same house with two brothers who had already converted a few years before because of a similar drug problem. However, his sibling relationship with them was so problematic that he said they never once tried to evangelize him:

> No, they didn't talk to me [about the Gospel]. One time I was consuming [drugs] in my room alone. They came in and instead of talking to me [about the Gospel] they started mocking me, throwing barbs at me. They would say, "Are you going to keep on [taking drugs]?" They didn't say, "Christ loves you," or preach to me. They never called out to me.

Nevertheless, when he did convert, his brothers' example was important for him:

> The Lord had manifested himself in them and pulled them out of where they were—because they were terrible. One would rob in the street. The other would steal at home. But the Lord, I mean, Glory to God; I'll give their testimony. I involve them here in this interview because they were an inspiration for me, seeing how the Lord had rescued them from the things they would do . . . and inspired, seeing everything that the Gospel was doing in the lives of those who were close to me, I realized that it was something supernatural, that it wasn't normal. And I said, "Hey, I have to try this."

Interestingly, although Ugeth's conversion got him to overcome his crack addiction, it seemed to have little effect on his distant relationship with his brothers. While I knew the three of them, his brothers came to church and sat together with their respective families. Ugeth had an entirely different circle of friends and sat elsewhere in the church. Ugeth clearly did not convert in order to conserve a relationship. Rather, his brothers' spatially present religious practice gave him the chance to closely consider its appropriateness for his life. We will see much more about Ugeth and his family in the next chapter.

Ecological Influence There are other mechanisms through which network influence can occur beyond social conformity. An Evangelical's religious practice may change the conditions to which a non-Evangelical responds (Marsden and Friedkin 1994). Wilkenman converted at the age of eighteen. Being a quiet, intellectual boy in one of the toughest, most violent neighborhoods in Caracas, he suffered severe personal and social adjustment problems. When he was a boy his mother separated from his father and began a new family. Because of frequent, acute conflict between his mother and stepfather, Wilkenman bounced between his "more or less" Evangelical mother's house and his Evangelical grandmother's house. According to his description, his mother was engrossed in her new family and small children and paid little attention to him. Wilkenman had no friends and would spend hours drawing or watching action movies on television. However, his mother and grandmother would both put Evangelical radio programs on at home. Once he started to listen, Wilkenman was hooked. He spent hours listening and even calling in to radio talk programs until he finally decided that becoming Evangelical would solve his problems. He went to church with his grandmother a few times and then started to go to Evangelical concerts and events he heard about on the radio. Wilkenman reports no attempts at Evangelization by his mother or grandmother; indeed, he eventually joined not his grandmother's church but the one he found with the most active youth program. Rather, he worked through the possibility of religious innovation in engagement with his radio. He explained, "It's the Holy Spirit that ministers to you through the radio. So I would listen to the church programs that were on at 9:00 P.M. and that talked about Venezuela's problems, people's problems, and Christ's solutions, how glorious the Lord is, this and that about the Lord. With the testimonies I heard, I found that Christ was the solution."

Roberto Alfonzo lived with his wife and children in his own house built as an addition to his mother's house—a common arrangement in the catacombs of Caracas's barrios. His brother and sister-in-law, who lived with Roberto Alfonzo's mother, converted to Evangelicalism before he did. When I asked Roberto Alfonzo if his brother talked to him about the Gospel he said, "Yeah, he talked to me about the Gospel. But not much. We come from a family where we respect each other a lot. When he'd go too far I'd say—in 'worldly' terms—'get lost' and he would stop immediately because there was personal respect in our family." Nevertheless, his brother and sister-in-law had services in their home and Roberto Alfonzo listened: "They would have services in my mother's house, and my house is below hers. So when they had their services, I would listen. They would have the [sound] equipment turned on and you could hear it since there is just one wall that separates us."[5] These services piqued his interest and led him to buy a Bible to study. He "surrendered" in a plaza service that he visited by himself one day on his way home from work.

The point of the cases of Bartolo, Ugeth, Wilkenman, and Roberto Alfonzo is not that spatially present Evangelical family members were irrelevant but rather *how* they were relevant. In these cases, and in others, describing the mechanism as social conformity seems false to the phenomenon. In none of these cases did the person appear preoccupied by coming into line with the beliefs of spatially present Evangelicals. Rather, either through modeling or by changing ecological conditions, spatially present Evangelicals exposed these respondents to Evangelical meanings and practices that came to make sense to them in their lives. In my data

5. It is customary for Venezuelan Evangelicals to use sound amplification even for a service attended by only a handful of people in a small space precisely for this effect: to get their message to others who might be interested but are not in attendance.

such indirect influence is evident in a substantial minority of cases of network influence (11 of 27, or 40.7%).

PROBLEMS, AGENCY, AND PURPOSES

The preceding explorations of Evangelical networks, countervailing networks, and structural availability clearly support the importance of a network perspective. My respondents who experienced problems only imagined religious alternatives when they had an Evangelical living in the household or when they did not live with family of origin that could provide social and cultural support and reinforce traditional meanings. However, it would be overdrawn to conclude from this that the attempt to address problems through religious meaning—the "deprivation-congruence hypothesis"—is causally irrelevant.

Problems

Network explanations of conversion are generally portrayed as alternatives to explanations based on problems or "deprivations." But this disregards important interactions between the individual experience of problems and the creation of structural location. It is generally assumed that structural availability is the product of happenstance, or at least issues irrelevant to conversion. So, for example, in their classic exploration of religious conversion and networks, Snow, Zurcher, and Ekland-Olson (1980) use the example of a twenty-five-year-old man whose luggage was lost on his flight to Los Angeles and who wound up living on the streets. This contingent misfortune left him open and receptive to recruitment to a religious movement. Indeed, in many of my cases, structural availability was caused by life course characteristics or contingencies. However, it should come as no surprise that frequently structural availability is *itself* caused by a problem that is involved in the conversion project. Among the men I interviewed, for example, Alberto, Jhony, and Melvin all lived on the street as a result of their involvement in drugs and crime. In other cases persistent problems had undermined the individual's place in the family of origin. Martín's mother forced him and his wife to leave because of their incessant fighting. Ernesto's mother threw him out of the house because of his constant involvement with drugs and violence. José Gregorio became structurally available when going to jail meant he was forced to be away from his mother's home. And Lenin voluntarily moved away from his family of origin because of inconformity and conflict. In all, in fifteen of the fifty cases of converts who experienced problems while not living with family of origin, it was the problem that would eventually lead to conversion that itself caused structural availability. Without these cases, the connection between not living at home and experiencing life problems is not significant (see appendix B). This leads to the conclusion that not living with family of origin is causally important not because it causes problems but because of what happens when problems occur. It also provides some sociological content to the common belief that an individual must "hit bottom" before getting serious about overcoming an addiction or other problem of the self (Irvine 1999: 56–57). In my data "hitting bottom" often amounted to individuals losing their most valued social relationships, which in turn simultaneously left them to their own problem-solving devices and freed them up for innovation.

Agency and Purposes

Structural explanations based on networks assume that people do not usually know why they do what they do and do not fully understand the consequences their action will produce (Giddens 1979: 59). Structural approaches do not deny that people experience agency in what they do, nor do they deny that they can provide agentive stories regarding what they have done. Rather, they argue that these vocabularies of motive are not scientific explanations because they leave out the real causes that determine who acts in which way (Emirbayer and Goodwin 1994; Burt 1986). From this perspective, taking the cases of Willian, who found Evangelicals to talk to at a lunch kiosk and cultivated the network, and of Ugeth, who decided to give Evangelicalism a try after seeing what it had done for his brothers, and using them as causal accounts would be simply be inadequate. However, there are three issues to keep in mind.

First, causal explanation of a particular outcome is not the same as causal explanation of a general type of outcome. If we are trying to explain who shops at a certain grocery store, the "need to buy food" will probably not be causally significant. Rather, geographic factors such as location of residence and the structure of transportation systems will be more causally important. But this does not mean that the need to buy food is insignificant. It simply means that it is a factor all people have in common and therefore cannot be used to distinguish who shops at a certain grocery store from who does not. In the same fashion, this analysis shows life problems to be neither sufficient nor necessary to cause Evangelical conversion (though they do stay in the equation as causally important; see appendix C). However, that should not be taken to mean that people do not convert in order to address problems. Rather, it simply means that significant life problems are so widely distributed that they are inadequate for explaining why people address them through *this* solution.

Second, in contemporary social theory, agency is not synonymous with purpose and intention. Anthony Giddens (1976: 77) defines agency as "the stream of actual or contemplated causal interventions of corporeal beings in the ongoing process of events-in-the-world," which is not confined to the intended consequences of an actors' action (see also Emirbayer and Mische 1998; Sewell 1992). Defined in these terms, the majority of the cases of conversion in which network location was causally effective demonstrate the respondents' agency in the construction of this location. In the great majority of the cases in which a respondent lived away from family of origin, he moved away due to life course considerations: marriage or employment. In contrast, respondents who lived with a spatially copresent Evangelical did so not by choice but because that was his family of origin or because the Evangelical in question converted after the respondent had joined the household. However, in ten cases the person intentionally moved into a household that had an Evangelical in it. Agency, thus defined, is quite compatible with the traditional network program. For networks to be key causal characteristics of social phenomena, it is not necessary for these networks to be uncaused, or even to be uncaused by the actors that eventually are constrained by them. Rather, the core claim is that they have important effects that function beyond (even contrary to) the conscious interests and intentions of actors. This would be like an actor who switches on the light to illuminate the room and unintentionally alerts the prowler (Giddens 1976: 77).

A third, more direct challenge to the exclusion of agency in network explanations, then, would be to demonstrate agency in which network effects are no longer unintended. This would be a purposive account in which an actor switches on the light to illuminate the room *in order to* alert the prowler. To inquire into this possibility, I looked at the cases in which the respondent intentionally created the network location, to determine if this agency was an integral part of the same project of change that resulted in conversion. In several cases I found evidence of such a process. Gregorio converted while living away from his family of origin and living with an Evangelical. However, he actively sought these conditions as part of a project of change. Two problems were affecting his life before his conversion: depression and loss of his job. While living at home with his family he became familiar with Evangelicalism at a revival and even had a religious experience. Nevertheless, despite his interest, he did not join a church. He met a number of Evangelicals from Caracas who invited him to stay with them if he ever came to the city, a move he was already considering. When he arrived in Caracas he looked up his Evangelical friends, and they found him a place to stay with several other Evangelicals. He immediately began to attend church with them. When his music career sputtered, he put all his energies into this Evangelical church. In this case, moving away from family of origin to Caracas to live with Evangelicals and pursue a music career were all part of a project of change, a new start that eventually led to religious conversion.

When José Gregorio went to prison for a cocaine binge that involved a car theft and shoot-out with police, he was assigned, beyond any intention of his own, to an Evangelical-controlled cell block. He converted within several weeks of his arrival. However, some months later he developed an attraction to a woman who frequently visited another inmate on weekends. When that inmate changed to a non-Evangelical cell block, José Gregorio changed along with him and promptly discontinued his religious practice. However, when the relationship with the woman did not lead anywhere, he intentionally moved back to the Evangelical cell block in order to return to his Evangelical participation. "The Devil tricked me and that girl got me to leave," he said. "She trapped me—I mean she captured me and I decided to change cell blocks, in order to maintain contact with her. And when I changed cell blocks and left the Gospel, she didn't visit the jail anymore. So she was an instrument intended to derail me. But I understood, and I went back." These are cases in which network location ends up looking like a mediating variable between individual motivations and conversion. It clearly has a causal impact, but the respondents themselves created that impact as part of a conscious project of change. The respondents did not necessarily see that a change in network location would lead to conversion in particular. But they did correctly perceive that, in more general terms, it would facilitate a project of change.

Something quite similar happens among men who have problems but do not choose to address them through an Evangelical project. They seem to understand clearly the support function of family of origin. Horangel, for example, married the proverbial girl next door and lived with his wife and baby in his in-laws' home. As is often the case, this living situation exacerbated marital conflict; Horangel complained that his mother-in-law meddled in their affairs and inevitably sided with his wife. The solution he found was to move back to his own mother's house just a few doors down. He and his wife are still married, and they get along fine, but he eats and sleeps at his mother's home rather than with his wife and child. Cristóbal, in contrast, was happily married with a new baby when his wife was diagnosed with cancer. In less than six months she was gone, leaving him with the long-term problem of how to raise a one-year-old boy on his own. "That's really why I came home," he explained, "because of my kid. I didn't have anybody to leave him with. That [where he lived] was a long ways away, and I worked in Los Palos Grandes [a relatively distant part of Caracas]." In each of these cases, the respondent had significant rapport with his family of origin and could count on their support, preventing any serious interest in a religious innovation such as Evangelicalism.

While these purposive constructions of network locations present a clear challenge to strong versions of the network project, it could hardly be otherwise. As people think about and imagine their social context, it would be surprising indeed if they never perceived the same causal sequences sociologists do. Nevertheless, it should be underlined that this process is limited. Such purposive construction happened in less than 10 percent of conversions related to networks. In more than 90 percent of cases there was no purposive relationship between the respondent's intentions and the network effects he was subject to.

CONCLUSION

The relationality of imagination we see in this chapter effectively tempers the implicit voluntarism of the imaginative rationality we saw in part 2. People act in the world, get things done, in part by creating concepts that remake, refigure, and reimagine the world in a way that makes it more amenable to their action. However, the possibilities and reach of imaginative rationality are strongly framed by the relational context. The particular network location of an individual strongly frames what can and cannot be imagined.

This analysis has been developed from data from eighty-four men, Evangelical and non-Evangelical. How would it look different if it had been carried out with women? On the one hand, the emphasis placed here on the relationality of religious and cultural practices is an analytic tendency central to feminist scholarship. In her classic work on gender and moral reasoning, Gilligan (1982) argued that women are more likely to engage in "relational reasoning" when thinking through ethical dilemmas rather than the "hierarchical reasoning" characteristic of men. Put differently, they are more likely to make decisions in terms of their impact on concrete others rather than in terms of fulfillment of abstract mandates (see also Smith 1990). My analysis here, then, represents an extension of feminists' theorization of relational reasoning to men, in this case marginal men in contexts in which social networks are key to survival. This being the case, it is plausible to think that the idea of relational imagination would also apply to women in this context. On the other hand, recent work by Penny Edgell (2006) has complicated this picture. In her study of congregational religion she showed that men were more likely to participate for family reasons and women were more likely to participate for reasons of the self. Clearly, only with further research will we be able to unpack the interaction of gender and relationality in religious practice.

The concrete character of network ties likely vary by gender. For example, among the men I interviewed the household was the relevant unit of analysis in deciding what counted as a network tie: an Evangelical in the household pulled people toward conversion; a member of the family of origin kept people away from it. With women this may well be different. In this context, stay-at-home women are more likely than men to have extrahousehold neighborhood ties. These ties could be causally significant for religious conversion in a way they are not for men. The conservative impact of family ties might be different as well. Women in this context are often seen as naturally religious, and non-Evangelical family members may bristle less at a daughter or sister becoming Evangelical than they would at a son or brother. But these ideas are little more than conjecture. Finding the network dynamics of female conversion would require actual data collection and analysis.

CHAPTER 7

Two Lives, Five Years Later

Chapter 6 provided a relational analysis of Evangelical conversion based on a comparable sample of Evangelical and non-Evangelical men. The relatively large size of this sample allowed me to render the variety of relational situations that facilitate or prevent Evangelical conversion. Here I want to look more deeply into these issues by focusing on two cases: Augusto and Ugeth. Each was in my original sample: Augusto was one of my non-Evangelical respondents; Ugeth was one of my Evangelical informants from the first days of my research. I reinterviewed each two more times, five and six years after our original interview. During that time, their trajectories crossed: Augusto had become Evangelical, and Ugeth had discontinued his Evangelical participation. I also interviewed significant others—family in Augusto's case, family and friends in Ugeth's.

With data from several sources and several points in time, I seek to provide a more nuanced view of the way both network influence and structural availability function. Augusto's case shows the subtle influence of networks and the power of Evangelical meanings to imagine alternatives in the most hopeless circumstances. Ugeth's case points to some limitations of Evangelical meanings and networks. Both cases reveal the plight of men coming of age in Venezuela's fading modernity.

AUGUSTO: "GOD DOES THESE THINGS"

I first interviewed Augusto as part of my sample of non-Evangelical men. Victor, a member of Emmanuel Church, and I were going door to door, and we knocked on Augusto's grandmother's door. Both he and his mother were living there because they had rented out their own apartment. When Victor and I explained what the interview was about through the bars covering their door, Augusto's mother became excited and asked us in. Probably under the biomedical conception that I was going to somehow provide Augusto with treatment, she said she would like her son to do it and called him out of his room. I explained the interview to him, and he acceded in a friendly, yet not enthusiastic manner. We conducted the interview in November 1998. Augusto was twenty-one years old. He had been suffering from devastating drug problems and involvement in delinquency since his early teens. This was a story that could be read without words: Augusto had a large scar over his left eye, numerous smaller scars on his face, and a permanent limp from a motorcycle accident. Lifting up his shirt would have revealed numerous scars from bullet and stab wounds. Though he was clearly intelligent, his conversation was marked by a distant gaze and an occasional irreverent smirk.

At the time of this first interview, Augusto's mother and aunt were both Evangelicals and would occasionally take him to church with them. But he usually found ways to avoid it and never went on his own initiative. I thought he might be cynical about Evangelicalism. But when I asked him about it in that first interview, his reaction seemed like a mixture of amusement and interest in a world very different from his own. When I asked him whether he liked to go to the youth group of his aunt's church or whether he just went to please her, he said:

> No, no, I do. I do because there are young people's groups there and there are young people and pretty girls who study and are getting ahead. They have their little projects, they make food and sell it. Others make stuff out of clay and sell it. They organize a lot of stuff, and you see that they don't have vices and don't spend money on vices. It's not bad. It's good.

It was evident at that time that he was interested but did not take it very seriously. Experiencing serious life problems, living with an Evangelical family member, yet unconverted, Augusto provided one of the contradictory cases presented in Table C3 (see appendix C).

When I followed up on my respondents five years later, I telephoned Victor and asked him about each of the young men I had interviewed in his building. When I got to Augusto, Victor excitedly told me that he had converted through Victory Outreach (VO), an Evangelical organization specializing in helping substance abusers. The Nuyorican Sonny Arguinzoni founded VO in East Los Angeles in the late 1960s. A heroine user who had spent time in jail before converting, Arguinzoni saw VO as an Evangelical mission with the specific goal of converting drug users. The organization is still headquartered in Los Angeles but now claims two hundred thousand members in five hundred churches or rehabilitation centers in twenty-four countries. Most Venezuelans' experience with VO comes through contact with young men selling pencils, bookmarks, or other items on public transportation to raise money for the organization.

I briefly interviewed Augusto in 2003 and then more thoroughly in 2004. I also interviewed his mother and aunt. During my first interview with Augusto, the importance of the latter two figures in his life was a recurring theme, and I focus on their versions of Augusto's biography to illuminate the functioning of network influence from the perspective of those doing the influencing. My interview with Augusto's mother, Margarita, revealed the heart-wrenching story of a mother raising children in a declining urban landscape and engaging in project after project to save her son from a life of violence and drugs. Margarita grew up in Carupano on the eastern Caribbean coast of Venezuela. She met her husband while in college; he completed his studies and became a laboratory researcher at the School of Dentistry at the Universidad Central de Venezuela. Margarita did not finish college but held a number of decent-paying semiprofessional white-collar jobs. The apartment complex where she and her husband raised their family is in the shadow of the modern Parque Central complex. When they bought it, it would have been considered well located in a downtown area close to governmental megaprojects of the oil boom years. But through the years of la crisis it became a run-down den of crime, drugs, and violence. As we will see, her husband's abuse, as well as Augusto's problems, progressively undermined the middle-class family Margarita sought to hold together.

The day we talked she was dressed in old work clothes, with her hair tied up with a handkerchief—ready to work after our interview in one of Victory Outreach's projects for the homeless. She explained that Augusto had behavioral problems from his early teens and went to jail for the first time at fourteen. She hired a lawyer to get him out and began a long series of attempts to reform Augusto. She explained:

> After that, looking for some sort of solution, I put him in a different school to see if he would change and nothing. I went and got the help of a cousin in Falcon [a state on Venezuela's western coast]. He was close to a school there. They enrolled him, and he was a good student. When I withdrew him, the principal was sad because in math and English he was their best student. He did his sophomore year in Falcon. Then one time my cousin [called and] said, "Look, Augusto left the house. Come and look for him. Come and see what you can do. I don't want to call the police because it would look bad if the police came here." So I had to go. I got time off from work—I worked in a bank office. I had to go find him and pull him from that high school. Since then he hasn't returned to high school. Later I put him in a rehabilitation center. He was there for a year and he told me, "Mom, I'm better. Get me out of here." It was a Christian center.
>
> *Was that rehab center for drugs or for behavior?*
>
> By that time it was for drugs and because he was involved in street crime. He would get together with some other kids and they would steal. They had a gang, and they would get together to rob people in the street; do all kinds of things; drink. He was getting further and further lost. So I put him in a Christian rehab center called Renacer [Rebirth]; that was in 1993–94. I talked to the leader, a pastor named José Silva—it was in a place outside of Caracas called Caucagua. So I had him there and there he met Pastor Daniel, the first "fruit" of Victory Outreach [in Venezuela]. He was there with him, and I've know him since then as well. He was there rehabilitating as well. He is the first pastor to come up through Victory Outreach in Venezuela. Augusto told me one day, "Mom, I'm better, I want to leave. I talked to the pastor and I'm better." Augusto had been there for a year, and they released him. I brought him back to Caracas and [said,] "Okay, let's get you studying or put you to work." Look. Within two weeks of leaving—One Monday I had the day off and we went to Caucagua to get his things. And on Tuesday I went to work. I worked my shift, and when I got home they told me that Augusto had been shot five times. Two weeks after leaving, he was already taking drugs and doing his thing in our neighborhood, but toward the southern part.
>
> *In San Agustín?*
>
> Yeah, underneath that [pedestrian] bridge they shot him five times. He was in the hospital for eleven days because of those gunshot wounds, but he survived.
>
> *Five shots? Was his life in danger?*
>
> Yes, his life was in danger. But the doctor told us that he was super drugged up. He had taken pills. He took a lot of pills, not other drugs, but lots of pills. He would throw them up, these white things. So that was in 1994.

That was ten years ago. It happened April 17, 1994. So from that point on, instead of getting better, he got worse because he had even more hate in his heart, revenge, desire for revenge. That was terrible. Our home was completely destroyed. His brother and sister didn't live with us anymore. He has a sister who graduated [from college] as a journalist, but she lived with her aunt. His dad didn't live with us. Our household was a disaster; a complete mess. My other son couldn't live there because they would fight, my oldest son with him [Augusto]. He wasn't a problem child. He worked and studied. He drank and used drugs but not the way Augusto did. Augusto had become a delinquent. [Augusto's brother] died three years ago. A car killed him. A car ran over him on Avenida Bolívar. *[Pauses and begins to cry softly]*

I spoke with Augusto in 1998. He told me that you went to Río Chico for a while too?

Yes, we went to Río Chico for fourteen months. In '96 he had already gone to trial. I don't know if he told you about his trial. In '95 he had gone to jail for a couple of months as well. Not to jail but rather a place called La Planta. But they didn't try him. He got out. We got him a lawyer who got him out, and he didn't go to prison. So in '96 he committed another crime. He and another guy robbed a kid. The kid went to the police, and they opened an investigation. So in '96 he was detained, and they let him go, I don't know how. I went and told the judge that he had a wound—because he had been stabbed during that same time period, in '96, and was in bad shape. He had been operated on and I went and told the judge, "Look, he can't come to the hearing because this and this happened, here's the doctor's note." So they let him go and the police [immediately] started looking for him. I was going crazy. I would say, "Okay, they're going to kill you right here or you're going to jail. I don't want to see you in jail, I'd prefer to see you dead." And I was getting divorced at that time, in 1995—if his father didn't look after us [I thought] it'd be better for him to leave. He didn't even represent a shoulder to lean on. So I got a divorce, I rented the apartment and went to Río Chico, to some houses in a new development—empty and brand-new. We went there to try and find a different life, so that Augusto could change—and fleeing [Caracas] so that he wouldn't go to jail. They caught his buddy who was involved with him and he was in jail for four years. The sentence was eight years, but they reduced it for good behavior. So we were in Río Chico doing well there; we lived on the rent from our apartment and my family also helped out. But then Augusto started drinking and committing crimes again. He got to the point that he would take drugs and was out all night. Somebody hit him here *[points to above her left eye]* and they left him on the highway almost dead—they busted open his left eye with a bottle. Terrible. A woman who lived right there [where they dumped him] gave him first aid. She was a nurse and she took him to the hospital in Río Chico and he was lucky. There was a nurse at the hospital who was one of his little girlfriends. She talked to the doctor and they did a good operation on him—I thought he was going to lose his eye.

Later he came to the Clínico [Universitario—the teaching hospital at the Central University] so that they could check out his eye and everything was perfect. . . .

As a result of that we came back to Caracas again. We left that house empty. In 1998 we were back here again. I found a clinic for him here. He was there for a month and escaped. It was a private detox clinic. After one month he escaped with thirteen other kids. I talked to the director, and she said no, he could not come back because he was one of those who slashed a male nurse to get out. I was going crazy trying to figure out what to do with Augusto. And he was running because he didn't want—He did all those things, but he didn't want to go to jail. Because he knew that people in jail had said they were going to kill him. He had done so many bad things and had so many problems that he got to the point that he was scared. If the people he had messed with didn't pay him back, the police would—he was living a life that wasn't a life. "I don't want to go to jail. That depresses me. I don't want to see more mothers suffering, no," [he would say]. One time in Maracaibo [in a prison] they cut a guy's head off and played soccer with it. They do drugs; they're armed. It's exactly the same [as being on the street].

So he went to Victory Outreach in 1999. I called Daniel [Ruiz]. I called him and said, "Daniel, take Augusto." At that time [VO] was in La Vega. I believe their first house was in Antimano when they began. So he was there, and one day he left because he didn't like the food, this and that. . . . [So he left.] [Later they shot him in the buttock.] He was shot because he was stealing a motorcycle with another kid in San Agustín. [The owners] found him in Parque Central and shot him. He survived that one too. I'm telling you, he's like a cat with nine lives.

So how did he get to Victory Outreach?

Because I knew Daniel. Augusto himself would say, "Mom, Daniel is [at VO]." [I would say,] "Go, Augusto. Get moving." He went to their center on Avenida Andrés Bello. He would go, but then he would leave and hit the street again. He wanted me to pay for a place for him to stay. My family didn't want him in the house. And how was I going to pay for a place for him? I would have to hide him from his brother so that he could sleep. He was in constant danger.

Then in 2001 they came looking for him where I lived, in his grandmother's house. . . . [T]hey knocked on the door and he was there. I was working for AVANZA, an NGO that works with abandoned children—something to keep me busy. I went to work and my mother wasn't at home. He stayed home alone and I didn't want to leave him the keys. He told me he wanted to wash his clothes. So he started washing there with his friend and the police came. . . . He lied about who he was [when they asked] and then said, "Just a minute, I'm going to get my ID," and shut the door. Get his ID? No, he went to escape. He broke the window frame and jumped. He came to Parque Central and hid. He was a little bit hurt, but they both [Augusto and Jefferson] got there. He called me at work and said, "Mom, come over here, I'm in the mezzanine of Parque Central and I have a problem." "What problem?" [I asked]. "When you get here I'll tell you. Bring me some food." He was all roughed up and he got a ride here [to VO] on a bicycle. Thank God since that time he hasn't left.

Somebody brought him here on a bicycle?

Yeah, he had some friends there, [at Parque Central] and they brought him here [Victory Outreach]. Thank God, he's been here for three years, since February 14, 2001. That was the last time, and he hasn't left. So he has been progressing, he is the youth leader, and he feels better. He started at the bottom [in the church hierarchy].

The history of Augusto's travails and his mother's series of projects aimed at reforming him finally found success in the form of Victory Outreach. But she was not the only network tie leading toward a project of Evangelical reform. The most important early influence stimulating his Evangelical imagination was Margarita's younger sister, Dalia. Hoping to capture his attention and spur his reform, Dalia frequently brought Augusto to the youth group of the Pentecostal church she attended in an affluent, old money sector of Caracas. In 2004 we spoke in a café below my office in Chacao. She arrived dressed stylishly but casually. Her interview gave a quite different perspective from her sister's and was frequently critical, revealing more of the family problems with which Augusto had grown up. Venezuelan families tend to be close, but this does not necessarily mean that siblings are generous with each other. Indeed, being close often seems to go hand-in-hand with being sympathetic, yet openly critical. Dalia related how she and Margarita would take Augusto to rehabilitation centers:

He would be there for a while and then he would leave. [My other sister and I] would always blame [Margarita], saying, "But you don't leave him. Leave him there!" But she would always be there. She's still dependent [on Augusto], it's like a sickness in their mother-son relationship. And I think she felt very guilty about her son's situation. . . . So how did she confront the problem? By trying to give Augusto to other people. For example, I don't know if she told you she sent him to a cousin's house. Then she sent him to another family. She tried to fix things her own way, not God's way. She should have surrendered to God and trusted in him that Augusto would change.

Dalia told me that she used to take Augusto to services and that she engaged in a spiritual battle to try to win him over. The entire narrative is told in the form of Evangelical testimony.

Since he was a child, I would take him to church—just like I've taken all my nieces and nephews to church. But each one of them has continued on with their lives [i.e., hasn't become an Evangelical]. We would go out and look for him. Margarita would tell me, "He said he would go! Go get your car to take him!" I would go get in my car and go find him. I would go to the places where he would hang out. And he would lie to us: "No Aunt, not today. Tomorrow I'll go." We would go into the areas where the malandros hung out. There was a girl who used to be in that world and she would go with me. We took him to [a rehab center in] Valencia and a couple of days later he left.

I would think to myself, "I'm not going to pray for him anymore," but I had some friends who would always remind me—the people I work with, who I have a ministry with. They would say to me, "Dalia, how's Augusto?" It was like a calling. "You have to pray, keep praying for him," they would say. And there was another lady who would also ask me about Augusto. So, among all of us, we were looking out for him in prayer. Meanwhile, Margarita would go to church, but she still wasn't firm. It's only now that she has begun to get stronger [in her faith]. She would go on and on trying to get him help with doctors and other things.

I think the most significant thing that happened was a dream I had. I would see Augusto as a child, a beautiful child, [his skin] all smooth—because now he has scars all over. I have a photo of him when he was a little boy, all clean and innocent. I dreamed of him as a little boy, a little baby. I had told my sister, "Margarita, why don't you think about when you were pregnant with Augusto, anything that happened. Ask the Lord for forgiveness if you did anything bad, something that might have affected Augusto. Think, think, because I dreamed about him—that might have been the moment when he started doing drugs." I told Margarita, "You have to think back and try to find the moment, find out what happened, why Augusto is so tangled up by drugs, why he wants to get out but can't.

After that dream, I was still sensitive.[1] The image would come back to me all the time. I got on my knees and said to the Lord, "But Lord, this is my son, this is my son"—because there were people who thought that Augusto was my son. Since they were little all three of [Margarita's kids] spent a lot of time with me—even more than my own oldest son. I would get on my knees and say, "But Lord," and demand, "Lord, if he is like my son and you say your covenant is with our children, do your work." Apparently that was the moment when Augusto definitely decided, "I'm going to surrender, I don't want this life anymore." Within a couple of days he went directly to VO, and he's still there. But that's the way it is. I think that when God has a plan—because you get tired of it. You say, "This is the same thing again and again, the same story, Augusto"—but when the Lord takes charge, you have to follow. [He took charge] through those people who would ask me about him without even knowing him except for my stories,

1. She is expressing here the idea that she was still in a state of special susceptibility to communication from God.

[and through] his friend Daniel who went to VO first. Daniel had been in the first rehab center—Renacer. He left and was lost again. Margarita accepted him in her house. And later she came across Daniel, and he was working with VO. Now he's a pastor in Colombia. He got married.

Why did an Evangelical project of self-reform work this time when it had failed before? What was different? I asked Dalia about Augusto's mother's religiosity. Dalia questioned whether Margarita had really been strongly Evangelical.

Augusto was a case that didn't fit in my previous analysis because he lived with his mother and his mother was Evangelical.

But that's not true. His mother wasn't Christian.

At that time she attended Renacer.

Going to church is one thing. Surrendering and having a devotional life and reading the Word is something else. She didn't [do that]. She would go looking for help. Here in Venezuela, Evangelical churches are the ones that have centers for drug addicts. She looked for help, and she would leave him there.

So how did Margarita become Evangelical?

Through Augusto's situation. . . . Margarita arrived after being hit hard by the problems he had. And really, it's only after Augusto becomes firm in the Lord that he brings her in, he shows her in. Augusto really brings his mother.

Dalia went on to talk about how people become Evangelicals. Although she spoke in Evangelical terms, she pointed out the essential relationality of the process:

Unfortunately, the price you pay to seek God is pretty high. The people who come to church have a covenant. Even though we don't see with our own eyes a change in our families, we have a covenant that God is there, looking for us everywhere. It's like God catches us at a certain point in time. And our families are protected. God has a promise with Evangelical families. Believe in the Lord Jesus and you and your family will be saved. Of course that depends, in the end, on a personal decision. But everything the Lord can do, he does. There's always one person in the family. For example, in my family, there were no Evangelicals. And then when I married for the second time, my husband's mother was Evangelical. Then I get married and I seek the Lord. I had asked myself [religious] questions but never was all that interested. And that's the way it always is. We are the product of prayer, of the efforts of another person.

Dalia clearly saw herself as the central figure in Augusto's conversion and Margarita's efforts as irrelevant or counterproductive. Margarita and Augusto both agreed that Dalia was the central figure. Nevertheless, they each independently told me that Margarita started attending Victory Outreach before Augusto became really committed. In other words, they did not corroborate Dalia's claim that Margarita became Evangelical through Augusto. In our 2004 interview I asked Margarita about her history of Evangelical participation. I was wondering about the sequence of events that brought them both to become members of VO.

How long have you been in the Gospel?

I attended Renacer since about 1993.

And before that did you go to the Catholic church?

I was Catholic. I was married by the Church. I baptized my kids in the Church; they did first communion. We did all of that religious stuff.

What brought you to Renacer Church?

Because I was looking—they have a rehab center—I was looking for help for Augusto. They would take [people with drug problems] in and attend to them. They would send them to their rehab center in Miranda. At that time they were in the Nuevo Circo and I would attend church there. I would go to their services on Sundays and get to know people. And in Río Chico I would go to Word of Life. There too they wanted to help. I would tell them about Augusto, and they would say, "Well, bring him to church with you. He will come to the feet of the Lord." And they tried to take him to a camp too.

Did you become a member at Renacer?

No, I just went to services.

Did Augusto go with you?

When he was at the rehab center they would go to their church. I would go to mine.

When did you switch from Renacer to VO?

When Augusto left. When he came back [from the Renacer rehab center] after asking me to take him home because he was better and felt cured. And look, that was when he got shot. Lots of times when a person is a sinner and then gets to know the Word, his fall is even worse. It's the Devil. After that, it was worse. After leaving Renacer, he got shot, and then he kept on going with his delinquency. It's amazing he's not dead or in jail.

So you switched to VO?

> In 1999, looking for help for him.
>
> *You started to attend here [VO]?*
>
> *[Nods]* Augusto would come and go. But I always stayed—Fridays and Sundays, praying for him. My sister too; she's like his spiritual mother. She has been very consistent. She's gone to Los Chorros Church for ten years. My sister was always praying for Augusto.
>
> *Would she take him to church?*
>
> Yes, she would invite him and sometimes he would obey. But God hadn't come to him yet at that time.

The explanations offered by Augusto, Margarita, and Dalia make sense in terms of the Evangelical discourse of supernatural agency effected through prayer and fasting; in terms of sociological discourse, I think Margarita's decision to become part of the VO community was the key. It was here that things finally "fit together" for Augusto. It is interesting to note that Augusto arrived at VO not because he had suddenly seen a light on the road to Damascus but because he saw it as a good place to hide out for a while. Nevertheless, while he was there he came in contact with some missionaries who captured his attention and spurred his imagination. Augusto told me about his conversion process:

> I had heard of VO and I didn't have any place to go. I couldn't rob anyone. I could hardly walk. I would get dizzy when I walked. . . . My idea was to let my foot heal, and in a month or two go live in a hotel. I knew I could get some money using my own methods. That was my intention. Stay here [VO] for a while. I couldn't go home to my family; they had shut the door on me. So I came here and the Word of God challenged me. There were men of testimony here. There were some missionaries from Mexico here. They had tattoos and used to inject heroin *[imitates them showing their forearms]*. And they would come and tell me how God had changed them, that God had washed them. That they had been terrible and that God could change me, that I could be somebody in life. And I started to believe it. I asked God, "Well, Lord, if you truly exist, I want you to change me." I started seeking God, and seeking God, and humbling myself before the Lord. And he did a miracle in my life. He touched me. He changed me. He washed me.

Augusto's problems with substance abuse and crime essentially got to the point that it made him structurally available. At this point he is essentially on his own, unable to depend on his family of origin. Although his mother would certainly have let him live at home again, his brother and grandmother did not want him there—in any case, the police were watching the apartment. And this time, living in a residence with other Evangelicals, he is confronted by some who do more than preach to him. They model Evangelical projects that began from circumstances similar to his. Augusto's aunt Dalia also pointed this out.

> *Since I first interviewed him six years ago, Augusto told me that you would take him to Los Chorros Church to the youth group, and he liked it but wasn't very steady. Why do you think now he has stuck to it, but in his first encounter he didn't?*
>
> Different environments. [At Los Chorros] he was in a church environment where the kids are different. They don't have the same— they might not understand his situation. But in Victory Outreach he is with people who have gone through the same things he has and who know how to treat him. Sometimes their way of treating people can be tough. In Victory Outreach there is a lot of tough talk because the person helping them rehabilitate has been through it. They don't fall for any manipulation. It's just you against you. It's a form of growing. That's the same thing he does now. He works with the young people now and he knows how to treat them. [People with drug problems] find other people there who have had the same problem and they become like family—remember, they actually live there.

In Augusto's case the persistent influence of his mother and aunt and innumerable failed attempts nevertheless created the social framework that would lead to his conversion. The friendship he developed with Daniel in the first rehabilitation center ended up being a key avenue for him to seek an Evangelical solution. After several tries, it appears that the right circumstances conspired to get him to stay. His mother's membership in Victory Outreach at the time of Augusto's crisis with the police effectively gave him entry into their residential program.

Whatever the explanation, the change I saw in Augusto was remarkable. From the troubled youth I had interviewed in 1998, he had become a respected church leader. When we spoke in 2003 Augusto told me that he was a youth pastor in the church. I have learned to be skeptical of any description of such titles or positions. Evangelicals are generally ambitious and often exaggerate their importance in their churches. I took for granted that this was true in this case. However, in 2004, after spending a day at the church with Augusto and his youth group engaging in an activity for neighborhood youth, it was clear that he had not exaggerated. Augusto not only had a striking rapport with them, but they seemed to revere his word. Over lunch he told me:

> I'm filled with happiness and satisfaction knowing that God can use me, knowing that [before] I wasn't worth anything—what does the Word say?

> "God chose the foolish to teach the wise." And it fulfills me; it satisfies me to see how young people listen to me. *[Pause]* Sometimes I ask myself why [this is happening]. But it's God. God does these things.

UGETH: "O LORD, DO NOT FORSAKE ME"

Ugeth was one of the first people I met during my fieldwork in 1996. He had converted just a few weeks before I started to go to Plaza El Venezolano. He was Ramiro's neighbor and frequently accompanied him to and from church, at the plaza, and on weekend evangelization jaunts. A big man, he weighed about 240 pounds when I first got to know him. Enthusiastic and likable, he would sing loudly during the plaza services and frequently assisted by reading the Bible. In the previous chapters there are several quotes from Ugeth describing how he came to convert under the influence of his brothers. He was not one of my main informants, but during the three years of my original fieldwork we crossed paths consistently, and he helped me carry out aspects of my research. I frequently gave Ramiro and him rides home from evening services.

I always regarded Ugeth as a solid and untroubled member of Emmanuel Church. His Bible was notable for the many bookmarks and highlighted verses he could easily appeal to in discussion. He would consistently attend services and had his own mission project in the barrio where he and Ramiro lived. I went with him once to his *campo blanco* (target congregation) and watched as he put the sound equipment together and earnestly led the service. Thus I was surprised when, in 2003, Ramiro told me that Ugeth had "fallen" about a year before and was using drugs again. I reinterviewed Ugeth in 2003 and 2004. In 2004 I interviewed family and friends. An in-depth examination of his case provides entrée to the processes and structures involved in akrasia. In Ugeth we see a case of social support that enables a man to avoid change and that works through cultural meanings that fail to engage his imagination.

In hindsight a few of my early field notes show signs of trouble. One of the first times we met, Ugeth showed me several bookmarks he had in his Bible:

> "The Lord is my rock, my fortress and my deliverer." (Psalms 18:2)
>
> "O Lord, do not forsake me; be not far from me." (Psalms 38:22)
>
> "No matter how long the night is, the sun always rises."
>
> "If things didn't go well yesterday, don't be discouraged. Today is a new day. Start again."

The two Psalms were on bookmarks the shape of a fat pencil. The two nonbiblical passages were published by an Evangelical publishing house and printed on colored scenic backgrounds. I jotted them down because they struck me as somewhat heavy for a person of such happy demeanor. In another note I described Ugeth's frustration as he told me that he does not argue with hermanos over who he is. He opened up his Bible and read to me 2 Corinthians 5:17: "Therefore if anyone is in Christ, he is a new creation; the old has gone and the new has come." I found these passages out of my hundreds of field notes by doing a word search through my database. In my original analysis they had not stood out enough to code them. But from what I know now, these notes seem to reveal the struggles of someone whose Evangelical project of self-reform was a daily battle.

During the two months of 2003 that I was in Caracas, Ramiro and I tried to find Ugeth. He was rarely at home as he spent most of his time in the street. One afternoon, after the plaza service was over, Ramiro and I were walking down one of the pedestrian malls north of Plaza Bolívar when Ramiro suddenly nudged me and said he saw Ugeth. We walked quickly until Ramiro said, "There he is." I had no idea who Ramiro was referring to among the dozens of people in my field of vision; then Ramiro started teasing a homeless person by pulling on the empty poster tube he was carrying. My immediate reaction was to think this was certainly a bizarre thing for Ramiro to do when we were trying to catch up with Ugeth. But then the obvious hit me, and I was speechless. This dirty, shabbily dressed skeleton weighing no more than 140 pounds was Ugeth. He was a hollow shell of his former self. His cheeks were sunken, making his strong jaw look absurd. His pants were precariously held up by a belt that made the waistband bunch up around the top. He looked dazed but clearly remembered me as we shook hands and embraced.

The three of us went into a restaurant to have coffee. Ugeth hinted that he was hungry, and I ordered him a *pabellón criollo*. When his food arrived Ugeth swirled the rice, black beans, shredded beef, and plantains altogether and sprinkled a packet of sugar on top of it. He gulped heaping spoonfuls of the mixture until it was gone. Still trying to hide my shock at the ghost sitting in front of me, I turned the tape recorder on and began the interview. Much of what Ugeth said was incoherent—either from recent drug use or from ambulating in the street for too long. Nevertheless, he spoke with the same authoritative, grandiose, and moralistic tone he had always used. He said little of substance and stayed as abstract as possible. He occasionally used Evangelical ideas for self-criticism but also to evade responsibility:

> I haven't allowed myself to be humbled; I haven't allowed myself to be carried by the things of God. The Lord has told me many times that he is the only one. He has demonstrated that when I am in the Gospel, when I persevere in the Lord, he blesses me. He completely changes me. Everyone—my community, my family, people—notices. . . . [But] your heart says one thing, and your mind says something else. I'm in that struggle. It's not easy; it's the enemy; it's a constant struggle. Things have happened to me that, you know, I really think, "Why do things have to be like this?"—People raising false testimony against me. But of course, it's the Enemy. Lots of times he uses a so-called Christian [to do his work]. And perhaps the Lord himself permits it to happen to test your faith, to see if you have genuine faith.

After we had eaten we began walking with Ramiro toward Plaza Bolívar. Ugeth called me aside and asked if I could offer him a "collaboration"—in Venezuelan Spanish this means a donation—so that he could take some necessities home. I gave him a Bs. 1,000 bill (about fifty cents at that time). Afterward Ramiro scolded me, saying Ugeth would simply use it for drugs. When Ramiro and I talked about what Ugeth had said, I realized I would have to dig deeper to get anywhere in this biography.

The ensuing year did not go well for Ugeth. In February 2004 he was shot four times in a drug dispute, briefly recovered his Evangelical participation, but then backslid into drug use. In June 2004 I was able to interview Ramiro, with whom Ugeth was living at the time; Ugeth's neighbor Belkis; his brother Yonathon; and finally Ugeth himself. Ramiro and Belkis talked about the circumstances in which Ugeth first dropped out of Emmanuel Church. Then his brother recounted what had happened since. Throughout we see their unsuccessful efforts to bring Ugeth back to Evangelicalism.

In Venezuela it is common for people to take a surplus they might earn and use it to buy a taxi. They then lease this taxi to one or two drivers in exchange for a flat rate. When they have paid off the vehicle they sell it for a profit or continue to lease it out. Ugeth appears to have started using drugs again while working in such an arrangement with his neighbor and fellow Evangelical, Alexander. Ugeth would drive the taxi, pay Alexander a flat rate, and keep whatever additional income he earned. Apparently, Alexander had set up a favorable arrangement as a way to help an hermano from Emmanuel Church. But the relatively good cash flow was too tempting for Ugeth, and he started using again. This led him not only to stop contributing to his household but also to stop paying the use fee Alexander and he had agreed on. A crisis ensued when Ugeth apparently went so far as to sell accessories from the car. Ramiro explained how the situation came to light:

> It seems that the car had been damaged and was in the shop. [Ugeth] left it in a shop and when [Alexander] went to get it, it didn't have the stereo, which cost Bs. 300,000 [at that time about $150], and the spare tire was missing. So he said he wanted to get the police to pick Ugeth up when he was sleeping at my house. I said, "No. Look. You know me. I haven't given a bad testimony here [in the barrio] like that for you to come and give me a bad testimony. Let me talk to him." So I waited for Ugeth in the middle of the night. I changed the lock because sometimes I didn't hear him come home—I had given him free rein in my home. So he had to call out to me from outside.
>
> "Hey, what happened? Why did you change the lock?" Ugeth said.
>
> "Because I want to talk to you and that's the only way I'm sure to hear you," I said. "Look, the owner of your taxi came here. Tell me if what he said is true."
>
> "No. No. That's a lie," Ugeth said.
>
> "Okay, let's go right now. He told me that whatever time you get in, we could knock on his door," I told him. [Alexander] lives close by.
>
> "No. Let's go tomorrow," Ugeth said.
>
> "No, no. If you are doing bad things, I want to help you. But if you don't want to admit it, then I can't have you in my house. He wants to get you here with the police while you're sleeping and I can't have that. I don't want you to ruin my testimony by causing problems here."
>
> "Okay, I'll get my clothes and go," Ugeth said. But then he said, "I'll come tomorrow and we will go talk to him." And I said, "Okay, good."
>
> He didn't come back to get his clothes until two weeks later when I wasn't home. He never went with me to confront Alexander. And Alexander and his wife would say, "That's fine, we will confront whatever [Ugeth has to say]. We're willing to go to the police." I was the one who had to mediate so that there wasn't a big problem in the barrio.
>
> But he must have already been getting into trouble. . . . One time Ugeth told me that he was going to Guarenas, taking a client, and the person had drugs on him. The guy left the drugs in the car [when he got out], and the police stopped [Ugeth]. He was detained until the next day and they let him go. And with stories like that I was starting to suspect [that something was wrong]. This was a man who had God [was Christian], and who had so many wonderful testimonies to tell. I let things go, but his wife would tell me, "He's not contributing to the house." And the hermano [the owner of the taxi] confirmed, "No, he's not paying me. This week he didn't pay me." And that led me to realize he was doing something wrong.

How long did he live in your house?

Two years.

. . .

So where did he go when he left your house?

[Belkis replies]: He was in the street. His brother [Yonathon] who attends Emmanuel said he was down in the lower part in the barrio. He was hanging out with all the drug addicts down there. His brother went and found him and tried to take him to Oasis [a drug rehab center] and he said, "Yeah, I'll go on Sunday, early. I'll be at my mother's house. Stop by to get me." But he never showed up. They say that down there there's a sort of cave that they [drug addicts] have where they consume. They just consume, they don't eat or anything. He disappeared for like a week. His family didn't see him at all.

Ugeth's family lives in an enormous rancho near Ramiro. One of the first families to establish themselves in the barrio some forty years ago, they have a much-valued street front. Whereas normal ranchos such as Ramiro's have only a couple of hundred square feet of living space, the Ávila house, built by the family over several decades, has four stories, a workshop on the roof, and about three thousand square feet of living space. It was hardly luxurious, however. Some divisions between rooms are walls and doors, but others consist of sheets hanging from the ceiling. Furnishings are cheap and sparse. Furthermore, at any given time there are anywhere from fifteen to thirty people living there as five of the nine adult children still live at home—some with spouses, children, and their own grandchildren. Manuel, the family patriarch, was able to build his house with his sons during the years of the oil boom. Coming of age during la crisis, none of his children could even consider replicating their father's feat. Of the ten Ávila siblings, one was killed in front of the house almost twenty years ago in a firefight he was apparently not involved in; three, including Ugeth, are drug addicts; and one of the two sisters supplements her income as a prostitute with a handful of regular clients. Verbal and physical violence are common if not fully accepted media of conflict. Ugeth's brother Yonathon, for example, had to move out of the house with his wife and baby on a day's notice because, after a serious argument, his brother-in-law threatened to burn them alive if they were there the next day. In this context such threats are not idle, and within twenty-four hours Yonathon got two hermanos with trucks to help him move his family and possessions to another hermano's house.

I interviewed Yonathon before a Sunday morning service at Emmanuel Church. What I thought would be a brief interview with a man not known for many words turned into a two-hour rap session during which he poured out his family problems, including Ugeth's situation:

> My brother is going through a really critical situation right now. My mother tells me that she has to continually hide everything, [like] the television. The last thing he did was sell all his wife's things. He sold her refrigerator, her stove, her bedroom set, her clothes.
>
> *And how is she getting by?*
>
> No, they're separated.
>
> *So he went in her house and sold her things?*
>
> No, there are some big rooms in [the Ávila family] house and he lived there with his wife. One of the things I always told Ugeth was that he should leave home. Even if it was hard, he should rent a place. But he didn't want to. I would tell him, you have to break yourself down, get independent, mature in that area.
>
> So my brother was basically out of control, drugs had him out of control. He would make things up, terrible schemes. He would call us by telephone to tell us about plans for my father's funeral. And I would say, "What happened? Who are you?" "Yes, Señor Manuel has died," he would say. That really affected me, and the whole family, because my brother was getting to the point that he would "kill" so that he could collect money for someone who hadn't died yet.[2] I don't know. This is something I don't usually talk about because it's too much. *[Speaking softly]* It's not easy to live with a person like that. *[Pause]*
>
> He "killed" his son. He asked for money for his son: "They shot my kid six times." He would go around collecting money. People would tell me, "I gave [Ugeth] this much, I gave him that much."
>
> *Why did his son get shot?*
>
> No, no. He would lie so that he could get money out of people, he said his son was in intensive care and needed a certain medicine. He has "killed" his wife, his father, his mother. It's incredible. He just lies too much. I don't understand how he could go that far.

Yonathon told me that their niece's boyfriend had tried to kill Ugeth over a drug debt. Their niece lives in the Avila house.

> I didn't even know it, but my niece's boyfriend sells drugs. . . . When I started looking into it, my brother was stealing drugs from him. I didn't

2. It is common in this context for people who suffer a family tragedy to go door-to-door passing the hat to collect money from neighbors for medical treatment or a funeral.

even know until the guy shot Ugeth five times. One of the shots was at his head. But when he shot at Ugeth's head, God's mercy is so great that the gate was in the way and that bullet ricocheted. The other bullets hit him in the back and in the legs. Ugeth was helping a guy named Carlos sell vegetables on Avenida San Luis and Avenida Fuerzas Armadas. He would get up at 3:00 A.M. to go get merchandise [at a municipal wholesale market]. There are some little walkways that are like a neighborhood that is locked.[3] He goes through to call the guy he works with to go to market. When he gets in and is going to close the gate, he sees [the niece's boyfriend] dressed all in black with a hood on. But he recognized him and said, "What's the matter, Carlitos?" And Carlos said, "Don't say my name. You know we have problems. You know that I've told you to pay me my money." He shoots at him to kill him, at his head. And we see the hand of God: the bullet ricocheted off of the gate. So neighbors start yelling and call my mother and we find him in a puddle of blood. One of the bullets perforated his kidney.

Thanks to God's mercy and to the doctors who did good work, we saw God's hand again and Ugeth was saved. His son, with whom he hadn't spoken in a long time, [came to visit] and Ugeth reconciled with his family. I told my brother, "Look what God is doing. I hope you can see what God is doing. Look what God does. God permits Satan to hurt you but doesn't touch your soul, so that you can make up with your family. God wants you to reconcile and mature." Ugeth cried with me. His son called me "uncle"—first time in years that he says "uncle" to me. He said "Uncle, can you pray for my dad and for me?" I said, "Of course, let's pray." And we started to pray. I could see that his son squeezed his hand and cried. And I said, "Ugeth, this is big. Don't waste this beautiful opportunity that God is offering you. I believe God works through mysterious ways. Take advantage of this blessing."

Ugeth is released. His son spent a lot of money on him in that hospital. My parents help him out. A real blessing. He starts attending a nearby church. It's an Assembly of God church but a campo blanco. The pastor tells me that Ugeth is a man of God. "Wow, look at the guy's Bible." Ugeth was helping him out in Sunday school. Incredible. Ugeth would take his granddaughter around with him, [and with] his wife and his son. His son started lending him his car. His son said, "Dad, how about if you help me drive the car? Let's use it as a taxi so that you can help yourself and you can help me. Since you know how [to drive a taxi]." It was incredible.

Then he came to the plaza one day—because we [Yonathon and another hermano] have a ministry in Plaza Miranda. He goes there and says, "I want to talk to you." He seemed recovered to me. He asked me for money. He said, "Yonathon, you know I don't have papers—I don't have identification. I don't have a license—and Franklin is going to lend me his car. I need you to lend me some money." And I said, "Okay, here you are, here's the money." When he leaves, the Holy Spirit tells me that that

3. This is the gate Aurelio put up (see chapter 1).

money was for drugs. But I said to myself, "May the Lord reprehend you Satan. You're not going to put doubts in me." So the Holy Spirit was alerting me, so that I could pray for him and watch out for him. But I really didn't think someone would be so persistent in backsliding. And he fell again. That was recent that he got shot—four months ago, in February or January. If you see Ugeth now, he is really deteriorated. My mother doesn't know what to do. I tell her, "Mother, take it easy, we're waiting for a miracle of God."

Ugeth has been in constant danger of death because he practically begs for drugs. Only God *[shakes his head]*—I've seen people get killed over that garbage. I believe what the Bible says: "Better a live dog than a dead lion." Ugeth is among the living. He has hope. I tell him, "Ugeth, you have hope. Fight. Struggle. But one thing I want you to do is to go to Emmanuel. Return to Emmanuel. Present yourself to the pastor and say Hermano Antonio I've come here so that you can help me. Go to church and subject yourself to the authorities because there is a principle. What's fallen on you is a spirit of rebellion . . . " And he cries with me and says, "It's too hard for me. I know the Gospel is too hard for me." I say, "No. That's not true. It's not the Gospel that is hard for you. What's hard for you is for you to subject yourself."

Yonathon asked my advice, and I suggested that they find a treatment center for Ugeth outside of Caracas where he could get away from all of his temptations. Yonathon said:

Rafael Mora has a really good rehab center [in Caucagua]. We took him there. [Rafael] gave his case to another person and said, "This is a special case. This is the brother of my hermano and friend. Let's help him. Let's help Ugeth." He stayed there and was happy; pleased with the welcome they gave him. But he couldn't get himself to stay. We've taken him to Guatire, but he doesn't stay. We've taken him to Victory Outreach, but he hasn't stayed either.

The problem with Ugeth is that he's too dependent. . . . I told my mother that the Bible says that the father who loves his child disciplines him. And if you have a program of discipline, you have to fulfill it. Discipline doesn't mean that you lay down the rules but then you go and open the door at 3:00 A.M. Ugeth needs some discipline, because he comes home, turns the TV on, and watches it until 5:00 A.M., lays down, and he's still there sleeping [at 9:00 A.M.]. His mind is a little workshop of evil. I think Ugeth needs to be talked to clearly, "these are the rules." . . . My mother has been very overprotective. That's her big problem. She has a hard time making decisions.

After three weeks of trying, Ramiro finally found Ugeth and told him I wanted to interview him. When he found out, Ugeth came to Emmanuel on Friday, Saturday, and Sunday to meet with me. I finally interviewed him on Sunday. He was cleaned up and dressed in his best—a baggy suit from before his backslide. I was hopeful. My interest had brought him back to Emmanuel for the first time in a long time. Would my interest and support perhaps spur him to recovery? During the interview, Ugeth said, referring to me, "I thought to myself, 'If this guy is looking for me, it's because God is interested. If he's interested, God is even more interested.'"

But my much sought after interview was largely useless other than to realize that Ugeth was not on the verge of self-reform: he denied the obvious, repeated lies and contradicted himself repeatedly. He was clearly still using. He repeated that he had left Emmanuel because of the confrontation over the taxi in which church leaders had unjustly ordered him to pay for the damages. "I thought to myself, 'If that's how they treat the green leaves, how do they treat the dry leaves?' and I decided to leave the church." In his version he left the Assembly of God church that Yonathon told me about because the pastor was fornicating: "Just being in that church you can get contaminated because when a pastor is in sin, the whole church is in sin." He left Rafael Mora's rehab center because he also saw things there that he did not agree with: "I didn't like their services. The stage would be lit up and the congregation would be dark. [I said to myself,] 'Hey, this isn't Godly, because we are the light.'" In his view his family unjustly blamed him for things his nieces steal: "For them, everything that goes wrong is the fault of this guy right here *[thumps his chest with his thumb]*. Because my mother has a problem, the Enemy puts it in her head that I steal things from home." Furthermore, his brothers, Yonathon and Andrés, never reached out to him because "they are immature in the Gospel. They don't have that capacity." When we ended the interview I offered to take him out for lunch, but he asked me for money instead. Incredibly, I was caught flat-footed and gave him some—momentarily deluding myself that it might actually go for the groceries he said he was going to buy.

Ugeth's biography is an open-ended narrative, so any explanation for his problems must be tentative. But I can point out a few relevant features about his ongoing failure to gain agency over his life. It is clear that Ugeth has a serious substance abuse problem and an accentuated capacity for deception. This was his tendency before he became Evangelical, and he apparently struggled with it while he was a participating Evangelical. Now he lies, schemes, and rarely owns up to his problems. Furthermore, Yonathon is probably right that continuing to live with his family would not help Ugeth. As discussed above, the support provided by family of origin does not necessarily help a person address life problems; it can also enable him to deny these problems and thereby prevent imaginative solutions. Ugeth never left his parents' house even when he was sober and solvent. Of course, this has a lot to do with the economic prospects of people of Ugeth's generation—most of his eight brothers and sisters still live in that house. But the effect is the same, and the level of dysfunction in the Ávila household is probably related to this.

Most relevant for the concerns of this book is that it seems as though Evangelicalism has become more of an impediment than a solution. I have argued in most of this book that Evangelical meanings and practices can be consciously used by people to portray their worlds in such a way that they can exercise a degree of agency over their immediate social context. But, of course, meaning can just as well be turned back against itself. It is clear from Ugeth's statements that while Evangelical meanings occasionally grab him and shore up his will, just as often he can use them to avoid responsibility.

Another way in which Evangelicalism seems to be impeding a solution is through the idea of miraculous change. The idea that when you "surrender" you become a new person often leads important network ties such as Yonathon to underestimate a recovering substance abuser's continuing susceptibility. Thus Yonathon lends Ugeth the money for his papers within a couple of weeks of his getting better, knowing that having money in his pocket is often Ugeth's downfall. This same focus on miraculous supernatural change also leads others to underestimate the importance of factors other than repentance—such as getting away from Caracas or urban environments generally (Emerson and Smith 2000). When Belkis tried to take Ugeth to a rehab center Ugeth said he would prefer to go to one outside of Caracas. Belkis told me how she reacted: "I got mad. I told him, 'The Devil is not going to place conditions on me. If you really want to change, you have to accept where God takes you.'" Evangelicalism does indeed contain symbolic resources with which to imagine Evangelical projects as processual, long-term struggles. But the dominant tendency is to think that all a person really needs is to get serious about God.

A final way that Evangelicalism seems to be an impediment is resignation to Ugeth's moral failures among Ugeth's family and friends. While Venezuelan Evangelicals often attend to people nobody else will—prisoners, the homeless, drug abusers—repeated failure can also lead to resignation. Ramiro, Belkis, and Yonathon (as well as Augusto's aunt

Dalia) at different points express the idea that they decided to "leave it to the Lord," since they were not getting anywhere. My good friend Ramiro, for example, spends vast amounts of time attending to all sorts of people in need. Yet his attitude toward a repeat backslider like Ugeth ranges from amusement to mocking. It is Augusto's mother and Ugeth's brother who seem to be the most persistent in their help, because of their deep personal tie.

Melvin, a non-Evangelical from Ugeth's barrio, presents a contrast to Ugeth. Melvin spent years in the street addicted to crack. He lived by collecting junk from garbage, refurbishing it, and selling it to different junk dealers in order to buy crack. He also, to a lesser degree (at least in his version of the story), begged and robbed to support his habit. Three years before our interview he became Evangelical under the influence of a neighbor and sobered up. But after only three months he had some bad experiences with certain hermanos and stopped participating. He said that he did not think he would fall back into drugs so easily. Soon he was using and living in the street again. About a year later some neighbors paid for him to take a Tadeo human development workshop sponsored by the Catholic Church. Melvin went high the first day. Nevertheless, he found the workshop a profound experience and quit doing drugs almost immediately. Since then he has continued doing workshops every couple of months. He said he found the members of his Tadeo workshops more sincere insofar as they did not try to implicate God in everything, as did Evangelicals. In Melvin's case a prior, ultimately failed experience with Evangelicalism became a part of his biography that made a different set of meanings and form of practice more helpful the second time around. It will probably take a different solution, like Tadeo, a rehabilitation program, or something else, for Ugeth to recover. An alternative solution seems unlikely, however, as he is currently networked into a circle of people for whom any solution other than Evangelical practice would be unacceptable.

COMPARING AUGUSTO AND UGETH

The cases of Augusto and Ugeth provide a nice review of the main issues of part 3. Their cases present a number of similarities. Both Augusto and Ugeth lived at home and were exposed to competing networks and associated meanings. They were each involved in, through their immediate surroundings, the world of drugs and delinquency. But they were each exposed to, through their immediate living situations, the discourse and practice of Evangelicalism. Augusto and Ugeth also had repeated exposure to Evangelical participation. Augusto lived in an Evangelical treatment center for a year and went to church with his aunt and mother; Ugeth was a practicing Evangelical for six years. What, then, can explain their diverging trajectories?

There are key differences. Ugeth's more extensive and voluntary Evangelical experience may make it *less* potent as a meaning system now. Ugeth decided to be baptized, participated actively, and had his own mission project in his neighborhood. This gave him a solid knowledge of the meaning system that he can now turn to almost any use. Augusto's previous engagement with the Evangelical meaning system, in contrast, was as a sixteen year old, interned in a rehabilitation center against his will, and later when his mother and aunt took him to a church to be with young people he could not relate to. When, at VO, he was exposed to the meaning system again at the age of twenty-five by people just like him, the meanings were powerful to him, engaged his attention, and spurred his project of self-reform.

There also seems to be a relevant difference in their relational contexts. Both Ugeth and Augusto appear to be in situations in which their mothers enable them to avoid addressing their problems. Yonathon tried to get Ugeth to live on his own—but even when he was solvent he lived at home—and he tried to get his mother to take a tougher line with Ugeth. However, this never seemed to happen. It probably would never have happened in Augusto's household either if the police had not been after him. Augusto in effect had run out of solutions; he could not go home and depend on his mother anymore. Thus Augusto's problems made him structurally available precisely at the same time that he encountered a set of meanings that engaged his attention, in the intimacy of his living space. Ugeth, on the other hand, was enabled to not address his problems in his living situation and in any case was networked into the same Evangelical meanings he knew well and had learned to manipulate.

CHAPTER 8

Toward a Relational Pragmatic Theory of Cultural Agency

My analysis suggests that the distinctions social scientists make between empowerment and moral order, self-interest and morality, calculation and contemplation need to be rethought. Among Evangelical men in Caracas, religion does not begin with disinterest. It begins with dis-ease that is consciously and rationally addressed through religious practice. And this pragmatic quality does nothing to challenge its viability or its sincerity. The smiles and tears, courage and fear are all real. It would be a mistake to regard this as unique to Latin American Evangelicalism. I suspect any close review of empirical research on contemporary religious and cultural practices around the world would reveal similar processes. Wherein, then, lies the persistence of these distinctions?

Postcolonial scholars argue that they are historical artifacts of Western cultural history. Asad (1993), for example, argues that the concept of religion as a symbolization of the general order of existence, autonomous from science, politics, and economics, was central to the constitution of a new kind of legal and moral subject in European modernity (see also Chakrabarty 2000). But this view of culture and religion still runs deep in contemporary scholarship. Whether one looks at the social sciences or the humanities, the default theory of meaning scholars use opposes the literal concepts used by natural science and everyday common sense to the figurative, expressive concepts of religion, poetry, and other cultural forms (Lakoff and Johnson 1980). In this view literal meanings are useful for goal-oriented action in the world, whereas figurative meanings provide a meaningful cosmos, including individual and collective identity and narratives about destiny. This dualistic view of meaning is so widely used not only because it has history behind it but also because it appeals both to scholars interested in culture and to those who are not. On the one hand, the image of literal meaning provides rationalistic perspectives with a handy solution to the methodological "problem of other minds"—the problem of how we understand the subjectivities of the people we study (Smelser 1997). Whether influenced by rational choice or practice theory, social scientists focusing on action are most intuitively convincing when they suppose that the actor has an objective and literal understanding of the situation—in other words, an understanding similar to that of the sociologist. So, for example, peasants resist agricultural innovations not because they are backward or ignorant but because they are rational maximizers for whom, because they live at subsistence levels, avoiding risk is more important than seeking additional profit (Scott 1976). Or impoverished women have children out of wedlock not because of a culture of poverty but because the social context is such that a permanent conjugal tie to a marginally employed man would be irrational (Stack 1974).

On the other hand, the image of figurative meaning cordons off culture from easy rationalist debunking. In the dualistic theory the meanings that the actor attaches to his or her cultural behavior are of a completely different order from the literal meanings used in everyday action. Social scientists working from a figurative view of culture then search for the real reasons for cultural practices in processes that operate behind the actor's back, such as collective effervescence, emotional needs, the need for identity and orientation, or simply the weight of tradition. The symbols themselves are substantially arbitrary and not connected with purposive engagement of the world, except to the extent that they might provide end values or limiting norms. Durkheim, for example, regarded religion as "true" in the sense that it symbolized something that was "real," that is, society. But actual religious ideas were clearly erroneous conceptualizations of reality. The nonscientific mind, in this view, has difficulty conceptualizing complex social forces and therefore looks for an external, easily graspable object with which to symbolize them. Any symbol at hand would do: a fish, a rock, the moon. For Durkheim, it is simply misdirected to try to understand the permanence of primitive religions by looking at the truth-value of their ideas, for it would be "incomprehensible that humanity should have remained obstinate in these errors through the ages, for experience should have quickly proven them false" (1915: 257). The real explanation for religious ideas is that they simply serve as sign vehicles for the power of society that the "primitive" feels.[1] The figurative view finds its logical conclusion in the structural view of culture in which cultural symbols gain their significance not with reference to the empirical world but with reference to each other (Kane 1992).

While the dualistic theory of meaning meets the needs both of rationalist scholars who want neither to deal with symbolic constructs nor to be accused of reductionism and cultural scholars who want to legitimate their field, it produces consistent problems in our understanding. Asad says the following with reference to religion:

> The separation of religion from science, common sense, aesthetics, politics, and so on, allows [Geertz] to defend it against charges of irrationality. If religion has a distinctive perspective (its own truth, as Durkheim would have said) and performs an indispensable function, it does not in essence compete with others and cannot, therefore, be accused of generating false consciousness. Yet in a way this defense is equivocal. . . . This kind of phenomenological approach doesn't make it easy to examine whether, and if so to what extent and in what ways, religious experience relates to something in the real world that believers inhabit. . . . Religious symbols are treated, in circular fashion, as the precondition for religious experience (which, like any experience, must, by definition, be genuine), rather than as one condition for engaging with life. (1993: 50–51)

The attempt to cordon off an autonomous cultural sphere or structure provides a Pyrrhic victory. While it protects it from debunking, it abstracts culture from life and relevancy. Understanding how people can get things done with culture becomes a problem rather than a base assumption.

For these reasons, criticism has been mounting from two different directions: from those who critique a lifeless, abstract concept of meaning and from those who critique a nonsymbolic concept of rationality. I take these up in this order.

1. There is indeed an often cited passage in which Durkheim asserts that religion provides a metaphor for society that translates everything essential (Durkheim 1915: 257). To that extent the analysis provided in this book would agree with him. But elsewhere he clearly asserts that for humans it provides a purely contemplative purpose, not one oriented to effective action in the world (Durkheim and Mauss 1963; see also Boudon 1994; Sahlins 1976; Smelser 1997).

AGAINST ABSTRACTION OF THE FIGURATIVE

The figurative side of the dualistic theory of meaning has been increasingly criticized by those who see a closer relationship between meaning and concrete action in the world. Eugene Halton (1995) refers to the attempt to preserve a cultural dimension by portraying it as a system in which signs gain their significance with reference to each other as "conventionalism." The base idea is one of "referential arbitrariness": cultural symbols have no necessary connection with any external, nonsymbolic reality and therefore cannot be reduced to it. Halton argues that although this indeed succeeds in portraying an irreducible structure we can call culture, the attempt at preservation effectively disengages culture from life. When culture is portrayed as a referentially arbitrary structure, it is difficult to understand how it is tied to action, desire, or bodily existence of any kind, how it can ever change, much less how it was created in the first place. In conventionalism, argues Halton, "the human creature, who, above all others both is open to and needs meaning, is denied the social capacity to germinate and body forth genuinely new feelings, perceptions, and ideas not reducible to, though growing out of, prior social norms" (92). Halton calls such conventionalism the "doughnut hole" theory of culture: it is empty at the center. Thus while Christian Smith, Jeffrey Alexander, and a line of scholars going all the way back to Kant are concerned about the moral being removed from the animal, Halton is concerned about the animal being removed from the moral. Halton calls for a return to a more "earthy" image of culture as "cultivation" or as "cultus." "Cultivation" emphasizes the way human beings cultivate meanings to further their goals. "Cultus" denotes the "living impulse to meaning" pursued through action. In Halton's perspective:

> Culture is a living, social metaboly of signs, not limited to a convention but in transaction with the inmost recesses of the person and with the qualitative, physical, and significant environment. The question is not whether culture is a "system" or not but whether we shall continue to conceive of culture as an inert, mechanical system or code, incapable of self-critical cultivation, or as a "living system"—a way of living fully open to contingency, spontaneity, purposive growth and decay. (Halton 1995: 82)

Halton's argument resonates with feminist theorists' critiques of scholarly prioritization of abstract meanings disengaged from the social reproduction of concrete individuals and especially the way in which this focus misportrays people in nondominant social positions.[2] In her critique of sociological theory, Dorothy Smith (1990: 17) distinguishes between a mode of knowing "located in the body and in the space it occupies and moves in" and "the governing mode," which "lifts actors out of the immediate, local, and particular place in which we are in the body," allowing them to develop abstract concepts that hold the appearance of autonomy. Because sociology is based on the governing mode and aims at extrasubjective, extralocal, extrahistorical concepts, when it looks at the way meaning is created by living individuals in concrete situations it conceives of it as the "sociology of knowledge." The latter uncovers and debunks knowledge as partial, interested, and subjective by uncovering its social determinants. Smith suggests a reorientation toward the "social organization of knowledge" that would look at "knowledge as socially and materially organized, as produced by individuals in actual settings, and as organized by and organizing definite social relations" (62). All knowledge, in this view, is created in the process of everyday activity in the world, and revealing that process does not debunk it but simply demystifies it.

Gilligan's (1982) classic research on gender and moral reasoning was motivated by theories of moral development that portrayed women's moral development as stunted and underdeveloped. Through presentation of moral dilemmas she shows that whereas the young men in her study reveal selves defined by separation and measured against abstract ideals, the young women reveal selves defined by connection and evaluated with reference to their care of particular others. When confronted with moral dilemmas, young men address them by fitting a particular case into an abstract moral logic, whereas young women address moral dilemmas through relational reasoning, by working out the consequences for concrete others in a concrete individual's network (Gilligan 1982: 35). Gilligan sees these as two different forms of moral reasoning, not as corresponding to the "essence" of male or female gender, but as diverging answers to basic contradictions of human experience: "These disparate visions in their tension reflect the paradoxical truths of human experience—that we know ourselves as separate only insofar as we live in connection with others, and that we experience relationship only insofar as we differentiate other from self" (63).

What can be taken from Smith and Gilligan for our purposes here is that a view of figurative meanings that are autonomous and disengaged

2. On this point see also Emirbayer and Mische 1997: 997.

from particular lives in the world corresponds most to the experience of people in dominant social positions. People in nondominant positions, who tend not to use meaning in this way, are often considered anomalous, deceptive, or somehow lacking in integrity or sincerity (Rosaldo 1974). While Smith, Gilligan, and others are concerned with the experience of women, the analysis provided here suggests that their view fits equally well with marginal peoples of either gender in places like Caracas's informal city. The way members of Latin America's popular sectors use meaning all too often becomes obfuscated by our concepts of culture as autonomous, abstract, and figurative.

AGAINST THE LITERALISM OF RATIONALITY

Scholars have also assaulted the literalist side of the dualistic theory of meaning, which assumes that successful action in the world must be pursued through literal meanings. First, work in cognitive linguistics and cultural anthropology has largely discredited the idea of a qualitative distinction between literal and figurative meanings. George Lakoff has persuasively argued that most scientific understanding of the physical world functions through metaphor. Others have argued that there is essentially no difference between literal and figurative meaning-making as they function through the same process: a better-known image from a source domain is predicated of a less well understood feature of a target domain and new meaning is constructed. In this view the literal and the figurative are seen as two ends of a continuum rather than as qualitatively distinct categories of meaning. A particular meaning's placement on this continuum is really just a matter of how "entrenched" it is in a given culture (Lakoff and Johnson 1980; Turner 1991). For example, while the notion of "market equilibrium" was taken to be figurative two hundred years ago, today it is considered literal (Bicchieri 1988).

Not only is there no qualitative distinction between figurative and literal meaning making, argues Lakoff, but the same standards of truth are applicable. He develops a pragmatist form of realism he calls "experientialist." "On the experientialist view, our conceptual system emerges from our constant successful functioning in our physical and cultural environment. Our categories of experience and the dimensions out of which they are constructed not only have emerged from our experience but are constantly being tested through ongoing successful functioning by all members of our culture" (Lakoff and Johnson 1980: 180). In Lakoff's view metaphors are "concepts we live by." Whether in science, common sense, poetry, or religion, metaphor unites reason and imagination in the thought process—and the proof is in the pudding. If they work for us, we believe them. Thus metaphors should not be defined in contradistinction to rationality. Rather they should be seen as a form of "imaginative rationality" (Lakoff and Johnson 1980: 193).

Debates over "realism" in social science methodology have also led away from literalist understandings of "truth." Although these debates focus on questions of social science epistemology, at stake are the same issues of meaning. "Theoretical realism" refers to the idea that a set of meanings persists to the degree that it is a true representation of the world. In terms of methodology this means that logical propositions are tested through empirical facts and survive to the degree that they are true. There is a growing movement among sociologists to articulate an alternative called "critical realism" (Steinmetz 1998). Critical realists believe that there is a reality that exists independent of our beliefs about it. They also believe we can fruitfully discuss better or worse conceptualizations of that independent reality. However, critical realism differs from theoretical realism's claim that concepts survive and persist to the degree that they are true images of independent reality. Rather, critical realists argue, "our judgements are conditioned by our circumstances, by what we know at the time and by the prevailing criteria of evaluation" (Archer, Collier, and Porpora 2004). Margaret Somers (1998) has forwarded an essentially similar realist methodology that she calls "relational pragmatic realism." In this form of realism a scientific concept survives not to the extent that it is a true, unmediated representation of phenomena but rather to the extent that there is evidence of the causal, practical, and relational significance of the postulated phenomena (Somers 1998: 743 ff.). If the concept works for us, we believe it.

Some recent work even takes issue with the classic assumption that literal meanings are more effective than figurative meanings in guiding successful action in the world. Raymond Boudon (1994) argues that there are any number of reasoning processes that, while not objectively valid, are *consistently* convincing to social actors (see also Cook and Levi 1990). In his work on the media and collective action, William Gamson (1992, 1995) argues that the meanings that successfully mobilize people to action are those that exaggerate the role of human actors and provide potential participants with a cognitive grasp of "abstract sociocultural forces" precisely by distorting the facts. Put differently, the "hot cognitions of misplaced concreteness" provide a sense of outrage, power, and agency in situations in which "an overdetermined structural analysis" would leave potential participants cold and unmobilized (Gamson 1995). Put differently, distorting "the facts" can increase successful agency in the world rather than undermine it.

CULTURAL AGENCY AS IMAGINATIVE RATIONALITY

In this book I have argued that neither a view of culture as a tool kit at the service of instrumental rationality nor a view of culture as a structure controlling humans behind their backs (or empowering them unintentionally) is adequate for understanding the agency involved in Evangelical conversion in Latin America. And I have argued that the dilemma posed by these two alternatives stems from the dualistic theory of meaning. I have offered instead a view of cultural agency as a process of imaginative rationality. This view, in turn, depends on a nondualistic, pragmatist perspective on meaning that I would like to fill out here. In the pragmatist perspective, human beings are creatures that can only relate to the world through the use of concepts. Concepts do their work by selecting out features from the infinity of experience. Like road maps that orient precisely through their poverty of detail, concepts enable action by reducing alternatives. Embodied in communicable form, they permit intersubjectivity through time and space. In other words, they permit communication between people and within the same person through time.

Humans create concepts as they confront dilemmas in the process of life. Concepts illuminate inchoate subjects (target domain or tenor)—which may consist of any recurring human experience—by attaching images or from a relatively better known domain (source domain or vehicle). To be potent, a concept needs to be "well stretched"; in other words, the feature abstracted from the source domain must be sufficiently different from the inchoate subject matter that it actually provides new meaning, yet not so different as to be irrelevant to the task of understanding (Friedrich 1991). Adequacy is determined by evidence of the causal, practical, and relational significance of a concept in action, as well as, in certain circumstances, its consistency with other concepts.[3]

Specifically *religious* meaning systems provide concepts in which images from a hypothesized and elaborated supernatural realm (source domain) are predicated of relatively inchoate aspects of everyday life (target

3. This clause needs to be added since, especially in the case of religion, many elaborate symbolizations may have the sole purpose of reconciling contradictory symbolizations. However, it should be pointed out that individuals and groups can easily maintain contradictory beliefs as long as these beliefs do not come into direct confrontation.

domain).[4] These concepts correspondingly direct action by constraining alternatives and interpreting experience in particular ways. The success of the system of meanings derives from evidence of its ability to conceptualize formerly inchoate phenomena in a way that facilitates practical action in everyday life. We can put all of this in the concrete terms of the empirical material reviewed above. So, for example, Venezuelan Evangelicals explain a man's inexplicable inability to stay away from drugs (target domain) as the work of Satan and his demons (source domain). They explain the overcoming of substance abuse (target domain) as the work of God facilitated by human fulfillment of "biblical" norms and prayer (source domain). As shown in chapter 5, if this conceptualization and the practice it implies delivers—a new believer does stay away from drugs—it receives powerful validation. That social scientists would identify different causal mechanisms from those identified by the religious convert does not mean the result is achieved by fluke. It simply means the causal mechanism is identified using alternative concepts.

The compartmentalization of culture is overcome in this theorization. *Any* recurrent situation that impinges on human beings will be addressed through concepts. And any conceptualization can potentially be religious—in other words, make use of a supernatural source domain. Thus religious meaning systems certainly *can* be dualistic in the way described by existing theories[5]—in the postmaterialist West it makes perfect sense for religion to be restricted to assuaging uncertainty about life after death, providing collective identity, or simply providing a general moral desire to be good for good sake. However, as shown above, spiritual and material do not need to be distinguished in the same way if at all. Among Venezuelan Evangelicals, religious meanings can be predicated of pressing life problems such as addiction, violence, and family conflict, and addressing these problems can be a religious goal. Seeking to address them through religious practice is no more instrumental than seeking eternal

4. It may seem ironic to argue that hypothetical supernatural beings and processes can function as a "better-known" source domain from which symbols can be taken to predicate aspects of the everyday social world. However, the beings and processes of this supernatural realm are generally anthropomorphisms consisting of selected, exaggerated aspects of human existence. Furthermore, this hypothetical supernatural domain can indeed be better known than everyday life insofar as there is a well-elaborated, often canonized system of ideas that can be studied and reflected on.

5. To avoid confusion, it is important to keep emic and etic meanings straight on this point. I have argued against dualistic theories of meaning used by social scientists (etic) and am providing a pragmatist alternative. This does not mean, however, that religious meaning systems (emic) cannot be dualistic. Put differently, there is no contradiction in a nondualistic theory of meaning being used to portray dualistic systems of religious meaning.

life through religious practice. And the predicative power of religion does not have to be confined to substantive issues of life. Religious concepts can just as easily be used to conceptualize the way people adopt religion. The convert's biography is described as a long-term hegemonic battle between Satan and God that culminates in the conversion period. God has chosen the convert, actively reaches out through an Evangelical preacher or witness, and the as yet unconverted soul merely assents to the outreach. In other words, religious meaning systems contain second-order concepts that make meaning about the meaning system itself. And all of this can be said about culture in general. Social movements develop narratives about who they are and where they came from. Rock-and-roll bands write about the life of rock-and-roll bands. Sociologists organize retrospectives about their careers as sociologists.

Many have warned against the intellectualist fallacy whereby religion and other forms of culture are seen as forms of pseudoscience. When discussing religion, Durkheim argued that if this were its central purpose, then we should not be able to understand how it has endured. Indeed, it would be ridiculous to explain the persistence of Hopi rain dances by looking at the meteorological record. However, assuming that cultural concepts therefore have no orienting function is not the only possible direction this concern can take. Lakoff argues that the choice of seeing a meaning system as completely disengaged in the world or as necessarily literally true is a false opposition:

> What the myths of objectivism and subjectivism both miss is the way we understand the world through our interactions with it. What objectivism misses is the fact that understanding, and therefore truth, is necessarily relative to our cultural conceptual systems and that it cannot be framed in any absolute or neutral conceptual system. Objectivism also misses the fact that human conceptual systems are metaphorical in nature and involve an imaginative understanding of one kind of thing in terms of another. What subjectivism specifically misses is that our understanding, even our most imaginative understanding, is given in terms of a conceptual system that is grounded in our successful functioning in our physical and cultural environments. It also misses the fact that metaphorical understanding involves metaphorical entailment, which is an imaginative form of rationality. (Lakoff and Johnson 1980: 194)

In other words, validity is in the eye of a beholder who lives and acts in the world. While most of this book looks at the way Venezuelan Evangelical meanings can actually work, in chapter 5 it is pointed out that the meaning system has resources for explaining failure. This culture work is the stuff of Evangelical discussions and the specialty of pastors who elaborate religious meaning (Weber 1968: 472). The most immediate resource derives from the fact that the pursuit of "this-worldly" goals through religious practice is a "project" that extends through time. It is never clear at any given point in time whether a project should be declared a failure or the deadline for success should be postponed. Like a student who trusts that her studies will lead to a good job, an activist who hopes mobilizing in the streets will lead to social change, or a scientist who is confident that further research will explain away a pesky anomaly, any given defeat can be overcome by postponing success to an unspecified future date. Persisting failure will lead Evangelicals to self-examination of their religious practice, to statements that emphasize God's mystery, to the idea that God tests and refines Christians through "trials of fire," or to statements that emphasize the continuing efficacy of Satan and the real rewards that will accrue in the next world.

Robert Orsi (2005) has recently argued against the focus on agency in the study of religion: "Religion is often enough cruel and dangerous, and the same impulses that result in a special kind of compassion also lead to destruction, often among the same people at the same time" (191). I address Orsi's objection more fully below, but first I want to point out that I agree with Orsi in the following, fundamental sense. Meaning *is* something. It is not just a general social value that provides an abstract sense of morale and motivation. Rather, it consists of concepts that have specific characteristics that lead to specific results (Edgell 2006; Lichterman 2005). Whether these results are beneficial or tragic will depend, in large part, on the evaluator's perspective. And the bag is inevitably mixed. In my fieldwork I have seen that while Evangelicals' reputation for honesty makes them desirable employees, their time-consuming religious commitments gives them a reputation for being unreliable. While their religiosity gives them a singular motivation for reaching out to the poor, disregarded, and imprisoned, it can also make them cruel and insensitive in the face of repeated failures of self-reform. While Evangelicalism presents perhaps the most dynamic element of civil society in Latin American countries such as Venezuela, from another perspective they might be seen as sapping strength from other social movements that could bring about "real" structural change. But it is indeed my claim in this book that, on balance, the Evangelical meanings studied here can empower and make agents of young Venezuelan men marginalized by the circumstances of their social context. Nevertheless, whether Evangelical meanings empower or hinder any particular individual depends on that person's microcontext. And whether individual-level empowerment aggregates into desirable social-level outcomes depends on the macrocontext and is the subject of an important debate beyond the scope of this book (see Austin-Broos 1997; Levine and Stoll 1997; Smilde 1998).

CULTURAL AGENCY AND RELATIONAL IMAGINATION

Orsi (2005: 170) argues that scholars of religion would do well to replace the meaning-making subject of much study of religion with a more tragic figure constrained by meanings: "This leads to a more chastened view of culture generally and of religion in particular, one that steers clear of words like empowerment, agency (simply), and transcendence and instead moves in the register of the tragic, of the limited and constrained, or what I would think of as the real." In agreement with Orsi, I would not extend the claims I am making about Venezuelan Evangelicals to "religion" in general. This is a study of recent converts, not people immersed in a religious tradition handed down through generations. When people are in the position to choose their meanings, they often choose meanings that successfully address enduring states of dis-ease. But more often than not, they do not have full liberty on this point. People are embedded in social structures that limit alternatives if they provide them at all. As discussed in chapter 6, in some cases people exercise conscious agency over their networks, but this process is limited. An innovation in meaning such as that implied by religious conversion strongly depends on network location. Having a network link to Evangelicalism is perhaps the most effective cause of conversion. But it is important to remember that networks do not only exist with reference to the outcome of interest. Networks also lead to alternative innovations. In Venezuela's faded modernity the form of imaginative rationality winning the most converts among young men is the complex of drugs, crime, and violence. Ugeth was originally converted by his brothers' example. But being embedded in his parents' household has kept him intimately exposed to drugs and crime in a way that makes them difficult to overcome. Indeed, the Ávila family provides a microcosm of the macrocontext. We could hold Ugeth's brother Yonathon up as an example of how poor Venezuelans are adjusting to new realities and gaining autonomy and individual responsibility through religious empowerment. But if we look at him in context we see that the modern prosperity of the Ávila patriarch has been followed by the postmodern scorecard of one dead, three drug addicts, one prostitute, and one Evangelical family man. We can go further with the case of Ugeth and see that the "alternative" Evangelical meanings his network offers him seem to have lost their potency for him. He is, in effect, networked into a circle. On the one hand, he is immersed in a network that provides a repertoire of projects involving drugs and crime; on the other, the network competing for his attention provides Evangelical projects that only momentarily capture his imagination and which quickly succumb to his manipulation.

The analysis of imaginative rationality developed here problematizes the neo-Marxist position of Castells in which the identity movements of marginalized groups are portrayed as reactive and inconsequential. It is clear that Venezuelan Evangelicals are able to gain agency over aspects of their immediate life circumstances through religious practice. But I think the analysis of relational imagination developed here problematizes the glib voluntarism of neoconservative scholars such as Amy Sherman, Peter Berger, and David Martin. People cannot willy-nilly adopt any culture, any time. In chapter 7 we saw that Augusto was exposed to the right meanings at the right time in the right social space. It could easily have been different. If he had not been forced from his home, or his mother had given up on her Evangelical project of reform for Augusto, he could easily have continued his life of drugs and delinquency, likely meeting the same fate as Gilberto, Erik, Yilber, Fredy, and Juan—friends of his who met violent deaths. In sum, the decline of Venezuela's state-led modernity has brought about as many "works of the flesh" as "fruit of the spirit." Hence, discussion of the implications of Evangelical growth for debates on poverty and culture in Latin America need to move beyond partisan metaphors and toward flat-footed, empirical research in particular historical contexts.

PROVINCIALIZING EUROPE

In his watershed 1993 article on a new paradigm in the study of religion, Stephan Warner argued that concepts created for the study of religion in Europe were empirically inappropriate for the study of religion in the United States. Instead of concentrating on sacred canopies that break and become secular, scholars in the United States found themselves looking at vibrant religious economies in which people choose their religion. Instead of looking at religion as provider of explanation and meaning, scholars in the United States found themselves looking at religion as provider of solidarity and morale (Warner 1993: 1052). As reviewed at the beginning of part 2, the new paradigm has recently come under fire as reductionistic, and scholars have urged a return to views of religion and culture as relatively autonomous moral orders that exercise independent impacts on social life (Alexander 2004; Smith 2003).

Interestingly, simultaneous to Warner's efforts to articulate a paradigm of study not based on the European experience, postcolonial scholars similarly urged their peers to "provincialize Europe." Chakrabarty argues that to understand postcolonial societies, rigorous distinctions between sacred and secular, poetic and prosaic, need to be overcome. In his native Bengali province, for example, supernatural figures and beliefs are routinely tied together into packages of this-worldly political projects. But the direction postcolonial scholars have taken skirts the Scylla of reductionism while avoiding the Charybdis of "culture as moral order." In tandem with the pragmatist and feminist theorists described above, postcolonial scholars' emphasis on cultural diaspora has required a move away from cultural coherence and consistency and toward a concept of culture as continually changing, multiple, contradictory, and inevitably embedded in action in the world (see Asad 1993; Clifford 1988).

This book can be seen as an argument precisely to merge these two provincializing projects. Classic secularization theory was based on a dualistic theory of meaning that reified the distinction between literal "rational" meanings and figurative, moral meanings. Here my argument is that the best way to conceptually address the failure of secularization theory is not by simply reaffirming the literal or reaffirming the figurative, as moral order theorists would have it, but by undermining the distinction itself. A concept of cultural agency as "imaginative rationality"—or "critical animism" as Halton would have it—will put us in a better position to understand religious vitality around the globe.

Properly pursued, this provincialization should work full circle. First, as several scholars have argued, not only the weight of world religiosity but also the weight of world religions such as Christianity and Islam are increasingly moving toward the global South (Jenkins 2002; Norris and Ingelhardt 2004). If sociologists of religion hope to keep up with this demographic trend away from the United States and Europe, then reassessing their theories of meaning will be an essential task. In contexts in which basic necessities often go unsatisfied, a theory of meaning that can incorporate need satisfaction through religious practice is essential. And this provincialization can be generalized beyond religion. It has become commonplace among North American scholars to argue that the culture work done by social movements in the United States and Europe might not be echoed in the developing world where grassroots mobilization presumably might be more guided by tradition or emotionally reactive (see, e.g., Oliver and Johnston 2000). But empirical research belies these cautions. Marginalized sectors as well as displaced local elites frequently turn to cultural identities and discourses as the basis for mobilizing political power. The success of indigenous identity politics provides an important example. In Ecuador, Bolivia, and elsewhere, indigenous groups have been able to mobilize ethnic identity into a formidable political force and to achieve many of the same goals they were not able to as peasant-based movements (Pallares 2003; Yashar 2005; for public protest more broadly, see López Maya, Smilde, Stephany 2002; Smilde 2004). All of these movements work through metaphors that describe their world and narratives of their own origin.

Of course, the charge to "provincialize Europe" is broader than the "southernization" of world religion and cultural mobilization. First, cultural diaspora is rapidly becoming a globalization of ethnicities as travel and communications technologies reduce the need for acculturation. Global cities significantly populated by immigrants still networked to their contexts of origin have, in many ways, made the distinctions between industrialized and developing worlds, center and periphery, largely irrelevant. Most of what is described in this book could be found in Latino Pentecostal churches in Chicago, Illinois, or Athens, Georgia. Indeed, recent books on religion in Latin America have taken to speaking of "religion in the Americas" and study Peruvians in New Jersey as well as former gang members from Washington, D.C., accommodating to life in San Salvador (see Peterson, Vásquez, and Williams 2001). Second, as pointed out in the introduction, the problem of agency through belief is a central one in any social context. The claim that "you gotta believe" in order to overcome substance abuse, win the big game, increase sales or defeat injustice, is all around us. It is our theory of meaning that needs to catch up.

Epilogue

My last visit to Caracas in January 2006 allowed me to catch up on some of the people and spaces analyzed in this book. Ramiro, his wife, and their two daughters moved to a small town in the Andes so that he could become the pastor of an Emmanuel Federation church—representing a radical change from the dangerous Caracas barrio they left. The move was made easier by the ongoing legal difficulties over the possession of Ramiro's rancho. During his previous marriage, he had built a two-story house on top of his wife's parents' rancho. When his wife left him he stayed there raising their son. Ten years later, when both Ramiro and his former wife had remarried, Ramiro's former in-laws began legal proceedings to gain ownership of Ramiro's rancho. The ensuing legal battle has lasted years during which Ramiro has had to vacate the premises several times. The property is still in legal limbo.

According to Belkis, whom I spoke with by phone, Ugeth was living essentially the same way as the last time I saw him, in 2004. He was still using crack, living in and out of his parents' house, and periodically practicing Evangelicalism only to backslide again.

In early 1999, soon after I ended this study, Enrique quit his job as a computer systems operator in a bank headquarters to became pastor of an Emmanuel church in Barquisimeto. By January 2006 it had become one of the biggest, most successful churches in the federation.

In 2004 the Emmanuel church split over a new discipleship program. Pastor Antonio decided to adopt the "method of twelve," a sort of pyramid structure that has the pastor at its peak and twelve disciples who seek twelve disciples who seek twelve, and so on. The method caused an upheaval in the church fought through a discourse of heresy. A large segment of the up-and-coming leadership, long frustrated by Pastor Antonio's failure to discuss his plans for retirement, as well as his ad lib organizational style, decided to split off and establish their own church. They took more than half of the church with them. The conflict ran through the federation as well, with more than half of the 120 churches leaving to join other federations or become independent. Those who left say Pastor Antonio has begun to follow a heretical doctrine created by men rather than the Holy Word. Those who stayed in the Emmanuel church say that those who left did so because of their own ambition, that the method of twelve is a form of organization and nothing else. Nevertheless, the members of the two churches in Caracas are on friendly terms and collaborate frequently in plaza and other interchurch events.

The daily service held in Plaza El Venezolano had to be discontinued when the plaza was restored and declared a national monument. Paradoxically, the service has now moved to the northeast corner of Plaza Bolívar, where political and philosophical discussion traditionally takes place. A contemporary description of Plaza El Venezolano would be different from the one I offer in chapter 5. The fountains work; the cement benches have been replaced with colonial-style wood benches. No street vendors are allowed. Indeed, after seven years of Hugo Chávez's "democratic revolution," my entire "tale of three cities" would be different. While there is no shortage of opinions, nobody knows whether "el proceso" will provide a viable alternative for Venezuela or implode under the centripetal forces of one-party rule. But by 2006 Chávez's nationalist policies, massive social spending, and political incorporation of popular sectors had revived not only the centrality of the modern nation-state but also the promise of an egalitarian modernity in which all Venezuelans would become citizens. At the same time, the postmodern realities of dramatic inequality, crime, and violence continued unabated.

Thus this book should be taken as ethnography of cultural agency among Venezuela's popular sectors in the period leading up to the Chávez administration. Many of the microsocial conditions that Evangelicalism helps men to address, such as crime, violence, and akrasia, seem to have changed little since then. Others, such as unemployment, economic difficulties, poor health, and opportunities for social activism, may have. But I would claim that the basic portrait of Evangelical belief and practice as imaginative rationality and the explanation of who converts through relational imagination remain valid.

APPENDIX A

Status of Evangelical Respondents after Five Years

Five years after finishing my original data collection for this book, I returned to Caracas to carry out follow-up research. Below is a list of all my Evangelical respondents, with leaders from the two churches I studied. It shows that after five years, 67 percent of my respondents were still participating either in the church that they attended when I interviewed them or at another Evangelical church. This finding contradicts the stereotype of revolving-door conversion among Latin American Evangelicals. The percentage is slightly higher than estimates in other contexts (Bowen 1996), perhaps in part because I include not only those who persist in the churches I studied but also those who are known to be attending other churches.

EMMANUEL CHURCH

Ramiro	Continues at same church
Alberto	Unknown
Enrique	Pastor at Emmanuel Church in Barquisimeto
Jhony	Continues at same church
Eric	Switched to Las Acacias Church
Guille	Discontinued
Manuel	Continues at another church
Ugeth	Discontinued
Davits	Continues at same church
Nelson	Founding a new church

José María	Continues at same church
Lenin	Founding new church with Nelson
Gregorio	Moved back to Ciudad Guyana but still works as evangelist
Inerio	Continues at same church
Miguel Vicente	Continues at same church
Willian	Discontinued consistent attendance
Luis	Unknown
Victor	Continues at same church
Henrique	Continues at same church
Juan Miguel	Unknown
Larry	Unknown
Pablo	Discontinued
Andrés	Continues at another church
Josué	Unknown
Iván	Continues elsewhere
José Gregorio	Youth pastor at Emmanuel
Carlos	Continues at same church
Juan Betancourt	Continues at another church
Juan Zerpa	Runs mission in another part of Caracas
Martín	Unknown
Darton	Continues at same church
Wilkenman	Discontinued
Juan Santiago	Continues at same church
Fernando	Unknown
Henry	Continues at another church
Simón	Continues at same church
Fabio	Continues at same church
Ernesto	Unknown
Juan	Continues at same church
Silvio	Continues at another church
Pedro	Continues at same church
Vincenzo	Unknown

Ernestillo	Continues at same church
Bartolo	Works at mission in Aragua

RAISE YOUR VOICE TO THE LORD CHURCH

Fredy	Continues at another church
Henry	Discontinued
Renlón	Continues at same church
Orent	Continues at another church
Jorge	Continues at same church
Carlos Gómez	Continues at same church
Ismael	Continues at same church
Roberto Alfonso	Continues at same church
Teodoro	Unknown
Ricardo	Discontinued
Agustín	Discontinued

APPENDIX B

Methods and Methodology

PARTICIPANT OBSERVATION

I chose to begin my fieldwork with Emmanuel Church not only because it was active, dynamic, and "representative" in relevant ways but also because it was readily accessible by car. I knew extensive participation in an Evangelical church would require attending evening services. As most churches in Caracas are in high crime areas with difficult access, there were few options. I found that although Emmanuel Church was also in a dangerous area, it was easily accessible by major roads, and parking was always available near the church door since few other members had cars. An added bonus of Emmanuel Church, I soon found out, was that members of the church held plaza services daily in downtown Caracas, which I attended frequently.

Most of my time in the field was spent engaged in participant observation. Much of this was in Evangelical services and events. However, I tried, as much as possible, to spend time with Evangelicals as they went about their daily routines. Ramiro helped me with repairs and remodeling in our apartment. I accompanied Enrique to political events. And both Ramiro and Enrique gave me key logistic help carrying out my research in their church and making contacts with non-Evangelical respondents. I, in turn, often assisted them with my car in their various activities—some related to Evangelicalism, some not. I also participated in numerous activities not related to the Emmanuel and RYVL Churches, such as Evangelical talk radio shows. During the course of my fieldwork I also visited most of the larger Evangelical churches in Caracas, including neo-Pentecostal, Lutheran, and Presbyterian.

Most of my data collection from this participant observation originated as notes taken on a small notepad, later turned into scenes at my computer. I tried to write down important phrases verbatim; for others I used the technique of writing down keywords for later reconstruction. When I had the chance to sit down soon after the field visit, I was able to reconstruct these phrases easily. However, when there was a delay or I felt that I had not written the phrase precisely as I heard it, I paraphrased. After reading Philippe Bourgeois's *In Search of Respect* and realizing the power of tape-recorded participant observation, I decided to keep my tape recorder on when I was with Ramiro and Enrique. By that time I had known them for two years and they were comfortable with my research and with me. The tape recorder was always kept in the open, both for reasons of recording quality and to comply with the ethics of informed consent. When another person entered the conversation, Ramiro, Enrique, or I would say something along the lines of "He's/I'm taping for research." However, sometimes when the conversation was brisk or urgent, we did not point out that the tape recorder was on, although it was always in plain view. This participant-observation recording provided some of the most important data for my analysis.

LIFE HISTORY INTERVIEWS

I developed and tested a first draft of the interview instrument in my first year of fieldwork with Evangelicals in Venezuela's interior. I modified it during my next year at the University of Chicago and again during the first eight months of my fieldwork with Emmanuel Church. I did a handful more practice interviews in November 1996 and revised the instrument again.

The art of qualitative interviewing is to direct the respondent toward topics of interest while not importantly affecting the respondent's way of expressing his or her thoughts. An interview with too little direction can result in long ramblings of little relevance and a respondent who becomes frustrated at the length of the interview. An interview with too much direction can produce data that are distorted and insensitive to unexpected events. The difficulty of striking an adequate balance led me to conduct all the interviews myself rather than train interviewers. As far as possible I have tried to present interview data as interactions in which my own cultural categories came into contact with those of the respondent.

At one point in the pretests of the instrument, nine of eleven interviewees broke down crying during the interview when painful moments of their past were touched on and probed. On hearing about this problem at a conference sponsored by one of my funding agencies, a senior social scientist optimistically pointed out that I was giving my interviewees an opportunity to come to terms with their biographical issues. My wife, a mental health professional, was less sanguine. She pointed out that because I had no training in counseling or therapy, it would be unethical for me to open people up to this point and then be unequipped to help them address their issues. In the interviews done in 1997 and 1998, then, I steered away from topics that seemed to be causing pain—relationship breakups, family deaths, persistent problems of self—once they were identified in outline. I would like to say that this turned into a win-win situation that benefited the analysis. It did not. As a piece of scholarship this book is lesser for the gaps in detail this occasionally produced. But it is a better work of sociology if the latter is conceived of as a practice whose ends do not justify doing harm to participants. Only one of the eighty-four respondents in this round of interviews broke down and cried (El Andino). However, there were many tense moments, red faces, watery eyes, and lowered, almost inaudible voices that led me to change the subject.

I began my research by interviewing fifty-five men from the two churches I studied. My interviews aimed to understand the conditions that precipitated conversion in each individual case. The central methodological challenge in working with life histories, of course, is to find a way to get at "the facts" in order to construct a causal account. Life history is not only a data collection method for social scientists; it is also a medium through which social actors construct the self, and their narratives are necessarily partial and embellished. This leads many researchers to argue that you simply cannot use life histories to obtain objective facts and can only treat life histories as cultural objects (see, e.g., Blee 2002; Irvine 1999). The problem can only be exacerbated in the case of religious conversions since these often accentuate narrative reconstruction of biographies (Csordas 1994; Smilde 2003). In Pentecostalism, for example, the "once was lost, but now am found" narrative structure may well lead to an exaggeration or even fabrication of problems in the respondent's past, leading to an overestimation of their causal importance.

Nevertheless, while they are reinterpreted, reconstructed, and overlaid with meaning, biographical facts such as addiction, divorce, and household composition do exist, and causal accounts can be constructed if these facts are painstakingly uncovered. Furthermore, in most field settings there are cultural tendencies that if comprehended can facilitate the sociologist's task. Among the respondents studied here, there were two such tendencies. First, I found that the "once was lost" narrative had a competitor. In what might be called the "chosen by God" narrative, a respondent cultivates an image of having converted beyond any self-interest or intention when he was abruptly chosen by God. This is a source of spiritual legitimacy just as powerful as the "once was lost" narrative. As a result I found no systematic bias. When concrete facts revealed inconsistencies, I found that underreporting of life problems was just as likely as overreporting.

Second, these Evangelicals place a high premium on honesty in the sense that an exposed outright lie would result in a tremendous loss of esteem. Distortions of the past, therefore, are usually produced through abstract scripted narratives that selectively omit specific facts or strategically obfuscate sequences of events. My interview strategy was to make this difficult by getting as concrete as possible. I did not ask respondents what caused them to convert, to tell me their life histories, or to tell me what their lives were like before their conversion. Rather, I guided respondents through the time period under study using a month-by-month event-history calendar to track twenty-one variables from three years before their conversion (or seven years before our interview in the case of nonconverts): religious participation, residence, education, employment, wife's employment, nonreligious participatory organization, relationship, personal health, family health, death of friends or family, family Evangelical contact, non-family Evangelical contact, victim of crime, alcohol abuse, drug abuse, gambling, problems with police/law, betrayal by or loss of friend(s), financial problems, fear for safety, family problems (Freedman et al. 1988). We started with those aspects of life, such as residence and conjugal relationships, about which memory was most likely to be accurate. Where memory faltered, I used temporal landmarks common to all, such as the riots in February 1989, the two coup attempts in 1992, the World Cup soccer tournaments of 1990 and 1994, or life events such as the birth of a child. Clearing up temporal ambiguity was the source of many modifications of personal history.[1] I made every effort to get the respondent to speak in concrete terms. For example, if he said he had a drinking problem I asked what concrete problems it caused him. In numerous cases the person claimed to have had a drinking problem before converting but could not give concrete descriptions of or tell stories about actual problems it had caused him. In these cases I did not code the interview as reflecting problems with substance abuse.

I have no illusions that in every case I got down to the "real" reasons for conversion. However, I do think the methodology was highly successful in breaking through the more common elements of Evangelicals' own narratives. In every case I was reasonably satisfied that I had been able to determine a constellation of causal factors that precipitated conversion. Respondents frequently attempted evasion through ambiguity, generality, or fudging on the temporality of their memories. This was especially true of embarrassing relationship problems, sexual problems, or being left by a woman. There is one aspect about which I am sure several Evangelical respondents were not truthful: committing murder. Several of those who talked about having been involved in acute problems of violence said that they had never pulled the trigger. This seemed implausible in many cases but in two in particular. Luis came to be the leader of a gang that, by his own description, specialized in murder, but he claimed never to have pulled the trigger. It seems exceedingly unlikely that he would become leader of the gang without this experience. Similarly, Ernestillo became Evangelical after being accused of murdering two students in front of his house. He said he had no idea why the police and his neighbors had pointed to him. His claim to have been in his room "sleeping" is the classic unconfirmable alibi. However, "involvement in violence" was the code used, not murder specifically. So these omissions did not affect the coding of the data. Such lies are understandable given how the justice system is viewed in Venezuela. Respondents who had been involved in crime but had not gone to jail frequently said that God had protected them. The idea of "turning oneself over" to the authorities to pay for one's crimes would simply not be understood in a context in which the justice system is seen as the embodiment of injustice itself.

While among the Evangelical respondents the challenge was overreporting, among non-Evangelicals it was underreporting, especially of drug use and involvement in criminal activity. Many of those in this group did talk to me about their drug use. Some others did not, but it was evident from their backgrounds that a period of drug use probably occurred. In two cases of individuals whom I

1. This methodological strategy closely resembles "objective hermeneutics" (Reichertz 2002). I disagree with Denzin's (1989) view that such an approach necessarily conflates data, sociological texts, and subjects' lives. Misplaced concreteness is not the weakness of any one methodological approach but a general pitfall all sociological thinking needs to avoid. I also disagree that it implies a linear view of biography. It is precisely biographical facts that often help us to demonstrate contingency despite respondents' efforts to construct linear narratives.

contacted but who declined to be interviewed, it was clear from what others close to them told me that they were deeply involved in drugs. In one case I found out that a respondent who said he had never used drugs in fact had a difficult drug past but had since straightened out. In this case I coded a suspicious period in his life in which he could not explain what he had been doing for several years as involvement in drugs and violence.

Pilot interviews made clear that conducting interviews in respondents' homes was not viable. Such an interview becomes a much-anticipated household if not neighborhood event, and it is very difficult to explain the need for privacy without causing offense. Even when there was understanding and a desire to comply, many respondents' homes simply did not have any private place in them. Windows frequently have no panes. Sheets rather than doors frequently are used at doorways. And asking for a room apart is simply too much to ask of a household where there may be several times more people than rooms. Thus I looked for another space to carry out the interviews. The first third of my interviews were conducted in office space I rented. When this proved time-consuming and Emmanuel Church built an addition to the church that housed classrooms, I began to do interviews there. In the smaller church I likewise did interviews in an upstairs classroom. On a few occasions when this was logistically impossible, interviews were conducted in my home or in a restaurant or other public places.

SAMPLE

Much of the work on Latin American Evangelicals has been based on understandably haphazard data collection. The exploratory nature of cross-cultural fieldwork on a relatively unknown topic has meant that researchers have largely engaged in snowball samples or simply asked for volunteers. Such samples with Latin American Evangelicals are subject to an extreme self-selection bias. For example, at several different points in my research when word got around that I was doing interviews, I was approached by individuals, usually with big smiles on their faces, asking to be interviewed. They were usually very disappointed when I said that they did not fit my sample and continued to try to convince me. (Occasionally the insistence got to the point that I obliged by conducting an impromptu interview on whatever topic occurred to me.) The tendency toward self-selection is likely to create a bias toward those interviewees who had preconversion problems that are not continuing sources of shame—substance abuse instead of, say, involvement in violent crime—and toward those who had successfully overcome their problems rather than those who were still struggling. The darker, more disturbing portrait contained in this book is in part the result of the violent context of Caracas; but it also has much to do with my pursuit of a representative sample that included those men who did not necessarily want to be interviewed.

Because I was interested not only in what had happened in their lives but also in how they described it, I did in-depth qualitative interviews rather than a large-sample survey. I sought to engage a sample of respondents representative of Evangelicals in general and with which I would be able to establish rapport in one-on-

one interviews. I decided to focus on men between the ages of fifteen and forty-five who were members of the church but had been baptized within the previous seven years. Concentrating on one age group and one gender would permit me to reach a level of saturation that might not have been the case with an unrestricted sample. I wanted men who were not simply visiting the church but were committed members. Because I would be doing life histories from before their period of conversion to the present, interviewing longtime members would have been too time consuming. Furthermore, pilot interviews demonstrated that the difficulty of recall, at the level of specificity I was looking for, greatly increased with time. I focused on men because of the highly personal subject matter of the interviews. Pilot interviews showed that doing one-on-one interviews with a woman behind closed doors was not an acceptable practice. Even if it had been, establishing rapport on sensitive personal issues such as sexuality was unlikely. The resulting sample is representative of Evangelical men of a Pentecostal tendency in large urban centers of Venezuela.

The interview data are derived from fifty-six interviews with Evangelical men from two churches. Forty-six of the interviews were carried out in Emmanuel Church, ten in RYVL Church. Both samples were complete in the sense that I attempted to interview every baptized male member between the ages of fifteen and forty-five who had converted within the previous seven years. In both cases, making full use of networks, being flexible regarding time and place, and old-fashioned persistence resulted in an exceedingly high response rate: over 90 percent in each church. In Emmanuel Church I was aware of five individuals who fit my description but with whom I was never able to make contact. In one case I completed the attitudinal part, but there was not enough time to finish the biographical case. And in another, the biographical part was completed but not the attitudinal. In RYVL Church one person who was on my list was away during the period of my interviews.

I originally had drawn a sample in Emmanuel Church from its membership list. However, it became evident that it not only was inaccurate regarding when people had converted, but it was also irrecoverably out of date, containing names of individuals who no longer attended the church. As Ramiro had helped me locate individuals on the list whom he knew, all the first twenty-one interviews were of members of the Sunday school class he taught. I decided to do a complete sample of those who attended Ramiro's class and who fit the description I was working with. This worked well in the sense that the smaller church I studied had a similarly defined Sunday school class for young men, and I was able to use a similar complete sample from them.

Despite having clearly articulated the criteria for interviewees, in several cases it became apparent after an interview began that the interviewee did not fit the criteria for inclusion. Given the logistic difficulty of actually converging in space, time, and desire, it was hard to pass up these opportunities. When the person was outside the age group (in each case, older), I conducted the interview anyway with the idea that it might show some relevant differences. They did not. In each of these three cases the life history evidenced situations indistinguishable from the rest of the group. Nevertheless, I excluded two of these interviews from the analysis in chapter 4 because they would have provided undue support for the conclusions, and age was likely a relevant factor in one of the independent variables (living with family of origin). I drew the line in cases in which the potential interviewee was not a baptized member of the church but was visiting from the interior or had just begun his Evangelical career. The one exception here was the case of Ricardo. At the time of our interview he had been Evangelical for a year and a half, was finishing his indoctrination classes, and was preparing for his baptism, which was to take place within a few weeks.

I selected the control group of non-Evangelical men to be comparable to the Evangelical sample based on social class as defined by residential location. Originally I had planned to do paired comparisons by selecting one non-Evangelical man who lived a certain fixed distance from each of my Evangelical respondents. But realizing the immense logistic difficulty of doing so, I decided to select four nuclei for interviews. Using the Evangelical sample as a base, I located four nuclei determined geographically using a map created by the Centro de Investigaciones en Ciencias Sociales that zones the city into 700+ sectors defined by social class. This strategy worked well with the two samples, resulting in almost identical means in social class. The following is a calculation of the mean and standard deviation of the social class score for 75 of the 84 members of the sample who lived in the metropolitan area of Caracas. (Excluded are 9 cases, or 10.7 percent of the participants: 7 Evangelicals who lived in satellite communities not included on the map, 1 non-Evangelical who lived in such a community, and 1 non-Evangelical who lived in the street.)

	MEAN	STD. DEV.	CASES
Entire Population	6.8400	1.9731	75
Non-Evangelical	6.7778	1.9677	27
Evangelical	6.8750	1.9960	48

In these four nuclei, I started from an arbitrarily selected point and went door-to-door asking whether there were any men in the household between the ages of eighteen and forty-five who would agree to participate in my study.[2] If there were, I arranged an interview (if there was more than one, I chose whoever was available). Two exceptions to this were two workers in the downtown informal economy. I had selected a nucleus in the neighborhood near the church since several of the Evangelical respondents were from that neighborhood. However, as I conducted these interviews I realized that they were all relatively more settled than some of the Evangelicals in this group who had converted while living in flophouses and working in the downtown informal economy. Thus I selected two respondents based on their participation in this economy. I offered the non-Evangelical respondents Bs. 10,000 (at that time about U.S.$17) for their participation. This was a considerable attraction for these men as it represented more than a day's pay for many of them—and was the only way to ensure an ac-

2. None of my Evangelical respondents were under eighteen years old, so I modified the age group for the non-Evangelical sample to reflect that.

ceptable response rate. The response rate varied from 50 to 100 percent between nuclei, with an overall response rate of 65 percent.

PROCESSING AND ANALYZING THE DATA

The interviews were transcribed by student research assistants in Caracas and then analyzed using a software package for qualitative data analysis named Atlas.ti. After experimenting with independent variables using logistic regression and then qualitative comparative analysis, I built up an explanation based on three causal conditions—the respondent's life problems, whether or not he lived with an Evangelical, and whether or not he lived with his family of origin—as well as the outcome variable of conversion. Below I provide the coding rules I used.

Life Problems

I use *problems* instead of alternative terms often used in studies of conversion or social movement mobilization. *Deprivations* only makes sense from a structural functional perspective in which one can make sense of a baseline equilibrium of need fulfillment. This is rarely feasible and even less so in a cross-cultural study. Instead I view problems as a persisting sense of *dis-ease* in an individual's experience. *Complaints* makes most sense when there is an adversary who has authority over or responsibility for the problem in question. That is rarely the case with the problems described here.

I coded as problematic those extensions of time during which the respondent told of having one or more problems that threatened valued aspects of his existence (e.g., family relationships, work or economic stability, personal safety) or that impeded aspects of his existence that he considered basic and important (e.g., forming a family, basic social interaction with peers). For example, a respondent who reported occasionally or frequently drinking more than he would like in a certain period but who did not tell convincing stories of how this jeopardized his health, marriage, work, or other important aspect of life was not coded as having a problem. If, on the other hand, the respondent told concrete stories about the ramifications this had (e.g., jeopardizing his marriage or his work), I coded it as a problem.

Living with an Evangelical

I coded a period in the respondent's life history as living with an Evangelical when he lived with one or more individuals who were participating Evangelicals at the time. In two of the thirty-four cases this was a religion other than Evangelicalism. I felt justified in this coding decision because they clearly functioned as equivalents. For example, Eric's sister was a member of a Seventh-day Adventist church, a religion rejected as "erroneous" by some Evangelicals but accepted by others because it accepts the doctrine of the Holy Trinity. Eric's sister provided a key stimulus to his conversion by giving religious meaning to the stillbirth of his child that relieved him from guilt. Eric converted to Pentecostal Evangelicalism but carried this same meaning with him. Agustín lived for a time with his mother and sister who were members of Sana Doctrina, a religion that is similar to Evangelicalism in its emphasis on perfectionism and millennialism and belief in the Holy Spirit but that does not emphasize spirit possession like Pentecostal Evangelicalism does. When Agustín converted again, it was during a home service that his mother had organized with members of her church. Nevertheless, he reinitiated his participation in the Evangelical church where he previously was a member. It is worth pointing out that this analytic move provides a case that contradicts the analysis provided here (Agustín) as well as a case that supports it (Eric).

Living with Family of Origin

I coded a period of time as "living with family of origin" when the respondent lived with one or more members of the family nucleus in which he grew up. I expanded this criterion by including those who lived within fifty feet of their families of origin. Because it is common among the popular classes in Venezuela for parents to permit their children to build on top of or next to their home, five cases were recoded (three had built on top of or adjacent to their parents' homes; two lived in homes within fifty feet of their parents' homes). Each of these cases increase fit with the model provided here. But I think the modification clearly fits with the substantive dynamics described. In one case, Teodoro, the "family of origin" was other than his biological nuclear family. Teodoro converted while living with his aunt and cousins with whom he had grown up. Indeed, he talked of this period as "living at home." Only later did it come out that they were not his biological family of origin. In any event, this does not affect the conclusions provided here since he was living with an Evangelical. I coded as "not living with family of origin" the four cases provided by Jhony and Melvin despite their "officially" living at home. Three of these cases support the analysis (the two from Jhony and one of Melvin's), and one contradicts it (one from Melvin). This analytic decision is justified insofar as each of them was heavily involved in drugs and petty crime and slept in the street, in flophouses, or in friends' places, only coming home occasionally to "crash," get some sleep and clean up. Each described these periods of his life as living "in the street."

Conversion

I coded a respondent as having converted to Evangelicalism if he not only "accepted the Lord" but also followed that up with sustained participation in an Evangelical church. Thus I did not count as conversion those often repeated cases in which the person "accepted the Lord" in a service or as a result of Evangelization but did not follow it up with participation. I did not require the person to have been baptized as it often takes months or even years to complete the indoctrination classes and reach the point at which the pastor decides he is ready.

APPENDIX C

Quantitative Analysis of Networks and Conversion

QUALITATIVE COMPARATIVE ANALYSIS

I used Charles Ragin's (1987, 2000) qualitative comparative analysis (QCA) to develop my causal explanation of conversion. QCA uses Boolean algebra to penetrate bodies of data that are not large enough for multivariate statistical analyses, yet are too large for simple eyeballing. Yet it also facilitates the dialogue between ideas and evidence that is the strength of qualitative data analysis. It works by presenting every possible combination of dichotomous independent variables in a truth table to see how these combinations line up with the dependent variable. Independent variables are tried and discarded, defined and redefined to increase fit. Focusing on contradictory cases, QCA amounts to a multi-iterated process of inference and updating. Rather than try to find which variable wins the battle of main effects, QCA can portray multiple causal combinations, including minority effects.

Not surprisingly, looking at the Evangelical life histories in isolation seems to corroborate views of their religious practice as caused by the experience of life problems. Fully 85 percent of the conversions to Evangelicalism among my respondents were preceded by addictive behavior, involvement in violence, relationship problems, or problems of personal adjustment. But the fact that these respondents appear to convert in order to address life problems does not mean these problems *explain* conversion. Other men with similar problems may address them in different ways or not address them at all. To figure out what factors can provide a causal account, we need to include the sample of nonconverts.

To work with this life history data in QCA, I segmented it into "spells" as used in event-history analysis (Allison 1984). A spell is a time segment whose duration is determined by unique combinations of the independent variables under review. In other words, when any one of the independent variables changes, the old spell ends and the new spell begins. Of course, the duration of

Table C1. Truth Table of Combinations of "Life Problems" and "Living with an Evangelical"

	Total	~C	C	Proportion	Outcome
~P~E	40	40	0	.00	~C
~PE	12	3	9	.75	C
P~E	65	31	34	.52	?
PE	21	2	19	.9	C
Total	138	76	62	.45	

NOTE: P=Life problems; E=Living with an Evangelical; C=Conversion.

spells varies—in this study anywhere from one month to several years—and the total number of spells depends on which and how many independent variables one chooses.

I began by looking at cases in which conversion took place in the absence of problems. In all these cases the person lived with another Evangelical. I then combined these two explanatory variables (Table C1) and followed up the contradictions among those cases in which the respondent was experiencing a problem but did not live with an Evangelical.

I tried a number of different variables to see whether they could successfully distinguish between those who committed and those who did not (Table C2). I found here that migration provided the most significant correlation. I added this variable to the truth table. But through following up on the contradictions I found that what was really at play in "migration" was whether or not the person lived with his family of origin. Changing the variable to simply whether or not the person was living with his family of origin increased its explanatory power.

Table C3 is a truth table of every combination of the three independent variables, the total number of cases in each combination, the number of conversions among these, the proportion this represents, and a judgment on the output value. Comparing the proportion of conversions that occur in each causal combination to the overall proportion of .431, we get clear, statistically significant tendencies in all but one combination: ~PFE.

Disregarding the ambiguous row (Ragin 1987: 116–17) and reducing the truth table to ask which combinations constitute *clear* causes of conversion, we get three causal combinations that can be used to guide qualitative analysis.

1. ~P~FE combines with P~FE to produce ~FE
2. P~F~E combines with P~FE to produce P~F
3. P~FE combines with PFE to produce PE

   C = ~FE + P~F + PE

Put substantively, conversion results from spells in which men (1) do not live with family of origin and live with an Evangelical; or (2) are experiencing life problems and do not live with family of origin; or (3) are experiencing life problems and live with an Evangelical. Preliminary analysis, then, shows that the ex-

Table C2. Comparison of Cases of Conversion and Nonconversion in Combination "Life Problems" and "Not Living with an Evangelical"

	Conversion (N=34)	Nonconversion (N=31)	p-value	Test[f]
Cohabitation[a]	15 (44%)	11 (35%)	1.0	CS
Migration[b]	17 (50%)	7 (23%)	.025	CS
Employment[c]	16 (47%)	13 (42%)	1.0	CS
Evangelistic contact[d]	6 (8%)	1 (3%)	.067	FER
Family of origin contact	5 (15%)	5 (16%)	.69	FER
Extended family contact	7 (21%)	4 (13%)	.312	FER
Any family contact	12 (35%)	9 (29%)	1.0	CS
Nonfamily personal contact[e]	23 (68%)	26 (84%)	.2	CS
Any family or personal contacts	29 (85%)	30 (97%)	.98	FER

[a] Lived with partner, either married or unmarried.
[b] Conversion occurred in place other than hometown.
[c] Employment status would benefit from conversion: unemployed, day worker, informal worker, entrepreneur.
[d] Exposed to Evangelicalism through evangelization, outdoor campaign, plaza service, or radio.
[e] Friend, coworker, neighbor.
[f] CS=chi-square; FER=Fisher's exact, right.

Table C3. Truth Table of Combinations of "Life Problems," "Living with Family of Origin," and "Living with an Evangelical"

P	F	E	Total	~C	C	Proportion of C	Output
~P	~F	~E	10	10	0	.000**	~C
~P	~F	E	7	1	6	.857*	C
~P	F	~E	30	30	0	.000**	~C
~P	F	E	6	3	3	.500	?
P	~F	~E	40	10	30	.750**	C
P	~F	E	10	1	9	.900**	C
P	F	~E	30	25	5	.167**	~C
P	F	E	11	2	9	.818**	C
			144	82	62	.431	

NOTES: P=Life problems; F=Living with at least one member of family of origin; E=Spatially present Evangelical; C=Conversion.
*Binomial probability < .05; **Binomial probability < .01.

perience of life problems is part of the story but is neither sufficient nor necessary for conversion. Rather, two variables fill out the picture by pointing toward a respondent's network position.

Using this table, I was able to gain sufficient orientation to carry out my qualitative analysis of causes. The goal was not to figure out which variable individually explains the most but rather to see how they work together.

Table C4. Cross-Tabulation of the Experience of "Life Problems" While "Not Living with Family of Origin"

	F	~F	Total
P	41	50	91
~P	36	17	53
Total	77	67	144

NOTES: P=Experience of life problems; F=Living with family of origin. Chi-square=7.04; *p* is less than or equal to 0.01.

ANALYSIS OF AGENCY IN NETWORKS

The last section of chapter 6 on agency in networks also relied on a multistaged quantitative analysis. It began by noting that the individual experience of life problems (P) stubbornly stays in the equation (see Table C2). Even if we were to code the output of ambiguous combination ~PFE as conversion, the causal significance of life problems would remain. While "Living with an Evangelical"(E) would become a sufficient condition, "not living with family of origin" (~F) would still need to combine with P to cause conversion. The reason P does not drop out of the equation is the very clear tendency for the combination ~P~F~E not to lead to conversion. In other words, if a respondent who lives away from family of origin (~F) does not experience problems (P), no conversion occurs.

But it is still possible to question the causal importance of problems. QCA is oriented toward causal diversity and counts all causal relationships with the same output as equal, no matter their numeric frequency. The combination P~F~E accounts for close to half of the conversions in the sample. We could argue, then, that while ~F does not *necessarily* cause P, and ~F is not the *exclusive* cause of P, there appears to be a *strong tendency* for ~F to cause P. If this were the case, problems would still not be spurious; for without them ~F does not lead to conversion. But we would better consider P a mediating variable. A simple cross-tabulation of all cases according to whether they were living with family of origin or not and whether they experienced life problems indeed shows a highly significant relationship (Table C4).

This is clearly consistent with the possibility that problems are a function of structural availability and therefore not as causally important as we might think. But, of course, correlation does not establish direction of causation, and in chapter 6 I suggested that structural availability *itself* could be caused by a problem involved in the conversion project. Table C5 shows that if we exclude these cases from the sample[1] in order to simply compare cases in which life problems clearly arise and are experienced while living *with* family of origin, versus cases in which life problems clearly arise and are experienced while living *apart from* family of origin, the connection does not meet generally accepted standards of significance

1. An alternative strategy would be to recode these cases as living with family of origin, which would reduce the significance even further. However, this would become substantively unintelligible in cases such as José Gregorio, who was in jail.

Table C5. Cross-Tabulation of the Experience of "Life Problems" While "Not Living with Family of Origin," Excluding Cases in Which "Life Problems" Caused "Not Living with Family of Origin"

	F	~F	Total
P	41	35	76
~P	36	17	53
Total	77	52	129

NOTES: P = Experience of life problems; F = Living with family of origin. Chi-square = 2.54; p is less than or equal to 0.20.

Table C6. Agency in Construction of Network Locations

	Intentionally Brought About	Not Intentionally Brought About	Total
Not living with family of origin (~F)	34	11	45
Living with an Evangelical (E)	10	17	27
Total	44	28	72

Table C7. Purposive Action in Construction of Network Locations

	Intentional but Not Integral to Project of Change	Intentional and Integral to Project of Change	Total
Not living with family of origin (~F)	31	3	34
Living with an Evangelical (E)	6	4	10
Total	37	7	44

for a sample of this size. This finding leads to the conclusion that ~F is causally important not because it causes P but because of what happens when P occurs.

In the last section on agency and purposes, the data show that in 61 percent of cases of conversion in which either E or ~F was causally effective, we can see respondents' agency in the construction of their network location (Table C6). To look into agency in the more restrictive sense of intentionally creating a network location as part of a project of change, I examined these forty-four cases identified in Table C7. In seven cases I found evidence of such a process.

Glossary of Spanish Terms

23 DE ENERO. Large housing project in western Caracas.
ABASTO. Mom-and-pop grocery store.
BARRIO. Poor neighborhood of self-constructed homes *(ranchos).*
BLOQUE. Apartment building in public housing project.
CADENA. Chain of vendetta murders.
CAÍDA. "Fall"; refers to "backsliding" from Evangelical commitment.
CAMPAÑA. Evangelical revival.
CAMPO BLANCO. Target congregation being organized by members of an existing church.
EL CARACAZO. Three-day period of rioting that started on February 27, 1989, in response to neoliberal reform measures.
CAUDILLO. De facto political leader ruling largely by force rather than ideology or institutions.
CENTRO HÍPICO. Bar-restaurant where men gather to drink and watch horse races.
LA CRISIS. "The crisis"; term Venezuelans use for the period of economic decline beginning in 1983.
CRISTIANOS. Christian; the most common term Evangelicals use to refer to each other. Implicitly denigrates Catholics as not truly Christian.
CULEBRA. "Snake"; refers to long-standing vendettas that have many twists and turns.
ENCULEBRADO. Involved in one or several vendettas.
EVANGÉLICOS. Evangelical Christians.
FIRME. "Firm"; the way in which Evangelicals describe themselves when they have succeeded in fulfilling Evangelical behavioral norms.
HERMANO. "Brother"; term male Evangelicals use to refer to one another. Often used instead of "Mr." or "Pastor."

MALANDRO. Gangbanger or delinquent; a youth who is involved in drugs, crime, and violence.

EL PROCESO. Term used by supporters of President Hugo Chávez to refer to the process of social change during his administration.

RANCHO. Self-constructed home in a barrio.

EL RANCHÓN. "Big rancho"; affectionate name given to the sanctuary of Emmanuel Church.

TADEO. Human development workshop organized by the Catholic Church.

VARÓN. Term used for a man that accentuates his masculinity.

VIVO. Clever, quick, tricky.

References

Ainslie, George. 1992. *Picoeconomics: The Strategic Interaction of Successive Motivational States within the Person.* New York: Cambridge University Press.

———. 2001. *Breakdown of Will.* New York: Cambridge University Press.

Albán Estrada, María, and Juan Pablo Muñoz. 1987. *Con Dios todo se puede: La invasión de las sectas al Ecuador.* Quito: Editorial Planeta.

Alexander, Jeffrey C. 1988. *Action and Its Environments: Toward a New Synthesis.* New York: Columbia University Press.

———. 1990. "Analytic Debates: Understanding the Relative Autonomy of Culture." In *Culture and Society: Contemporary Debates,* ed. Jeffrey C. Alexander and Steven Seidman, 1–29. New York: Cambridge University Press.

———. 2003. The *Meanings of Social Life: A Cultural Sociology.* New York: Oxford University Press

Allison, Paul. 1984. *Event History Analysis.* Thousand Oaks, CA: Sage.

Althauser, Robert. 1990. "Paradox in Popular Religion: The Limits of Instrumental Faith." *Social Forces* 69(2): 585–602.

Anderson, Benedict. 1993. *Imagined Communities: Reflections on the Origin and Spread of Nationalism.* London: Verso.

Annis, Sheldon. 1987. *God and Production in a Guatemalan Town.* Austin: University of Texas Press.

Ansell, Christopher K. 1997. "Symbolic Networks: The Realignment of the French Working Class, 1887–1894." *American Journal of Sociology* 103(2): 359–90.

Archer, Margaret S., Andrew Collier, and Douglas V. Porpora. 2004. *Transcendence: Critical Realism and God.* New York: Routledge.

Asad, Talal. 1993. *Genealogies of Religion: Discipline and Reasons of Power in Christianity and Islam.* Baltimore: Johns Hopkins University Press.

Austin-Broos, Diane J. 1997. *Jamaica Genesis: Religion and the Politics of Moral Order.* Chicago: University of Chicago Press.

Bakhtin, Mikhail. 1981. *The Dialogic Imagination: Four Essays.* Ed. Michael Holquist, trans. Caryl Emerson and Michael Holquist. Austin: University of Texas Press.

Bankston, Carl L., III, and Min Zhou. 1996. "The Ethnic Church, Ethnic Identification, and the Social Adjustment of Vietnamese Adolescents." *Review of Religious Research* 38(1): 18–37.

Barrantes, César. 1997. *El apoyo a la economía popular en Venezuela: Hacía una política social orgánica del Estado?* Caracas: Ediciones FACES/UCV.

Barrios de Chungara, Domitila, with Moema Viezzer. 1978. *Let Me Speak! Testimony of Domitila, a Woman of the Bolivian Mines.* Trans. Victoria Ortiz. New York: Monthly Review Press.

Bastian, Jean Pierre. 1994. *Protestantismos y modernidad latinoamericana: Historia de unas minorías religiosas activas en América Latina.* Mexico City: Fondo de Cultura Económica.

Becker, Penny Edgell, and Pawan H. Dhingra. 2001. "Religious Involvement and Volunteering: Implications for Civil Society." *Sociology of Religion* 62: 315–35.

Bender, Courtney. 2003. *Heaven's Kitchen: Living Religion at God's Love We Deliver.* Chicago: University of Chicago Press.

Berger, Brigitte. 1991. *The Culture of Entrepreneurship.* San Francisco: Center for Self-Governance.

Berger, Peter. 1990. Foreword to *Tongues of Fire: The Explosion of Protestantism in Latin America,* by David Martin. Oxford: Basil Blackwell.

Bicchieri, Cristiana.1988. "Should a Scientist Abstain from Metaphor?" In *The Consequences of Economic Rhetoric,* ed. Arjo Klamer, Donald M. McCloskey, and Robert M. Solow, 100–115. Cambridge: Cambridge University Press.

Blee, Kathleen. 2002. *Inside Organized Racism: Women in the Hate Movement.* Berkeley: University of California Press.

Boudon, Raymond. 1994. *The Art of Self-Persuasion.* Trans. Malcolm Slater. Cambridge: Polity Press.

Bourdieu, Pierre. 1977. *Outline of a Theory of Practice.* Cambridge: Cambridge University Press.

Bourgois, Philippe. 2001. "In Search of Masculinity: Violence, Respect, and Sexuality among Puerto Rican Crack Dealers in East Harlem." In *Men's Lives,* 5th ed., ed. Michael S. Kimmel and Michael A. Messner, 24–32. Boston: Allyn and Bacon.

Bowen, Kurt. 1996. *Evangelism and Apostasy: The Evolution and Impact of Evangelicals in Modern Mexico.* Montreal: McGill-Queen's University Press.

Briceño León, Roberto, Alberto Camardiel, Olga Avila Fuenmayor, and Edoardo De Armas. 2002. "Un alálisis social de ser víctima." In *Morir en Caracas: Violencia y ciudadanía en Venezuela,* ed. Roberto Briceño León and Rogelioi Perez Perdomo, 31–50. Caracas: Universidad Central de Venezuela.

Briceño León, Roberto, and Rogelio Pérez Perdomo, eds. 2002. *Morir en Caracas: Violencia y ciudadanía en Venezuela.* Caracas: Universidad Central de Venezuela.

Brown, Karen McCarthy. 1991. *Mama Lola: A Vodou Priestess in Brooklyn.* Berkeley: University of California Press.

Bruner, Jerome. 1991. "The Narrative Construction of Reality." *Critical Inquiry* 18: 1–21.

Brusco, Elizabeth. 1995. *The Reformation of Machismo.* Austin: University of Texas Press.

Burdick, John. 1993. *Looking for God in Brazil.* Berkeley: University of California Press.

Burke, Kenneth. 1957. *The Philosophy of Literary Form.* Rev. ed. New York: Vintage Books.

———. 1969. *A Grammar of Motives.* Berkeley: University of California Press.

———. 1989. *On Symbols and Society.* Ed. Joseph R. Gusfield. Chicago: University of Chicago Press.

Burt, Ronald S. 1986. "Comment." In *Approaches to Social Theory,* ed. Siegwart Lindenberg, James S. Coleman, and Stefan Nowak, 105–7. New York: Russell Sage Foundation.

Calhoun, Craig, Edward LiPuma, and Moishe Postone. 1993. *Bourdieu: Critical Perspectives.* Chicago: University of Chicago Press.

Cariola, C., M. Lacabana, L. Bethencourt, G. Darwich, B. Fernández, and A. T. Gutiérrez. 1989. *Crisis, sobrevivencia y sector informal.* Caracas: Editorial Nueva Sociedad.

Cartaya, Vanessa, and Yolanda D'Elía. 1991. *Pobreza en Venezuela: Realidad y políticas.* Caracas: Cesap-Cisor.

Castells, Manuel. 1997. *The Power of Identity: Economy, Society and Culture.* Cambridge: Blackwell.

Castillo, Anabel. 1997. *Jóvenes transgresores: En búsqueda de aceptación social.* Caracas: Universidad Central de Venezuela.

Chakrabarty, Dipesh. 2000. *Provincializing Europe: Postcolonial Thought and Historical Difference.* Princeton: Princeton University Press.

Chen, Chi-Yi, and Michel Picouet. 1979. *Dinámica de la población: Caso de Venezuela.* Caracas: UCAB-ORSTROM Edición.

Chesnut, Andrew R. 1997. *Born Again in Brazil: The Pentecostal Boom and the Pathogens of Poverty.* New Brunswick, NJ: Rutgers University Press.

Cleary, Edward L. 1997. "Introduction: Pentecostals, Prominence, and Politics." In *Power, Politics, and Pentecostals in Latin America,* ed. E. L. Cleary and H. W. Stewart-Gambino, 1–24. Boulder, CO: Westview Press.

Comaroff, Jean, and John L. Comaroff. 1991. *Of Revelation and Revolution: Christianity, Colonialism, and Consciousness in South Africa.* Chicago: University of Chicago Press.

Connell, Robert W. 1987. *Gender and Power.* Stanford: Stanford University Press.

Consejo Episcopal Latinoamericano. 1982. *Sectas en América Latina.* Guatemala City: Imprenta Gutenberg.

Cook, Karen S., and Margaret Levi. 1990. *The Limits of Rationality*. Chicago: University of Chicago Press.

Cook, Karen, and Joel Whitmeyer. 1992. "Two Approaches to Social Structure: Exchange Theory and Network Analysis." *Annual Review of Sociology* 18: 109–27.

Coronil, Fernando. 1997. *The Magical State: Nature, Money and Modernity in Venezuela*. Chicago: University of Chicago Press.

Crisp, Brian F., Daniel H. Levine, and Juan Carlos Rey. 1995. "The Legitimacy Problem." In *Venezuelan Democracy Under Stress*, ed. Jennifer McCoy, Andrés Serbin, William C. Smith, and Andrés Stambouli, 139–70. New Brunswick, NJ: Transaction Publishers.

Csordas, Thomas. 1994. *The Sacred Self: A Cultural Phenomenology of Charismatic Healing*. Berkeley: University of California Press.

Davis, Joseph E. 2005. *Accounts of Innocence: Sexual Abuse, Trauma, and the Self*. Chicago: University of Chicago Press

Dayton, Donald W. 1987. *The Theological Roots of Pentecostalism*. Grand Rapids, MI: Francis Asbury.

Denzin, Norman. 1987. *The Alcoholic Self*. Newbury Park, CA: Sage.

———. 1989. *Interpretive Biography*. Newbury Park, CA: Sage.

De Soto, Hernando. 1989. *The Other Path: The Invisible Revolution in the Third World*. New York: Harper & Row.

Dewey, John. 1922. *Human Nature and Conduct: An Introduction to Social Psychology*. New York: Random House.

Douglas, Mary. 1986. *How Institutions Think*. Syracuse, NY: Syracuse University Press.

Duque, José Roberto, and Boris Muñoz. 1995. *La ley de la calle: Testimonios de jóvenes protagonistas de la violencia en Caracas*. Caracas: Fundarte, Alcaldía de Caracas.

Durkheim, Émile. 1915. *The Elementary Forms of the Religious Life*. Trans. Joseph Ward Swain. New York: Free Press.

———. 1951. *Suicide: A Study in Sociology*. Trans. John A. Spaulding and George Simpson. New York: Free Press.

———. [1914] 1973. "The Dualism of Human Nature and Its Social Conditions." In *Emile Durkheim, 1858–1917*, ed. Kurt Wolff, 325–40. Columbus: Ohio State University Press.

Durkheim, Émile, and Marcel Mauss. 1963. *Primitive Classification*. Trans. Rodney Needham. Chicago: University of Chicago Press.

Ebaugh, Helen Rose, and Paula Pipes. 2001. "Immigrant Congregations as Social Service Providers: Are They Safety Nets for Welfare Reform?" In *Religion and Social Policy*, ed. Paula Nesbitt, 95–110. Walnut Creek, CA: AltaMira.

Edgell, Penny. 2006. *Religion and Family in a Changing Society*. Princeton: Princeton University Press.

Ellingson, Steve. 1995. "Understanding the Dialectic of Discourse and Collective Action: Public Debate and Rioting in Antebellum Cincinnati." *American Journal of Sociology* 101: 100–144.

Ellison, Christopher G. 1997. "Religious Involvement and the Subjective Quality of Family Life among African Americans." In *Family Life in Black Amer-*

ica, ed. Robert J. Taylor, James S. Jackson, and Linda Chatters, 117–31. Thousand Oaks, CA: Sage.

Elshtain, Jean Bethke. 1981. *Public Man, Private Woman: Women in Social and Political Thought.* Princeton: Princeton University Press.

Elster, Jon. 1979. *Ulysses and the Sirens: Studies in Rationality and Irrationality.* Cambridge: Cambridge University Press.

———. 1983. *Sour Grapes: Studies in the Subversion of Rationality.* Cambridge: Cambridge University Press.

———. 1987. *The Cement of Society.* Cambridge: Cambridge University Press.

Emerson, Michael O., and Christian Smith. *Divided by Faith: Evangelical Religion and the Problem of Race in America.* New York: Oxford University Press, 2000.

Emirbayer, Mustafa. 1997. "Manifesto for a Relational Sociology." *American Journal of Sociology* 103(2): 281–317.

Emirbayer, Mustafa, and Jeff Goodwin. 1994. "Network Analysis, Culture, and the Problem of Agency." *American Journal of Sociology* 99(6): 1411–54.

Emirbayer, Mustafa, and Ann Mische. 1998. "What Is Agency?" *American Journal of Sociology* 103: 962–1023.

Fajnzylber, Pablo, Daniel Lederman, and Norman Loayza. 1998. *Determinants of Crime Rates in Latin America and the World: An Empirical Assessment.* Washington, DC: World Bank.

Farrer, James. 2002. *Opening Up: Youth Sex Culture and Market Reform in Shanghai.* Chicago: University of Chicago Press.

Fernandez, James W. 1991. *Beyond Metaphor: The Theory of Tropes in Anthropology.* Stanford: Stanford University Press.

Festinger, Leon. 1962. *A Theory of Cognitive Dissonance.* Stanford: Stanford University Press

Flora, Cornelia Butler. 1976. *Pentecostalism in Colombia.* Cranbury, NJ: Associated University Presses.

Foley, Michael W., John D. McCarthy, and Mark Chaves. 2001. "Social Capital, Religious Institutions, and Poor Communities." In *Social Capital and Poor Communities,* ed. Susan Saegert, Phillip J. Thompson, and Mark R. Warren, 215–45. New York: Russell Sage Foundation.

Fonseca, Claudia. 1991. "Spouses, Siblings and Sex-Linked Bonding: A Look at Kinship Organization in a Brazilian Slum." In *Family, Household and Gender Relations in Latin America,* ed. Elizabeth Jelin, 133–60. London: Kegan Paul International.

Fraser, Lyndon. 2002. "To Tara via Holyhead: The Emergence of Irish Catholic Ethnicity in Nineteenth-Century Christchurch, New Zealand." *Journal of Social History* 36(2): 431–58.

Freedman, Deborah, Arland Thornton, Donald Cambum, Duane Alwin, and Linda Young-Marco 1988. "The Life History Calendar: A Technique for Collecting Retrospective Data." In *Sociological Methodology,* vol. 18, ed. C. C. Clogg, 37–68. Washington, DC: American Sociological Association.

Freston, Paul. 2001. *Evangelicals and Politics in Asia, Africa and Latin America.* New York: Cambridge University Press.

———. 2004. *Protestant Political Parties: A Global Survey.* Burlington, VT: Ashgate.

Friedrich, Paul. 1991. "Polytropy." In *Beyond Metaphor: The Theory of Tropes in Anthropology*, ed. James Fernandez, 17–55. Stanford: Stanford University Press.

Froehle, Bryan. 1997. "Pentecostals and Evangelicals in Venezuela: Consolidating Gains, Moving in New Directions." Pp.201–225 in *Power, Politics, and Pentecostals in Latin America*. Edited by Edward L. Cleary and Hannah Stewart Gambino. Boulder CO: Westview Press.

Gamson, William. 1992. *Talking Politics*. Cambridge: Cambridge University Press.

———. 1995. "Constructing Social Protest." In *Social Movements and Culture*, ed. Hank Johnston and Bert Klandermans, 85–106. Minneapolis: University of Minnesota Press.

Gamuza, Juan Miguel. 1988. *Las sectas nos invaden*. Caracas: San Pablo.

Giddens, Anthony. 1976. *New Rules of Sociological Method: A Positive Critique of Interpretative Sociologies*. New York: Basic Books.

———. 1979. *Central Problems in Social Theory: Action, Structure and Contradiction in Social Analysis*. Berkeley: University of California Press.

Gilligan, Carol. 1982. *In a Different Voice: Psychological Theory and Women's Development*. Cambridge, MA: Harvard University Press.

González Casas, Lorenzo. 2002. "Caracas: Territory, Architecture and Urban Space." In *Planning Latin America's Capital Cities, 1850–1950*, ed. Arturo Almandoz, 214–40. London: Routledge.

Gould, Roger V. 2003. "Why Do Networks Matter? Rationalist and Structuralist Interpretations." In *Social Movement Networks: Relational Approaches to Collective Action*, ed. Mario Diani and Doug McAdam, 233–57. New York: Oxford University Press.

Greeley, Andrew. 1995. *Religion as Poetry*. New Brunswick, NJ: Transaction Publishers.

Griswold, Wendy. 1987. "A Methodological Framework for the Sociology of Culture." *Sociological Methodology* 17: 1–35.

Gutiérrez, Ana Teresa. 1990. *Sobrevivencia y sectores populares en Venezuela*. Caracas: CENDES.

Haines, Valerie A., Jeanne S. Hurlbert, and John J. Beggs. 1996. "Exploring the Determinants of Support Provision: Provider Characteristics, Personal Networks, Community Contexts, and Support following Life Events." *Journal of Health and Social Behavior* 37(3): 252–64.

Halton, Eugene. 1995. *Bereft of Reason: On the Decline of Social Thought and Prospects for Its Renewal*. Chicago: University of Chicago Press.

Hansen, Karen V. 2005. *Not-So-Nuclear Families: Class, Gender, and Networks of Care*. New Brunswick, NJ: Rutgers University Press.

Hardin, Russell. 1995. *One for All: The Logic of Group Conflict*. Princeton: Princeton University Press.

Harding, Susan Friend. 2000. *The Book of Jerry Falwell: Fundamentalist Language and Politics*. Princeton: Princeton University Press.

Harrison, Lawrence E. [1985] 2000. *Underdevelopment Is a State of Mind: The Latin American Case*. Updated ed. New York: Madison Books.

Harrison, Lawrence E., and Samuel P. Huntington. 2000. *Culture Matters: How Values Shape Human Progress*. New York: Basic Books.

Hobbes, Thomas. 1962. *Leviathan.* Ed. Richard S. Peters. New York: Collier Books.

Hoge, Dean R., Benton Johnson, and Donald A. Luidens. 1995. "Types of Denominational Switching among Protestant Young Adults." *Journal for the Scientific Study of Religion* 34(2): 253–58.

Hurtado, Samuel. 1999. *La sociedad tomada por la familia.* Caracas: Ediciones de la Biblioteca de la Universidad Central de Venezuela.

Irvine, Leslie. 1999. *Codependent Forevermore: The Invention of Self in a Twelve-Step Group.* Chicago: University of Chicago Press.

James, William. 1961. *The Varieties of Religious Experience.* New York: Macmillan.

Jenkins, Philip. 2002. *The Next Christendom: The Coming of Global Christianity.* New York: Oxford University Press.

Joas, Hans. 1993. *Pragmatism and Social Theory.* Chicago: University of Chicago Press.

Kane, Anne. 1992. "Cultural Analysis in Historical Sociology: The Analytic and Concrete Forms of the Autonomy of Culture." *Sociological Theory* 9(1): 53–69.

Karl, Terry L. 1995. "The Venezuelan Petro-State and the Crisis of 'Its' Democracy." In *Venezuelan Democracy under Stress,* ed. Jennifer McCoy, Andres Serpin, William C. Smith, and Andres Stambouli, 33–55. New Brunswick, NJ: Transaction Books.

Kuhn, Thomas S. [1962] 1970. *The Structure of Scientific Revolutions.* 2d ed. Chicago: University of Chicago Press.

Lakoff, George, and Mark Johnson. 1980. *Metaphors We Live By.* Chicago: University of Chicago Press.

Lalive d'Epinay, Christian. 1969 *Haven of the Masses: A Study of the Pentecostal Movement in Chile.* London: Lutterworth.

Lamont, Michele. 2000. *The Dignity of Working Men: Morality and the Boundaries of Race, Class, and Immigration.* New York: Russell Sage Foundation; Cambridge, MA: Havard University Press.

Lander, Edgardo. 1995. *Neoliberalismo, sociedad civil y democracia: Ensayos sobre América Latina y Venezuela.* Caracas: Universidad Central de Venezuela.

Levine, Daniel. 1973. *Conflict and Political Change in Venezuela.* Princeton: Princeton University Press.

———. 1992. *Popular Voices in Latin American Catholicism.* Princeton: Princeton University Press.

Levine, Daniel, and David Stoll. 1997. "Bridging the Gap between Empowerment and Power in Latin America." In *Fading States and Transnational Religious Regimes,* ed. Susanne Hoelber Rudolph and Joseph Piscatori, 63–103. Boulder, CO: Westview Press.

Levine, Donald N. 1995. *Visions of the Sociological Tradition.* Chicago: University of Chicago Press.

Lichterman, Paul. 2005. *Elusive Togetherness: Church Groups Trying to Bridge America's Divisions.* Princeton: Princeton University Press.

Liebow, Elliot. 1967. *Tally's Corner: A Study of Negro Streetcorner Men.* Boston: Little, Brown.

Linger, Daniel. 1993. *Dangerous Encounters: Meanings of Violence in a Brazilian City.* Stanford: Stanford University Press.

Lofland, John, and Rodney Stark. 1965. "Becoming a World-Saver: A Theory of Conversion to a Deviant Perspective." *American Journal of Sociology* 30: 862–74.

Lomnitz, Larissa Adler. 1977. *Networks and Marginality: Life in a Mexican Shantytown.* New York: Academic Press.

López Maya, Margarita. 1996. "Nuevas representaciones populares en Venezuela." *Nueva Sociedad,* no. 144 (July–August): 143–51.

———. 1997. "El repertorio de la protesta popular en Venezuela, 1989–1994." *Cuadernos del CENDES,* no. 36 (September–December):109–30.

———. 2004. "Exposición con motivo del reconocimiento en la Asamblea Nacional de la ratificación del presidente." Presentation to the Nacional Assembly of the Bolívarian Republic of Venezuela, August 27.

López Maya, Margarita, David Smilde, and Keta Stephany. 2002. *Protesta y cultura en Venezuela: Los marcos de acción colectiva en 1999.* Caracas: FACES-UCV, CENDES, FONACIT.

Machiavelli, Niccolo. 1950. *The Prince and the Discourses.* Trans. Luigi Ricci and Christian E. Detmold. New York: Random House.

Malinowski, Bronislaw. 1954. *Magic, Science and Religion, and Other Essays.* New York: Anchor Books.

Mariz, Cecilia. 1994. *Coping with Poverty: Pentecostals and Christian Base Communities in Brazil.* Philadelphia: Temple University Press.

Marquez, Patricia. 1999. *The Street Is My Home: Youth and Violence in Caracas.* Stanford: Stanford University Press.

Marsden, Peter V., and Noah E. Friedkin. 1994. "Network Studies of Social Influence." pp. 3–25 In *Advances in Social Network Analysis: Research in the Social and Behavioral Sciences,* ed. Stanley Wasserman and Joseph Galaskiewicz, 3–25. Thousand Oaks, CA: Sage.

Martin, David. 1990. *Tongues of Fire: The Explosion of Protestantism in Latin America.* Oxford: Basil Blackwell.

———. 1991. "The Economic Fruits of the Spirit." In *The Culture of Entrepreneurship,* ed. Brigitte Berger, 73–84. San Francisco: Institute for Contemporary Studies.

Mauss, Marcel. 1990. *The Gift: The Form and Reason for Exchange in Archaic Societies.* Trans. W. D. Halls. New York: Norton.

Maust, John. 1984. *Urban Growth and God's People in Ten Latin American Cities.* Coral Gables, FL: Latin American Mission.

McAdam, Doug. 2003. "Beyond Structural Analysis: Toward a More Dynamic Understanding of Social Movements." In *Social Movement Networks: Relational Approaches to Collective Action,* ed. Mario Diani and Doug McAdam, 281–98. New York: Oxford University Press.

McAdam, Doug, and Ronnelle Paulsen. 1993. "Specifying the Relationship between Social Ties and Activism." *American Journal of Sociology* 99(3): 640–67.

McGrath, Alister E. 2002. *The Future of Christianity.* Malden, MA: Blackwell.

McLean, Paul D. 1998. "A Frame Analysis of Favor Seeking in the Renaissance:

Agency, Networks, and Political Culture." *American Journal of Sociology* 104(1): 51–90.
Mead, George Herbert. 1964. *On Social Psychology; Selected Papers.* Ed. Anselm Strauss. Chicago: University of Chicago Press.
Mears, Daniel P., and Christopher G. Ellison. 2000. "Who Buys New Age Materials? Exploring Sociodemographic, Religious, Network, and Contextual Correlates of New Age Consumption." *Sociology of Religion* 61(3): 289–313.
Meirelles, Fernando, and Kátia Lund, dirs. 2002. *City of God.* O2 Filmes e VideoFilmes, Rio de Janeiro.
Mische, Ann. 2003. "Cross-Talk in Movements: Reconceiving the Culture-Network Link." pp.258–280 In *Social Movement Networks: Relational Approaches to Collective Action,* ed. Mario Diani and Doug McAdam, 258–80. New York: Oxford University Press.
Mische, Ann, and Harrison White. 1998. "Between Conversation and Situation: Public Switching Dynamics across Network Domains." *Social Research* 65(3): 695–724.
Montero, Maritza. 1984. *Ideología, alienación e identidad nacional: Una aproximación psicosocial al ser venezolano.* Caracas: Ediciones UCV, 1984.
El Nacional. 1996. "Venezuela esta entre los países mas corruptos." June 2.
Navarro, Juan Carlos. 1995. "In Search of the Lost Pact: Consensus Lost in the 1980s and 1990s." In *Venezuelan Democracy under Stress,* ed. Jennifer McCoy, Andres Serpin, William C. Smith, and Andres Stambouli, 13–31. New Brunswick, NJ: Transaction Publishers.
Nepstad, Sharon Erickson. 2004. *Convictions of the Soul: Religion, Culture and Agency in the Central American Solidarity Movement.* New York: Oxford University Press.
Nepstad, Sharon Erickson, and Christian Smith. 2001. "The Social Structure of Moral Outrage in Recruitment to the U.S. Central America Peace Movement." In *Passionate Politics: Emotions and Social Movements,* ed. Jeff Goodwin, James M Jasper, and Francesca Polletta, 158–74. Chicago: University of Chicago Press.
Neuhouser, Kevin. 1992. "Democratic Stability in Venezuela: Elite Consensus or Class Compromise?" *American Sociological Review* 57: 117–35.
Nisbett, Richard E., and Dov Cohen. 1996. *Culture of Honor: The Psychology of Violence in the South.* Boulder, CO: Westview Press.
Obeyesekere, Gananath. 1981. *Medusa's Hair: An Essay on Personal Symbols and Religious Experience.* Chicago: University of Chicago Press.
Ocampo, José Antonio, and Juan Martín, eds. 2003. *A Decade of Light and Shadow: Latin America and the Caribbean in the 1990s.* Santiago, Chile: Economic Commission for Latin America and the Caribbean.
Oliver, Pamela, and Hank Johnston. 2000. "What a Good Idea: Frames and Ideologies in Social Movements Research." *Mobilization: An International Journal* 5(1): 37–54.
Orsi, Robert. 2005. *Between Heaven and Earth: The Religious Worlds People Make and the Scholars Who Study Them.* Princeton, NJ: Princeton University Press.

Ortner, Sherry. 1984 "Theory in Anthropology since the Sixties." *Comparative Studies in Society and History* 26: 126–66.

Padgett, John F., and Christopher K. Ansell. 1993. "Robust Action and the Rise of the Medici, 1400–1434." *American Journal of Sociology* 98(6): 1259–1319.

Pallares, Amalia. 2003. *From Peasant Struggles to Indian Resistance: The Ecuadorian Andes in the Late Twentieth Century.* Norman: University of Oklahoma Press.

Parsons, Talcott. 1937. *The Structure of Social Action.* Vol. 1. New York: Free Press.

Peirce, Charles S. 1877. "The Fixation of Belief." *Popular Science Monthly* 12(November): 1–15.

Pérez Schael, María Sol. 1993. *Petróleo, cultura y poder en Venezuela.* Caracas: Monteávila Editores.

Peterson, Anna, Manuel Vásquez, and Philip Williams. 2001. *Christianity, Social Change, and Globalization in the Americas.* New Brunswick, NJ: Rutgers University Press.

Poewe, Karla, ed. 1994. *Charismatic Christianity as a Global Culture.* Columbia: University of South Carolina Press.

Polkinghorne, Donald. 1988. *Narrative Knowing and the Human Sciences.* Albany: State University of New York Press.

Pollak-Eltz, Angelina. 1994. *La religiosidad popular en Venezuela: Un estudio fenomenológico de la religiosidad en Venezuela.* Caracas: San Pablo.

Polletta, Francesca. 1998. "Contending Stories: Narrative in Social Movements." *Qualitative Sociology* 21(4): 419–46.

Portes, Alejandro, and Kathy Hoffman. 2003. "Latin American Class Structures: Their Composition and Change during the Neoliberal Era." *Latin American Research Review* 38(1): 41–82.

Ptacek, James. [1988] 1998. "Why Do Men Batter Their Wives?" In *Families in the U.S.: Kinship and Domestic Politics,* ed. Karen V. Hansen and Anita Ilta Garey, 619–33. Philadelphia: Temple University Press.

Ragin, Charles. 1987. *The Comparative Method: Moving beyond Qualitative and Quantitative Strategies.* Berkeley: University of California Press.

———. 2000. *Fuzzy-Set Social Science.* Chicago: University of Chicago Press.

Reich, Otto. 1983. "Foreign Aid Policy and Latin American Development." *Trade, Aid, and U.S. Economic Policy in Latin America.* Occasional Paper Series No. 6. Washington, DC: Center for Hemispheric Studies, American Enterprise Institute.

Reichertz, Jo. 2002. "Objective Hermeneutics and Hermeneutic Sociology of Knowledge." In *A Companion to Qualitative Research,* ed. Uwe Flick, Ernst von Kardorff, and Ines Steinke, 290–95. London: Sage.

Ricoeur, Paul. 1984. *Time and Narrative.* Vol. 1. Chicago: University of Chicago Press.

Ríos Troconis, Asdrúbal. 1986. *Desde los pequeños principios a las grandes realizaciones.* Maracaibo: Editorial Patmos.

Roberts, Bryan R. 1968. "Protestant Groups and Coping with Urban Life in Guatemala City." *American Journal of Sociology* 73: 753–67.

Rosaldo, Michelle Zimbalist. 1974. "Women, Culture, and Society: A Theoretical Overview." In *Women, Culture and Society,* ed. Michelle Zimbalist Rosaldo and Louise Lamphere, 17–42. Stanford: Stanford University Press.

Saegert, Susan, Phillip J. Thompson, and Mark R. Warren, eds. 2001. *Social Capital and Poor Communities.* New York: Russell Sage Foundation.

Sahlins, Marshall. 1976. *Culture and Practical Reason.* Chicago: University of Chicago Press.

———. 1985. *Islands of History.* Chicago: University of Chicago Press.

Salamanca, Luis. 1997. *Crisis de la modernización y crisis de la democracia en Venezuela.* Caracas: Universidad Central de Venezuela.

Sampson, Robert J., Jeffrey D. Morenhoff, and Thomas Gannon-Rowley. 2002. "Assessing 'Neighborhood Effects': Social Processes and New Directions in Research." *Annual Review of Sociology* 28: 443–78.

Sarbin, Theodore R. 1998. "Believed-In Imaginings: A Narrative Approach." In *Believed-In Imaginings: The Narrative Construction of Reality,* ed. Joseph De Rivera and Theodore Sarbin, 15–30. Washington, DC: American Psychological Association.

Schelling, Thomas. 1960. *The Strategy of Conflict.* Cambridge, MA: Harvard University Press.

Scheper-Hughes, Nancy. 1992. *Death without Weeping: The Violence of Everyday Life in Brazil.* Berkeley: University of California Press.

Schneider, Louis, and Sanford M. Dornbusch. 1958. *Popular Religion: Inspirational Books in America.* Chicago: University of Chicago Press.

Schneider, Elia, dir. 1999. *Gluesniffer: Law of the Street.* Centro Nacional Autónomo de Cinematográfica CNAC, Unity Films, Tango Bravo. Credesca (Venezuela). Filmart P.C. (Spain).

Scott, James. 1976. *The Moral Economy of the Peasant: Rebellion and Subsistence in Southeast Asia.* New Haven: Yale University Press.

Sewell, William H., Jr. 1992. "A Theory of Structure: Duality, Agency, and Transformation." *American Journal of Sociology* 98: 1–29.

Sherkat, Darren E., and John Wilson. 1995. "Preferences, Constraints, and Choices in Religious Markets: An Examination of Religious Switching and Apostasy." *Social Forces* 73(3): 993–1026.

Sherman, Amy L. 1997. *The Soul of Development: Biblical Christianity and Economic Transformation in Guatemala.* Oxford: Oxford University Press.

Silletta, Alfredo. 1987. *Las sectas invaden la Argentina.* Buenos Aires: Editorial Contrapunto.

Silveira, Ellen, and Peter Allebeck. 2001. "Migration, Ageing and Mental Health: An Ethnographic Study on Perceptions of Life Satisfaction, Anxiety and Depression in Older Somali Men in East London." *International Journal of Social Welfare* 10(4): 309–20.

Simmel, Georg. 1971. *On Individuality and Social Forms.* Ed. Donald N. Levine. Chicago: University of Chicago Press.

Smelser, Neil J. 1997. *Problems in Social Theory.* Berkeley: University of California Press.

Smilde, David. 1994. "Gender Relations and Social Change in Latin American

Evangelicalism." In *Coming of Age: Protestantism in Contemporary Latin America,* 39–64. New York: University Press of America.

———. 1997. "The Fundamental Unity of the Conservative and Revolutionary Tendencies in Venezuelan Evangelicalism: The Case of Conjugal Relations." *Religion* 27: 343–59.

———. 1998. Review of *The Soul of Development: Biblical Christianity and Economic Transformation in Guatemala. American Journal of Sociology* 104(1): 273–74.

———. 1999. "Venezuela—Nationhood, Patronage and the Conflict over New Religious Movements." In *Religious Freedom and Evangelization in Latin America: The Challenge of Religious Pluralism,* ed. Paul Sigmund, 269–83. Maryknoll, NY: Orbis Books.

———. 2003. "Skirting the Instrumental Paradox: Intentional Belief Through Narrative in Latin American Pentecostalism." *Qualitative Sociology* 26(3): 313–29.

———. 2004. "Contradiction without Paradox: Evangelical Political Culture in the 1998 Venezuelan Elections." *Latin American Politics and Society* 46(1): 75–102.

Smith, Christian. 2003. *Moral Believing Animals: Human Personhood and Culture.* Oxford: Oxford University Press.

Smith, Dorothy E. 1990. *The Conceptual Practices of Power: A Feminist Sociology of Knowledge.* Boston: Northeastern University Press.

Smith, Jonathon T. 1982. *Imagining Religion: From Babylon to Jonestown.* Chicago: University of Chicago Press.

Smith, Raymond T. 1973. "The Matrifocal Family." In *The Character of Kinship,* ed. J. Goody, 121–44. Cambridge: Cambridge University Press.

Snow, David A., and Cynthia L. Phillips. 1980. "The Lofland-Stark Conversion Model: A Critical Reassessment." *Social Problems* 27(4): 430–47.

Snow, David, Burke Rochford, Steven K. Worden, and Robert Benford. 1986. "Frame Alignment Processes, Micromobilization and Movement Participation." *American Sociological Review* 51: 456–81.

Snow, David A., Louis A. Zurcher Jr., and Sheldon Ekland-Olson. 1980. "Social Networks and Social Movements: A Microstructural Approach to Differential Recruitment." *American Sociological Review* 45: 787–801.

Somers, Margaret R. 1993. "Citizenship and the Place of the Public Sphere: Law, Community, and Political Culture in the Transition to Democracy." *American Sociological Review* 58: 587–620.

———. 1998. " 'We're No Angels': Realism, Rational Choice, and Relationality in Social Sciences." *American Journal of Sociology* 104(3): 722–84.

———, ed. 2006. *Cultural Agency in the Americas.* Durham, NC: Duke University Press.

Stack, Carol B. 1975. *All Our Kin: Strategies for Survival in a Black Community.* New York: Harper and Row.

Stark, Rodney. 1996. *The Rise of Christianity: How the Obscure, Marginal Jesus Movement Became the Dominant Religious Forces in the Western World in a Few Centuries.* Princeton: Princeton University Press.

Stark, Rodney, and William Sims Bainbridge. 1980. "Networks of Faith: Inter-

personal Bonds and Recruitment to Cults and Sects." *American Journal of Sociology* 85(6): 1376–95.
———. 1987. *A Theory of Religion.* New York: Peter Lang.
Stark, Rodney, and Roger Finke. 2000. *Acts of Faith: Explaining the Human Side of Religion.* Berkeley: University of California Press.
Stark, Rodney, and Laurence R. Iannaccone. 1997. "Why the Jehovah's Witnesses Grow So Rapidly: A Theoretical Application." *Journal of Contemporary Religion* 12(2): 133–57.
Statistical Abstract of Latin America. Reference series (1955–2001). Los Angeles: University of California, Los Angeles, Latin American Center.
Steinberg, Marc. 1999. "The Talk and Back Talk of Collective Action: A Dialogic Analysis of Repertoires of Discourse among Nineteenth-Century English Cotton Spinners." *American Journal of Sociology* 105(3): 736–80.
Steinmetz, George. 1998. "Critical Realism and Historical Sociology: A Review Article." *Comparative Studies of Society and History* 40(1): 170–86.
Stiglitz, Joseph E. 2002. *Globalization and Its Discontents.* New York: Norton.
Stinchcombe, Arthur. 1968. *Constructing Social Theories.* New York: Harcourt Brace and World.
Stoll, David. 1990. *Is Latin America Turning Protestant? The Politics of Evangelical Growth.* Berkeley: University of California Press.
———. 1993. *Between Two Armies in the Ixil Towns of Guatemala.* New York: Columbia University Press.
Stromberg, Peter G. 1993. *Language and Self-Transformation: A Study of the Christian Conversion Narrative.* New York: Cambridge University Press.
Swidler, Ann. 1986. "Culture in Action: Symbols and Strategies." *American Sociological Review* 51: 273–86.
———. 2001. *Talk of Love: How Culture Matters.* Chicago: University of Chicago Press.
Tanner, Nancy. 1974. "Matrifocality in Indonesia and Africa and among Black Americans." In *Women, Culture, and Society,* ed. Michelle Zimbalist Rosaldo and Louise Lamphere, 129–56. Stanford: Stanford University Press.
Taylor, Verta. 1989. "Social Movement Continuity: The Women's Movement in Abeyance." *American Sociological Review* 54(5): 761–75.
Tramontin Querales, Rafael Arturo. 1999. *Aproximación al estudio de la familia Venezolana: Rol del trabajador social como dinamizador de procesos interactivos y comunicacionales.* Caracas: Ediciones FACES/UCV.
Turner, Terrance. 1991. " 'We are Parrots,' 'Twins are Birds': Play of Tropes as Operational Structure." In *Beyond Metaphor: The Theory of Tropes in Anthropology,* ed. James Fernandez, 121–58. Stanford: Stanford University Press.
Ugalde O., Luis, S.J., Luis Pedro España, Carmen Scotto, Anabel Castillo, Tulio Hernández, Néstor Luis Luengo, Marcelinao Bisbal, and María Gabriela Ponce. 1994. *La violencia en Venezuela.* Caracas: Monte Avila Editores Latinoamericana.
United Nations Development Program. 2000. *Report on Human Development in Venezuela, 2000: Ways to Overcome Poverty.* Caracas.
Uribe, Gabriela, and Edgardo Lander. [1988] 1995. "Acción social, efectividad simbólica y nuevos ámbitos de lo político." In *Neoliberalismo, sociedad civil*

y democracia: Ensayos sobre América Latina y Venezuela, ed. Edgardo Lander, 15–58. Caracas: Universidad Central de Venezuela.

U.S. Census Bureau International Data Base. 2004. ww.census.gov/ipc/www/idbnew.html.

Walker, Michael E., Stanley Wasserman, and Barry Wellman. 1994. "Statistical Models of Social Support Networks." In *Advances in Social Network Analysis: Research in the Social and Behavioral Sciences,* ed. Stanley Wasserman and Joseph Galaskiewicz, 71–98. Thousand Oaks, CA: Sage.

Walker Bynum, Caroline. 1987. *Holy Feast and Holy Fast: The Religious Significance of Food to Medieval Women.* Berkeley: University of California Press.

Wallach Bologh, Roslyn. 1990. *Love or Greatness: Max Weber and Masculine Thinking, a Feminist Inquiry.* Boston: Unwin Hyman.

Warner, R. Stephan. 1993. "Work in Progress toward a New Paradigm for the Sociological Study of Religion in the United States." *American Journal of Sociology* 98(5): 1044–93.

Watters, Mary. 1933. *A History of the Church in Venezuela: 1810–1930.* Chapel Hill: University of North Carolina Press.

Weber, Max. 1946. "The Protestant Sects and the Spirit of Capitalism." In *From Max Weber,* trans. and ed. Hans Gerth and C. W. Mills, 302–22. New York: Oxford University Press.

———. 1968. *Economy and Society.* Berkeley: University of California Press.

Wellman, Barry. 1982. "Studying Personal Communities." In *Social Structure and Network Analysis,* ed. Peter V. Marsden and Nan Lin, 61–80. Beverly Hills, CA: Sage.

Wiarda, Howard J., 2001. *The Soul of Latin America.* New Haven: Yale University Press.

Wiesenfeld, Esther, and Euclides Sánchez, eds. 1995. *Psicología social comunitaria: Contribuciones latinoamericanas.* Caracas: Fondo Editorial Tropykos.

Wilcox, W. Bradford. 2004. *Soft Patriarchs, New Men: How Christianity Shapes Fathers and Husbands.* Chicago: University of Chicago Press.

Wood, Richard L. 2002. *Faith in Action: Religion, Race and Democratic Organizing in America.* Chicago: University of Chicago Press.

Wuthnow, Robert. 1987. *Meaning and Moral Order: Explorations in Cultural Analysis.* Berkeley: University of California Press.

———, ed. 1994. *"I Come Away Stronger": How Small Groups Are Shaping American Religion.* Grand Rapids, MI: Eerdmans.

Yashar, Deborah J. 2005. *Contesting Citizenship in Latin America.* New York: Cambridge University Press.

Young, Alford. 2003. *The Minds of Marginalized Black Men: Making Sense of Mobility, Opportunity, and Future Life Chances.* Princeton: Princeton University Press.

Zubillaga, Veronica, and Ángel Cisneros. 2002. "El miedo en Caracas: El contraste en la experiencia del temer. Relatos y vivencias de amenaza en barrios y urbanizaciones de Caracas." In *Morir en Caracas: Violencia y ciudadanía en Venezuela,* ed. Roberto Briceño Leon and Rogelio Pérez Perdomo, 68–101. Caracas: Universidad Central de Venezuela.

Index

Compositor: Binghamton Valley Composition
Text: 10/13 Sabon
Display: Sabon
Printer and binder: Maple-Vail Manufacturing Group

The Groaning of Creation